Learning Networks

Learning Networks
A Field Guide to Teaching and Learning Online

Linda Harasim, Starr Roxanne Hiltz, Lucio Teles,
and Murray Turoff

The MIT Press
Cambridge, Massachusetts
London, England

1995

This book was set in Sabon by Asco Trade Typesetting Ltd., Hong Kong and was printed and bound in the United States of America.

Library of Congress Cataloging-in-Publication Data

Learning networks : a field guide to teaching and learning online /
Linda Harasim ... [et al.].
    p. cm.
Includes bibliographical references and index.
ISBN 0-262-08236-5
1. Education—Data processing. 2. Computer networks. I. Harasim,
Linda M. (Linda Marie), 1949– .
LB1028.43.L43   1995
371.3'34—dc20   94-46599
                                                           CIP

To the millions of learners now using networks and the hundreds of millions who will join them in the future

Contents

Preface

Learning networks use computer networks for educational activity—in primary, secondary, university, and adult education. They depend on the hardware and software that form the communications network, but they consist of the communities of learners who work together in the online environment.

Learning networks introduce new educational options to strengthen and transform teaching and learning practices, opportunities, and outcomes. They generate enthusiastic response from participants, who find that networking technologies can improve traditional ways of teaching and learning, and open up entirely new avenues of communication, collaboration, and knowledge building. There are as well potential pitfalls and disadvantages to network-based learning, as compared to the traditional classroom. This book draws on the experience of all four authors of teaching and learning online and incorporates examples and information from a wide variety of online and published sources. It is meant to serve as a guide to both educators and learners in this new, fascinating, and challenging environment.

Our online students, who taught us most of what we have written to share with others, contributed in many ways to this book. We thank as well the staff of The MIT Press, especially Bob Prior for his support of this book, Beth LaFortune-Gies for her assistance, and Sandra Minkkinen for her editorial expertise. We also are very grateful to Amy Mahan for her assistance and suggestions for improving the book and to Rosanna LePiane for her enthusiasm, support, and word processing skills.

I

The Field

1

Learning Networks: An Introduction

1.1 An Overview: What Are Learning Networks and Who Is Using Them?

Imagine learning with peers, expertise, and resources that are available whenever you want or need them. These "classmates" are from Moscow and Mexico City, New York and Hong Kong, Vancouver and Sydney—from urban centers and rural and remote areas. And they, like you, never need to leave home. You are all learning together not in a place in the ordinary sense but in a shared space, a "cyberspace," using network systems that connect people all over the globe. Your learning network "classroom" is anywhere that you have a personal computer, a modem, and a telephone line, satellite dish, or radio link. Dialing into the network turns your computer screen into a window on the world of learning.

Network is the descriptive name for these shared spaces. Telephone and satellite signals form a vast web or net that can join a computer to any other computer in the world. Supported by these networks, educators can create effective learning environments whereby teachers and learners in different locations work together to build their understanding and skills related to a particular subject matter.

Most of the systems that support Learning Networks are text only (some also support audio or graphics communication). The written word is uniquely suited to the construction, group revision, and sharing of knowledge. Practically all education is built around textbooks and written assignments, and computer-mediated communication (CMC) networks introduce an *interactive* text to enable information sharing and group knowledge building. Most CMC networks are asynchronous, a feature that, with the text-based nature of the communication, allows each participant to work at his or her individual learning pace and take as long as needed to read, reflect, write, and revise before sharing questions, insights, or information with others.

With attention to instructional design and facilitation, these shared spaces can become the locus of rich and satisfying experiences in collaborative learning, an interactive group knowledge-building process in which the learners actively construct knowledge by formulating ideas into words that are shared with and built upon through the reactions and responses of others.

Learning together can be much more engaging and effective than learning alone. Think of one of the earliest collaborative learning structures that most of us have experienced: the spelling bee. Remember concentrating and thinking along with the other members of your team as they tried to spell the words they were given? You "worked" harder than if you were just given a list of words to memorize all by yourself, and had more fun at the same time. Or, take the example of role playing to learn how to deal with an ethical problem or how to save a rainforest or run a business. This is what collaborative learning is all about: working together in teams that may vary from two people to a whole class or a whole school.

Computer-mediated learning networks are used at all levels and in all fields of education. From kindergarten to grade 12, entire classrooms of students are networked. At the university level, students use networks to enhance course activities, participate in courses delivered online, or enroll in entire degree programs offered through "virtual campuses" available on computer networks. Corporate and government training programs for employees are offered online or through a combination of media, including CMC. Noncredit, continuing education, and self-enrichment learning circles are also taking advantage of this new educational option. (See appendixes A and B for lists of learning network resources.)

In short, learning networks are groups of people who use CMC networks to learn together, at the time, place, and pace that best suits them and is appropriate to the task. The use of computer networks in primary, secondary, tertiary, and adult education introduces new options to transform teaching and learning relationships and outcomes. Use of these networks is generating enthusiastic responses from educators and learners, who find that networking technologies can improve upon traditional ways of teaching and learning as well as open entirely new opportunities for communication, collaboration, and knowledge building. In a world where lifelong learning is made both possible and necessary by the quick pace of technological and social change, the convenience and effectiveness of this new mode of learning make it a major educational force for the twenty-first century.

1.2 Historic Overview of Computer Learning Networks

Communication over computer networks first occurred in the 1960s with electronic mail on time-sharing computers. People communicated by sending messages using the same mainframe computers through dumb terminals connected to the mainframe or dial-up telephone lines (local and long distance). In 1969, ARPANET (Advanced Research Projects Agency Network) was developed as a U.S. government experiment in multisite packet switching (dedicated telephone lines for data communication), initially to link researchers with remote computer centers for sharing of hardware and software resources, such as computer disk space, processing power, databases, and computers (LaQuey 1993; Quarterman 1993). Users quickly realized that they wanted to use the networks to send messages to each other about the status of their projects (Quarterman 1993). In the early 1970s, an email function was added, and it soon became the most-used service on the network. Mailing lists (or distribution lists) were next implemented, because users found that they frequently wanted to send mail not just to specific individuals on the network but also to fixed groups of people, such as everyone involved in a certain implementation or participating in a particular team. In 1983 ARPANET split into ARPANET and MILNet (the latter an unclassified military network), but communications between the two continued; their linking and interconnecting became the basis for the Internet, the now worldwide "network of networks" that links millions of people and tens of thousands of computer resources.

In the early years, academics and educators had limited access to computer networks. Access to ARPANET was limited to military and contracts and universities working on defense research. Networks with other applications such as the UUCP, a cooperative, decentralized worldwide Unix communication network, and USENET (User's Network) were developed in the late 1970s, initially to serve the university community and later for commercial organizations. BITNET (Because It's Time Network) and CSNET (the Computer Science Network) were launched in the early 1980s to provide nationwide networking to the academic and research communities. These networks were not initially part of the Internet, but special connections subsequently were developed to enable the exchange of information and messaging between the various communities. This interconnection of networks was the beginning of the Internet. In 1986, the American NSFNet (National Science Foundation Network) was created to link researchers and subsequently academics across the United States with five supercomputer centers. NSFNet, the backbone network of the Internet, began to replace ARPANET, which was dismantled in 1990, and CSNET, which ceased operation in 1991. The Internet, a global network of networks, consists of over 8,000 smaller networks around the world covering all continents. It is the largest and fastest global network today.

The first computer conferencing system was designed and implemented by Murray Turoff in 1970 (Hiltz and Turoff 1978). Computer conferences create a permanent transcript of a group discussion and usually support group roles, such as moderator or leader. The first system, which involved twenty people spread around the United States, conducted over a period of thirteen weeks, was structured as a Delphi discussion process, an iterative series of questionnaires and feedback whereby knowledgeable respondents explore a complex topic (Linstone and Turoff 1975). This was the beginning of EMISARI (Emergency Management Information System and Reference Index), which evolved into a full-scale conferencing system, with personal messaging capabilities, discussion conferences, and a real-time messaging feature. Other conferencing systems were subsequently developed, among them, EIES, Forum, Confer, Planet, Participate, COM, CoSy, and Lotus Notes. Many still exist today and are used for organizational, scientific, community, or educational applications (see appendix C for a list of commercial vendors). The first-generation computer conferencing systems required a large mainframe or minicomputer to serve as the central host for the conference.

The creation of the first bulletin board system (BBS) for personal computers is generally attributed to Ward Christensen and Randy Seuss in February 1978 in Chicago (Sterling 1992). The first bulletin boards had only one common space or "board" for posting public messages and allowed only one user to be connected at a time. With rapid transformation of bulletin board software into better-designed and faster systems, the public acceptance of bulletin board systems led to the existence of around 30,000 boards by 1990 in the United States alone and tens of thousands in Canada and overseas.

An overview of the history of networking technology
- 1960s: networking and email developed on timesharing computers.
- Early 1970s: first email on packet-switched networks.
- 1970: EMISARI, the first computer conferencing system was designed and implemented.
- 1971: first commercial computer conferencing system developed.
- 1978: creation of first personal computer bulletin board system.

Educational uses of computer networks can be traced to the late 1960s, such as PLATO, a computer-assisted instruction (CAI) system developed for use on time-sharing computers. As early as 1969, Stanford University began delivering mathematics education to low-income students in Mississippi, Kentucky, and California using time-sharing computer networks (Hunter 1992). While these approaches were primarily CAI applications, some email interaction occurred, facilitating human-to-human networking on educational topics. By the mid-1970s, the availability of email on packet-switched networks enabled more generalized educational adoption of computer networking (Hunter 1992). Email was first used in the early 1970s for academic information exchange; by the late 1970s, it was being used for supplementing university-level courses as well. School-based applications of email networks followed as teachers and learners from kindergarten through grade 12 launched joint writing or research projects and cross-cultural exchanges, such as electronic penpals.

Computer conferencing systems were first used for course activity and delivery in the early 1980s, when the availability of packet-switched networks like the US Telenet and Tymnet made the cost of accessing these systems more affordable for educators and learners (Feenberg 1993). Interest in educational networking increased with the introduction of computer conferencing and bulletin boards, more sophisticated media for group communication, which offered educators better tools for defining learning structures and groups. The first educational uses of computer conferencing were for noncredit mini-courses and executive training programs and for classroom-based courses at the college level. Today, learning networks have been successfully adopted at all levels of education.

Over the past two decades, three basic approaches have emerged for educational applications of computer networks. Learning networks are used as an enhancement to traditional (face-to-face or distance) courses, as the primary teaching medium for a portion of, or an entire course, or as a forum for knowledge networking, participation in discussion groups, or information exchange with peers or experts and/or access to online resources.

1.2.1   Networked Classrooms As Course Enhancements

The networked classroom approach links classes in different geographical locations (local and global) for sharing information and resources, joint projects, and social interaction. This approach has been used from kindergarten up to adult education. One of the earliest examples was a network of secondary schools linked by Dartmouth College's time-sharing computer in 1969 (Hunter 1992). The InterCultural Learning Network (ICLN), implemented in 1983, used email to link schoolchildren in San Diego, California, with peers in Alaska and other states and eventually in Japan, Mexico, Puerto Rico, and Israel (Levin, Kim, and Riel 1990). The ICLN also introduced a research component into the networking activities. The research question was whether writing to real audiences on the network improved writing. The conclusion of writing experts was that it did. Access to real audiences was found to be more motivational than writing for assignments only and contributed to improved writing skills (Cohen and Riel, 1989).

The Canadian RAPPI network (1985–1987) linked schoolchildren and teachers in over seventy schools in Canada, France, England, and Italy to enable information exchange with peers in different regions and countries (Hart 1987). The RAPPI Project (Réseau d'Ateliers Pédagogique Pilote International—the International Educational Network Pilot Project) originated at the Versailles Economic Summit in 1982. RAPPI used the computer conferencing system at the University of British Columbia, Canada, to facilitate information exchange among schoolchildren in different regions and countries. The curricular focus was social studies and writing; through the network students learned about other cultures, life-styles, and perspectives, gaining increased knowledge about themselves and how they fit into a larger global community.

Applications of networked classrooms have flourished. They take advantage of the new communication networks to incorporate discussion and projects related to current events, research and scientific activities, environmental problems, and social, political, economic, and cultural issues.

1.2.2 Online Course Delivery

The computer network environment can serve as the classroom or campus—that is, the primary medium for class activity and interaction in credit and noncredit courses. Postsecondary institutions began experimenting with the use of computer conferencing for undergraduate course delivery (either total or partial delivery of course activities and group work) in the 1980s. In one of the most prominent of these experiments, the Virtual Classroom project, computer conferencing was proved to be a viable option for course delivery. In matched classes in subjects as different as sociology, computer science, management, and statistics, there was generally no difference in outcomes as measured by exam scores; additionally, students reported that they learned more online. In 1985, the Ontario Institute for Studies in Education (the graduate school in education for the University of Toronto) and Connected Education (affiliated with the New School for Social Research, New York) began offering graduate-level courses online, using computer conferencing as the principal mode of delivery (Harasim 1987b; Levinson 1989). Students log on to designated computer conferences to participate in class discussions, debates, seminars, individual and group assignments, and virtual "cafes" (online spaces for socializing) and libraries (resources such as bibliographies and articles available on computers on the network).

More recently, entire university programs have come to be based on CMC (see chapter 3). Online programs augment the range of possibilities for teaching and learning, adding another option to the palette offered by traditional face-to-face or distance education programs.

1.2.3 Distance Education and Open Learning

Distance education and open learning programs are adopting computer networking and conferencing media to enhance communication between the learner and the tutor and, increasingly, to explore a new option for distance education: collaborative learning, involving group projects and discussion among distance learners. The American Open University was a pioneer in the use of computer conferencing for distance education, introducing computer conferencing in 1983 as a tool to supplement learner-tutor communication. In 1989, the British Open University implemented computer conferencing for another pioneering distance education application: computer conferencing as part of a mass-based distance education course. The British Open University gave computer conferencing accounts to 1,300 students in one course. The advent of networking technologies such as computer conferencing together with examples of school and university applications have encouraged distance education instructional designers to introduce a collaborative learning approach that has hitherto not been possible in distance programming.

1.2.4 Knowledge Networking: The Internet

Knowledge networking describes the use of electronic linkages among different teaching and learning communities to facilitate information acquisition and knowledge building. Perhaps the most dramatic example is on the Internet. Thousands of discussions on topics ranging from the aardvark to zen are available to anyone with an Internet account (Krol 1992). Millions of academics, students, scientists, researchers, professionals, and educators participate twenty-four hours a day, seven days a week, exchanging tens of millions of messages across the globe daily on the Internet. These user groups represent an active forum of informal learning and information exchange: a knowledge network. By spring 1994, approximately 20 million people were using the Internet, primarily for social and knowledge networking. Originally developed for scientists and researchers, not only the numbers of users but the breadth of applications is expanding tremendously. Today the population size is growing exponentially; worldwide growth of the number of networks is doubling annually, and in Europe it is increasing by a factor of four annually (Quarterman 1993). This population includes elementary school to postsecondary students and teachers and a range of professionals and business users.

Regardless of their background, sophistication, or technical expertise, knowledge networkers share the same goal: they seek information and ways to understand and apply that information. Information may be obtained through access to other individuals or to files on the Internet and becomes knowledge as people interact with others to learn how to integrate and use that information. Knowledge networks are an informal way to accomplish the goal. Some user groups are loose and very informal, perhaps without a group moderator to organize the discussion flows or membership. Others are focused and may require applying to the moderator for permission to join. Potential knowledge networkers might include:

• An eighth-grade science teacher seeking information or resources on a particular topic, suggestions on how to develop the curriculum, or general peer or subject area support.

• Doctors sharing information on new treatments, approaches, medical issues, and professional challenges.

• High school students interested in space travel participating in discussion groups with scientists, astronauts, and science fiction writers.

• Hobbyists wanting to share or get tips and information.

• Seniors seeking support and information while also offering their own expertise and insights.

Knowledge networking is based on self-directed learning and growth through the pursuit of information, skills, and knowledge. There is no prescribed curriculum; learning occurs through interaction with peers and experts on any subject or field that the user is interested in—related to work, leisure, personal relationships, or community activities. The learner may construct a curriculum, tapping into the extraordinary array of resources available on the Internet or on any other network.

1.3   What Can Educators and Learners Expect from Taking Part?

Most of the examples of learning networks already described were not research experiments in the typical sense, rather, they were real applications endeavoring to extend and expand teaching and learning opportunities.

Early experiences with learning networks have demonstrated the potential for significant educational gains. Networking technologies can be easy to learn, and using them makes learning and teaching richer and more effective. Networks offer learners and teachers access to new ideas, perspectives, cultures, and information—enriching locally available resources. The group input enables multiple perspectives on a topic. Cross-cultural communication and global understanding are also facilitated. A better understanding of the interconnectivity of the world's population can contribute to learning how to respond to problems—global, political, social, and environmental.

With learning networks, the time, place, and pace of education are expanded and become more individualized while peer interaction and collaboration are emphasized. Students and teachers with access to a computer, modem, telephone line, and network service can access expertise, resources, and peers whenever they need or wish.

The quality of the interaction is also improved. Eisenberg and Ely (1993) note that "interaction through networks helps break down communication barriers and inhibitions that often stifle the open exchange of ideas in traditional classrooms" (p. 2). There are also important motivational benefits. "Network use is highly motivational for both students and teachers: kids interact with computer networks with energy and enthusiasm often missing in more conventional classroom students, and teachers are stimulated by the ability to share ideas, concerns, and solutions with colleagues across the country as easily as if they were in the next room" (ibid., 2–3).

Learning networks are also used effectively by students and teachers who are blind and/or deaf. Norm Coombs, a professor at the Rochester Institute of Technology who is blind, has taught courses using computer conferencing since 1986. As he notes: "The handicapped, once having learned the basic technologies, can participate equally with their disability being invisible" (Coombs 1989). Computer networking has also been used to teach writing skills for deaf and hearing students at Gallaudet University. According to Peyton and Batson (1986) and Thompson (1988), a network such as the real-time conferencing system used at Gallaudet allows students to be immersed in written language, just as they might be immersed in spoken language. Writing online can be used for many purposes, ranging from informal conversation to discussing reading texts or students' compositions, to composing extended texts together online. For students at the beginning stages of learning written English (beginning literates or English as a second language students), the teacher's writing can serve as immediate feedback and a model of correct usage. For students working at more advanced levels, the network interactions provide opportunities to think and write collaboratively with one another and with the teacher as model or coach.

Wells's (1992) review of the literature reveals a range of purposes for educational adoption of networking. Some of the principal reasons that educators have introduced networks into their class activities are to expand student opportunities for convenient course-related or social interaction with peers (Kaye 1991); to enable or enhance opportunities for group work for students in either face-to-face or distance education (Davie and Wells 1991); and to provide student access to online resources and relevant information (Teles and Duxbury 1991).

Honey and Henriquez (1993) surveyed 550 elementary, middle, and high school educators in the United States who were active users of telecommunications technology for professional development and student learning. The most highly rated incentives for using telecommunications as a professional resource was communicating with other educators, accessing information, and combating professional isolation. Over two-thirds of these educators reported that integrating telecommunications into their teaching made a significant and positive difference in how they teach. Conducting telecommunications activities with students enabled teachers to spend more time with individual students and less time lecturing to the whole class, and allowed students to carry out more independent work. The most highly rated incentives for using telecommunications with students include expanding students' awareness about the world, accessing information, and increasing students' inquiry-based and analytical skills.

According to the researchers the three most important factors influencing these teachers in selecting telecommunication services are service offerings (providing teacher resources, learner activities, or both), expense, and ease of use. The highest rated barriers to effective telecommunications use were insufficient telephone lines, lack of time in the school schedule, inadequate communication about school and district communications activities, and lack of money to cover the cost of network services. Lack of time in the school schedule and inadequate financial resources were found to be the most persistent barriers to effective telecommunications use.

Riel (1993) reported a survey of 110 teachers that studied the outcomes they saw for students who participated on the AT&T Learning Network. The goal was to see how teachers assessed the development of student skills that were related to the U.S. secretary of labor's Commission on Achieving Necessary Skills (SCANS) competencies. The teachers were asked to evaluate increases in student skills and competencies in a number of areas using a five-point scale. Teachers indicated strong gains in the SCANS foundational skills—reading and writing skills, collaborative learning skills, motivation to learn, self-esteem, and responsibility—and SCANS competencies—ability to work in a team, effective use of technology, research and organizational skills, knowledge of geography, and awareness of other cultures. The two most highly rated items were "developed ability to work in a team" and "promoted collaborative learning skills," important skills identified by the SCANS report that are not addressed in more traditional approaches to education.

In a recent survey of 240 teachers and learners on the Internet, 70 percent noted that using computer networks has changed how they viewed education (Harasim and Yung 1993). Of 176 respondents to the question on whether CMC is different from the traditional classroom, 90 percent responded yes. They noted that:

• The role of the teacher changes to that of facilitator and mentor.
• Students become active participants; discussions become more detailed and deeper.
• Access to resources is expanded significantly.
• Learners become more independent.

• Access to teachers becomes equal and direct.

• Interactions among teachers are increased significantly.

• Education becomes learner centered; learning becomes self-paced.

• Learning opportunities for all students are more equal; learner-learner group interactions are significantly increased.

• Personal communication among participants is increased.

• Teaching and learning is collaborative.

• There is more time to reflect on ideas; students can explore on the networks; exchange of ideas and thoughts is expanded; the classroom becomes global.

• The teacher-learner hierarchy is broken down. Teachers become learners, and learners become teachers.

Respondents also noted negative aspects of learning online: there is more preparation work for teachers, and learners have to work hard to stay current with the topic in order to participate thoughtfully and actively. Networks encourage, even require, active rather than passive participation. In order to be "present," users must make some comment and keep up with the interaction. Students report information overload, communication anxiety in relation to the delayed responses in an asynchronous environment, increased work and responsibility, difficulty in navigating online and following the discussion threads, loss of visual cues, and concerns about health issues related to computer use (Harasim 1987).

There are challenges to teaching and learning online successfully. Important questions need to be considered, such as which network technologies are appropriate, how to integrate networking into the curriculum, how to "teach" and "learn" on a networking system, and how to transform the network into an effective educational environment. The following chapters address these questions and consider the opportunities and the challenges.

1.4   Network Technologies

The technologies that support learning networks are simple and straightforward to use. Although more complex and advanced technologies are available, it is not a matter of very complex systems being better than very simple systems. Rather, the issue is what is suited to the learning objectives and the budget. A great deal can be accomplished with fairly simple and economical systems. In this section we introduce the network technologies that comprise the vast majority of learning networks, from primary school applications up to graduate schools and professional training.

Learning networks are composed of hardware, software, and tele-communications lines. The basic hardware components of the technology are a personal computer or workstation and a modem (a modem translates digital signals into analog signals that can travel over telephone lines and other media, and translates them back into digital signals when they reach the designated computer). The second component is the software used for group interaction: bulletin boards, electronic mail, or computer conferencing systems. A final component is the networks themselves, which link the computers to enable large groups of people to use the common software system to communicate and learn together.

Most educational CMC today is text based, so a very simple personal computer that can display text is sufficient. However, almost all media can be digitized and transmitted—sounds and pictures as well as words. In the future, as costs of hardware and software decrease and digital highways to carry signals at high speeds are built, learning networks increasingly will be a multimedia environment.

1.4.1   Bulletin Board Systems

A simple bulletin board system is a shared communication space for a small group, usually implemented on a single personal computer. It might have only one communication line available (i.e., if busy, try later) and represent merely a shared posting board where any participant can see or review anything that anyone else has already entered, or it may have only limited and very simple group communication facilities.

Many high school students have created bulletin boards on their own computers to share material and exchange communications with their friends. Student-run, student-initiated bulletin boards providing collaboration on homework and socializing may outnumber bulletin board systems set up by educators. High school teachers set up bulletin boards relating to classroom activities. And educational institutions set up bulletin boards for use by students, for example, to support specific student clubs. However, only a few public school institutions have set up bulletin boards, probably because of a limited awareness of the potential benefits and applications for this technology on the part of educators and administrators rather than concern with the costs of personal computers and associated software.

Bulletin board technology is a suitable starting point for learning groups of twenty to fifty individuals who are located in a local telephone calling area. Bulletin board systems are appropriate as well for the support of specific courses or clubs in the public school communities and may be used to support counseling and tutoring.

The newer generations of personal computers can support more versatile types of communication than the shared type of posting evident on the earlier systems. As the size of the population and the amount of communications grows, there is a need, however, for richer communication structures (such as conferencing systems) to support a wider range of learning activities.

1.4.2   Electronic Mail Systems

An email system is an electronic data transfer tool to send or receive messages over networks. Additionally, more advanced email systems have Append File capabilities for attaching binary files to messages to facilitate the exchange of large amounts of information.

Most universities and colleges have campus-wide digital networks to connect all the major computers on the campus. A significant number of public school systems have them as well and have plans to provide hardware network connectivity among all educational institutions in their jurisdiction. The economic justification is usually based on the savings in communication costs and processing costs in passing the large amounts of administrative data that flow among various administrative bodies. However, it is quite common and easy to support a network-wide message capability once the hardware network is in place.

Today most universities are part of a worldwide network that allows anyone at any university to message anyone at any other university. In general, these hardware networks with email software allow communications among individuals anywhere the network extends at much cheaper rates than by telephone or even mail. In many instances, local school systems are linked to the university-based networks and, through them, to the international networks. The numerous newspaper reports of grammar school students in North America communicating with grammar school students in Japan or Russia are an example of such network economics.

The large population size and the geographical spread of these academic networks enable new and unique learning communities and learning applications. For example, students taking environmental science in different high school courses within a region, country, or continent can exchange local measurements of acid rainfall, to understand conditions, large impacts, and thereby consider sources and causes. An educator trying to use a software package can message the author for advice.

Email systems are useful for reaching specific individuals and exchanging timely information among small groups. However, any active use of message systems quickly leads to the problem of information overload. There is a certain frequency of incoming traffic above which individuals can no longer cope with a lack of organization of the material flowing in. Another limitation of message systems for educational activities is the difficulty of facilitating group work online. Email systems do not automatically organize messages according to topic or group; a record and a shared object are not available to coordinate and unify online group communication.

1.4.3   News and Topic Services

Many networks have established databases for posting messages on a particular topic, giving individuals the ability to control whether they want to access information themselves or sign up for regular delivery of the information under a topic or message group. Many academic research communities in North America now have such message news services.

The message group capability enables a dynamic group newsletter, to which any member can add information for other members. The benefits for groups (e.g., all high school biology teachers within a geographical region) are apparent; the network provides a mechanism for ongoing, interactive peer group exchange that motivates and enhances professionalism and accomplishment among educators. The problem of the geographical spread of public school teachers by specialty areas can be resolved with the technology of learning networks.

1.4.4 Computer Conferencing

The email system model lacks any mechanism to enable a group to collaborate on a joint undertaking other than exchanging isolated items of information. Computer conferencing is based on the concept that software facilities can be built into the computer to allow groups to coordinate and organize the material in a manner appropriate to their communication objectives. It thus provides groups with specific "spaces" inside the software that can be tailored to their needs. In a sense it is a virtual reality, since the tailoring of group communication structures is really the creation of a particular social system.

A computer conference is a stored transcript of a discussion by a group in easily accessible format. Each conference has access privileges set by the person who opens (creates) the conference, specifying, for example, who can be a member of the conference. Each conference provides a membership list that allows participants to tell who has read what material, so one can know where everyone is in the discussion. Some systems allow people to make changes to their earlier contributions and notify the members of any changes. Others are structured to allow different individuals to edit the same contributions or to enter anonymous contributions. Conferencing systems may also allow such functions as various types of voting. In more advanced computer conferencing systems, the person who opens a conference can designate the type of structures and facilities he or she wants to make available in a particular conference. Some systems provide sophisticated information management tools or retrieval capabilities, so the material can be reorganized to reflect different review requirements.

Computer conferencing systems can be used in face-to-face classes or to serve as the environment for classes offered entirely online. A face-to-face class might use a computer conference to augment time available for class discussion or group work. Conferencing might also be used to link students in different classes or schools. Conferences might be designated as seminars for large or small group discussion, or subgroups of students might have their own private conference to do collaborative assignments. Students across different courses might have a Student Lounge on the system for socializing; the instructors might have a Teachers' Lounge as well. A computer conferencing system serving an educational community can be designed and set up to service the particular needs of that community.

1.4.5   Directory

Learning networks need a directory service to identify the other members of the network, the types of conferences available, and the topics being explored by mutual interest groups. When one starts talking about educational populations of many hundreds or thousands, the computer must facilitate the ability of individuals to find those groups in which they wish to participate.

There are some promising advances in the field, such as Internet sites that provide directories with electronic addresses and a brief description of all Internet resources. Also, a public domain software, WEB, provides direct and easy access to all Internet sites. More resourceful directories are still needed.

1.4.6   Customized Educational Environments

Some educational institutions and private companies have begun to develop customized network environments for education, with special tools such as group support and facilitation features or decision support features. One such customized approach is the Virtual Classroom which provides several key educational facilities or controls to instructors. For example, an instructor can ask a discussion question but require that the computer prevent students from seeing the answers by others until they have made their own independent response. This constraint is easier to do in the electronic environment than in the face-to-face classroom, and it imposes equal participation by all the students in the discussion. With the incorporation of an electronic gradebook, the system can automatically notify the student of grade entries or changes, so that the instructor does not have to write separate messages to each student.

Awakening Technology, another example of a customized system, has a tailorable groupware (computer conferencing) system for pioneering online self-development seminars. It offers a full range of computer conferencing services, including custom-tailored meeting spaces and experienced facilitation for client groups. The software enables easy tailoring to implement and adjust decision support and group flow tools to fit evolving dialogue needs (see Appendix C for vendor information).

1.4.7   Computer Networks: The Internet

Computer networks are the digital highways on which CMC travels. They consist of computers linked by high-speed lines that allow signals to travel at the speed of light. Information passed from one machine to another is divided into "packets," with each packet having an origin address and a destination address, as well as contents. Packets of information from hundreds or thousands of users at a time can share the same transmission line, with the computers that are nodes in the network sorting out the packets and passing them on to their correct destination machines.

One example of a computer network is the Internet, an international network of networks, that links hundreds of smaller computer networks spanning North America, Europe, Africa, Latin America, Australia, and Asia. This vast interconnection of computers provides an extremely rich set of resources to teachers and learners. There are three main services provided by the Internet: remote log-in (Telnet), file transfer (FTP), and email.

Telnet enables remote log-in to another computer on the Internet. By giving the command Telnet and the destination, a user can remotely log into another machine on the network and run the programs on that machine. For example, a conferencing program on a remote computer can be accessed through Telnet, assuming that one has a valid membership (ID and password) to join that conferencing system. (Many systems offer a restricted "guest" log-in status for users wanting to check out the available information.)

The Internet is run as a cooperative with a membership fee for each organization based on its size. When an organization joins, it makes its system available as a transfer point and as a node that others might potentially use for remote log-ins. There are no communications charges for the user (unlike a long-distance telephone call). With such access, instructors can locate materials for use in courses. For example, they might log into an online public access catalog, of which there are more than 200 on Internet.

The FTP is used as an alternative to email to move large files (e.g., software programs, digitized pictures, digitized sound) between computers. When downloading software or information, one must respect any copyright protections. For example, some software available via FTP is called "shareware": a potential user may download it and try it out free of charge, but if he or she decides to keep and use it, there is a fee or charge, sent to its creator or copyright holder.

Electronic mail is one of the Internet's most frequently used services. Indeed, many business cards now include an email address. Email can even be sent between machines that are part of a different network, with a gateway machine linking the two networks.

Although there are no comprehensive directories that list all or even most Internet information and interpersonal resources, there are many tools that can greatly assist in locating information on the Internet. Here we look at four such tools: Gopher, Veronica, Archie, and Jughead. (For further information, see Appendix E, or consult columns such as "Mining the Internet" in the journal *Computing Teacher*.)

Gopher is a user-friendly menu-driven information organizer that will "go-for" or "dig around"and retrieve whatever information the user seeks, even if the user does not know where that information may be located on the Internet. With Gopher, a user can travel around various Internet sites without needing to know their specific addresses. Gophers are multilevel menu systems that automatically make connections to other Internet sites to obtain the information requested. Users can browse the information available, save that information to a file on a local account, or capture the session to a log file. There are many Gopher sites on the Internet that are open for public use, accessible by Telnet or by a Gopher residing on one's local system.

Archie, another information location tool that is now resident on many Gopher servers, was developed at McGill University to allow users to locate information in file archives on the Internet by file name. Archie tools can be accessed using Telnet commands or by accessing Gophers that list Archie as a menu option. The user need only know part of the file name, and the Archie tool will help retrieve it. If the user does not know the file name as it is listed in the file archive, then the related tools, named for Archie's comic book companions Veronica and Jughead, can help.

Veronica, also available on Gopher servers, allows users to search for information by topic. Users can also use simple Boolean operators such as *and*, *or*, and *not*, to focus their search. Jughead is a related information tool that allows users to search for Gopher subdirectory names that include specified search terms.

1.4.8   National Research and Education Network

Although the Internet is growing exponentially, many education, academic, and research organizations are not connected. The U.S. National Research and Education Network (NREN), currently being developed, should be fully operational in the next decade, to be the successor to the research and education portion of the Internet in the United States.

When operational, NREN will provide data transmission at very high speeds, over hair-thin glass fibers at thousands of times the speed of the Internet. From home-based computers, users will be able to contact a variety of online services, from email to a selection and home delivery of videos, music, and entertainment. The NREN will raise the capacity of the Internet to more than 3 billion bits per second—the equivalent of 300 copies of *Moby Dick* or an entire encyclopedia could be transferred in 3 seconds, up from the Internet's current capacity of 45 million bits. New communications applications are also being developed to operate over the high-speed data highways.

1.4.9   Learning Networks

The application of any or all of these CMC technologies to the learning process is accomplished by learning networks. The basic building block of a learning network is the CMC system that sustains it. Learning networks may be launched successfully with basic CMC tools such as email. However, as a learning network can represent an entire educational institution or infrastructure (for online course activity, etc.) integrating other computer and information resources along with the communications capabilities will provide a richer array of tools for students and teachers. Along with the capabilities offered by email, bulletin boards, news services, directories, and computer conferencing, there is a need for such facilities as databases, analysis capabilities, information management facilities, and multimedia tools to support all the processes that can take place in a learning environment. Such integrated systems may be somewhat costly for many educational institutions, but costs are coming down at a fairly rapid rate. Moreover, learning networks range from simple text communication networks to sophisticated, powerful multimedia systems.

1.5   Fits and Misfits: The Medium and the Message

Some types of course material and teaching techniques are so perfectly matched to the characteristics of network learning that once an educator has tried it, she or he will not want to be without it. Others are manageable but are best undertaken with a combination of media.

A wide variety of subject matter, from anthropology to engineering, has been successfully offered online, including some that might at first seem difficult to do via this medium. The real question, though, is not whether a course *can* be done online but what is the best media mix to achieve the goals of the course within the constraints of the available resources or geographic dispersion of the students. More fundamentally, how should the media be used? What approaches to teaching and learning are most effective in a computer networking environment?

To address the latter question first, a learner-centered (rather than teacher-centered) model has been found as the best fit online. CMC is meant for the sharing and building of ideas, information, and skills among the participants to strengthen knowledge building, integration, and application of conceptual information. CMC is not suited to using the computer in a drill-and-practice mode, whereby the student interacts only with the computer. Drill-and-practice tasks that aid memorization by repetition are more appropriately conducted by CAI or CBT (computer-based training) programs.

CMC can be used for the transmission of lengthy lecture-type material, but because reading, screen after screen of material, with no opportunity to respond, is difficult and boring, this form of communication is better accomplished by textbooks or printed materials. And obviously, as a text-based medium, CMC does not easily transmit visual or auditory material. This is better done with videotapes, audiotapes, or CD-ROM and videodiscs, particularly if face-to-face meetings cannot be combined with online work.

Any course that emphasizes in-depth coverage and discussion of materials can be effectively conducted entirely online, as can any course with extensive writing assignments. The sharing of ideas and collaborative tasks, such as seminars or joint writing, are particularly effective online. Generally these activities use discussion, brainstorming, problem solving, group work, and reflective or analytical contributions based on special projects or research. Courses that use computer tools that can be installed on the PCs of participants (such as a spreadsheet program for courses in accounting or a Pascal compiler for courses in computer science) are also successful online. Even a course in music appreciation can be taught online: students might receive audiocassettes with the various arrangements and use the computer conferencing system for group discussions and group assignments. Audio conferences might be incorporated to supplement the audiocassettes and computer conferencing activities.

For foreign language learning, students must acquire the ability not only to read and write in the language, which can be done online, but also to speak and to understand the spoken language. Verbal and listening skills can be fostered by combining media. For instance, at Arizona State University, Spanish courses are offered through a combination of computer conferencing for written language skills, and audiotapes with workbooks, to listen to the language and to send tapes to the instructor with spoken-language exercises for evaluation. At Oklahoma State University, two versions of a French course were planned: one that would use videotapes to teach the spoken language, in combination with computer conferencing, for distance education students; and one for on-campus students that would use a limited number of face-to-face class meetings to teach spoken language skills. Both would use computer conferencing for practice with the written language, with all online communication carried out in French.

In Canada, high school teachers have used a bilingual (French/English) computer conferencing system to encourage student writing and language arts. Anglophone students in a Toronto high school communicated online with Francophone counterparts in a Montreal high school, in both languages. The opportunity to communicate with peers in a different city motivated students to pursue, with significant enthusiasm, what is typically a difficult and tedious task: writing and reading in a foreign language. The language classes became a source of great excitement and effort by the students; peer networking made foreign language learning come alive.

Mathematics and statistics might at first seem difficult to teach online. Two totally online courses in statistics, one at Upsala College and one at the New Jersey Institute of Technology (NJIT), handled the problem of mathematical symbols in different ways. At NJIT, students used a special PC-based "front end" that allowed them to type and read mathematical symbols from their keyboard, for some assignments that required mathematical notation. All NJIT students had the same IBM-compatible microcomputer, so they could simply be given the program. Upsala students did not have their own computers, and the equipment they used was very mixed (Apple IIs, IBM-PCs, and Macintoshes), so for the portions of the course that required the use of mathematical symbols, the instructor sent photocopies of the lecture-type material and homework problems through the mail, and the students mailed back their individual assignments.

No advanced computer skills are needed in these uses. Students who are unfamiliar with computers need an extra week or two at the beginning of the course to become comfortable with the technology, but almost everybody can begin to use these systems productively after a few hours of practice. Instructors should be comfortable with the basic operations of the system before the course begins, so they can help students who encounter difficulties.

With the aid of special equipment, disabled students and teachers can benefit from using this medium. For instance, students with cerebral palsy were provided with special keyboard guards to help prevent accidental keystrokes and with various input devices to serve as an alternative for those who could not use their hands. And in colleges and universities around the world, blind students participate actively, using Braille keyboards and voice-output devices.

The most important characteristic for student success in this medium is motivation. If the student wants to learn the subject enough to make the time to sign on and if the student has adequate reading and writing skills, the outlook is for success. There is no subject matter that cannot benefit from being taught partially or wholly online. A second factor is the creativity and effort of instructors to create a course design that involves active learning by the students and incorporates collaborative learning components.

1.6   Learning Outcomes

The traditional face-to-face classroom learning situation is generally-assumed to be the best to support learning, with other learning modes perhaps perceived as less effective. There is no evidence to support this assumption. In fact, quite the opposite is true: Online environments facilitate learning outcomes that are equal or superior to those generated in the face-to-face situation (Hiltz 1988a, 1994; Wells 1990).

Online interactions share many characteristics with face-to-face education: input of ideas, class discussions, debates, and other forms of knowledge building through interaction and exchange. The content of the curriculum can be organized topically and sequentially, over time, and students can work in full class groups, small groups, dyads, or individually. Teachers have access to the various forms of discussions and course activities. They have as well features distinct from those of face-to-face interactions: participants are geographically dispersed and share their expertise and ideas in a many-to-many, text-based, and asynchronous environment (Harasim 1990a).

The asynchronicity of online interactions allows participants time to reflect on a topic before commenting or carrying out online tasks. In some network systems, the learner can participate in group discussion only through making an initial comment on the topic. This "introduction" to group discussion with a first thoughtful comment (neither a response nor a critique to someone else's comments) promotes active participation of members.

In research on online graduate courses in education, students identified the following benefits in learning (Harasim 1987):

• Increased interaction: quantity and intensity

"To me, the major success of this course has been the truly interactive involvement through the medium. There was always a large support group (including peers and instructors) to respond to technical, academic, and even emotional (morale-boosting) needs. I've never been involved in a course in which I've learned so much from other students. This was because there was no competition for the floor and therefore everyone was able to have her say. Also, as remarks were all documented, they were subject to more in-depth consideration than in the normal classroom."

• Better access to group knowledge and support

"The information exchange is more diverse in that input is coming from everyone rather than only from the instructor." "I learned much more than in a regular three-hour course because of the interaction of all the students in the course. It is much more enriching this way. Through this medium we could tap the combined knowledge of the group."

• More democratic environment

"In online discussions, I think that there is a tendency to respond to content rather than to personalities."
"Conferencing as a course vehicle promotes more equal interaction among participants, dropping barriers of geography, urban/rural styles, social skills, mannerisms."

• Convenience of access

"I find myself thinking about the ideas in the online class more because there is no three-hour limit of class time."
"Being able to bring course material and participants into my own environment has allowed me to make it more a part of my life than one in which I participate at a great distance, in time and space, from my own setting. My reflections from the course are interacting constantly with my everyday life, at home and at the school where I teach."

• Increased motivation

"I am cold. I need to clean my lenses and I am thirsty. Yet, I'm still here. Know why this is better than TV—the anticipation of a good show, great cast of characters, fast-moving plot, thought-provoking and, like a serial, the end is not in view."

1.6.1   Active Learning

Active learning is a major outcome of learning networks. "Attendance" in a learning network activity both requires and enables active input. Even at the level of mechanics, the learner must keep actively involved: paying attention, pressing keys. However, active learning is more than just pressing keys: it is social and cognitive engagement. Participation is based on making input, responding to peers, and sharing ideas. A learner is socially present online only when she or he makes a comment. Those who read but do not comment are sometimes referred to as "lurkers," and other members of the conference are likely to cajole or encourage lurkers into active participation. Teachers may allocate a grade for online participation, thereby providing incentives and acknowledging student effort to learn the system and formulate a comment.

Active participation strengthens learning. Putting ideas or information into written form requires intellectual effort and generally aids comprehension and retention. Formulating and articulating a statement is a cognitive act, a process that is particularly valuable if comments such as "I don't agree" or "I do agree" are followed by "because . . ."

Making comments requires the learner to pull ideas and thoughts into a coherent form; this is intellectual work. Once the statement has been made and presented in the public forum of a conference or email network, it may well receive follow-up comments, such as requesting clarification and expansion or expressing disagreement for various reasons. Such exchange on an idea will require that the original author or another participant defend, refine, or acknowledge some fault in the position in a process of cognitive restructuring. The interaction activates intellectual processing and reflection on the idea.

Because online learning communities are always open, there is wide opportunity to participate and to refine and reflect on ideas. In the traditional classroom, only one person at a time may speak, and many people who would like to contribute are never called on. In the online environment each student can comment whenever he or she wants.

Moreover, ideas can be developed interactively, over time. Unlike the one-time-only chance to speak up in a typical lecture class, an online student can make many comments over the course of several hours or

days. Primary and secondary school students similarly have the opportunity to pursue and develop an idea. The result is that many discussions
may be proceeding simultaneously. The online classroom is always open.
This expanded access to learning peers and activities encourages reflection and interaction on ideas and building of knowledge.

1.6.2   Collaborative Learning

Collaborative learning refers to any activity in which two or more people work together to create meaning, explore a topic, or improve skills.
In a traditional course environment, most assignments are carried out as
private communications between an individual learner and the teacher.
There is a clear division of labor and authority between the "teacher"
and the "learner," and learning is usually a solitary activity. Since most
homework is done outside class, it is difficult to have groups of students
work together. Collaborative learning activities are possible face to face,
but they are limited by the logistics of students' being able to arrange to
meet. With CMC, practically all course activities can be designed as collaborative activities. Through formulating information or ideas in their
own words, and receiving feedback and evaluation on these formula-
tions from peers, knowledge, thinking skills, and meanings are socially
constructed. (Table 1.1 compares the collaborative and traditional
approaches.)

A practical definition of collaborative learning is any learning activity
that is carried out using peer interaction, evaluation, and/or cooperation,
with at least some structuring and monitoring by the instructor. In
designing an online course, the creative challenge to the instructor is to
rethink the syllabus in order to build in as many collaborative activities
as possible. These can range from full-class discussions and projects to
pairs of students working together on an assignment. At Upsala College,
a statistics course for freshmen was taught online. In the traditional
classroom, students were given a data set and asked to carry out a series
of assignments individually on this data set, such as finding the frequency distributions, means, and standard deviations of the variables. In
the online mode, one of the first activities was to take an online survey
about the characteristics and opinions of the students. The students thus
created the information that became the sample data for their practice.
For the first assignment, the instructor did not give the students a for-

Table 1.1
Collaborative versus traditional approaches to teaching: A writing course (based on Clifford 1981).

	Collaborative	Traditional
Role of instructor	Goal-setter Instructional designer Facilitator Resource Model Learner	Teacher Evaluator
Class structure	Students in groups from two to whole class	Individual students seated in rows
Text	Contributions generated by students and teacher in addition to textbooks	Commercial textbooks and published works
Audience	Students writing for each other	Students writing only for the instructor
Lecturing	Student-centered approach based on discussion of issues and questions raised by students	Formal lessons (e.g., grammar and rhetoric)
Revision	An ongoing process based on feedback from group members	Suggestions given by instructor after completed paper has been submitted
Evaluation	Evaluated by class members, including the instructor	Evaluated by instructor alone
Collaboration	Students work with peers guided and advised by instructor	Students work alone or with instructor only

mula or step-by-step instructions. Rather he gave them an objective and a reference to chapters in their text and asked them to suggest which statistics would be appropriate to the data and the objective, and why. The group thus arrived at an understanding of which statistics to use and why, rather than being told what to do by the instructor.

Collaborative learning changes the whole nature of the teaching-learning process and the teacher-student relationship. The educator becomes less an authority figure and more a resource and facilitator for the learning activities of the group.

1.6.3   Learning Communities

The community that forms among network users can be both personally and educationally enriching. Many people who enter a learning network for the first time fear they will find an impersonal, dehumanized space. The social reality of the environment frequently comes as a complete surprise. The communication flows enabled by the networks bring friendship, comradeship, intellectual stimulation, and personal satisfaction. Friendships are formed as the network becomes a "place" to share insights and concerns, problems and solutions, enthusiasms and fears.

Traditional face-to-face courses are short and time to interact is scarce, but the learning network is always available and always there when needed. Since everyone has a chance to "speak," students report that online environments enable them to communicate with their colleagues more than in face-to-face classes. This is especially true for students at the high school and tertiary education levels. The text-based nature of the medium has been credited with contributing to personalizing the medium; there is a letter-writing and sometimes even diary-like quality to online communication. Users personalize the medium by sharing information about themselves and focusing on shared interests. Community members come to know one another as individuals and friends. Text-based interactions focus on the meaning of the message rather than the physical cues such as race, gender, age, physical appearance, or dress of the sender, thereby reducing some of the discriminatory cues of face-to-face communication.

The place-independent nature of network communication offers an opportunity to learn about others and about oneself. An example from the RAPPI network is illustrative. Two classrooms were linked for exchange and discussion: a high school in northern Ontario and a high school in northern Italy. The students began with the typical greetings and self-introductions. Questions soon followed: What is your favorite food? Who is your favorite singer? Describe your city. Penpals in both countries came to realize that they knew little about their own culture as distinct from another culture. They had taken their world and their ideas for granted, as representing how the world really was. Now they sought to gather more information about themselves to share with their electronic penpals. The students in both schools developed a poll to collect data from schoolmates on their interests, concerns, favorite singers, and fashions. In describing their community, the students in northern Ontario discovered that the oldest structure was about 100 years old; the students in northern Italy noted that the oldest structure in their city was an aqueduct, over 1,000 years old.

As the exchanges continued, the level of discussion deepened, each side curious to discuss issues that confronted them and to learn how these same issues were viewed by counterparts in different cultures. Their exploration of political, social, and personal issues illuminated the other culture and way of seeing things and made each side more aware of its own identity and views.

Educational researchers have noted that learning networks linking urban and rural schools in different parts of the country or the world offer advantages for promoting students' writing:

• They create a functional environment for writing, one in which clear and interesting writing is essential for communicating with other students.

• The differences in life-styles and beliefs among students make it important to write good descriptive accounts of their everyday activities.

• The joint production of an electronic newsletter promotes collaboration among students and necessitates careful reading, revising, and editing (Riel 1983; Levin et al., 1984).

Bilingual networks of students can provide authentic contexts for writing in the native language and in the second language (Sayers 1989).

For students in universities, colleges, distance education programs, or training courses, learning networks may be the only opportunity for a learning community that they will encounter. Because the majority of students are working and/or have families and commute to campus, they typically never get to talk to classmates and instructors outside class settings. For example, at NJIT, only a minority of students live on campus. At graduation, individual students and their families form the social groupings; few bonds among the students are developed even in the years of face-to-face classes. On the other hand, students from an online management course had formed such close bonds that they gathered for a farewell party after the graduation ceremony. The online learning community that had formed on the network had been more lasting for the students than bonds formed through traditional courses.

There is growing recognition that learning is enhanced by small-group activities and by the ability of individual learners to work in heterogeneous groups to gain differing perspectives and experiences. This is as true for primary school children in Kansas interacting with peers in Russia as it is for a university student in engineering interacting with a sociology student. The development of learning communities provides the realization of group learning processes on a scale previously inconceivable.

2

Networks for Schools: Exemplars and Experiences

2.1 Models for Network School Learning

Network learning uses a variety of learning models, designs, and approaches that aim at structuring and sequencing the learning process and providing support to the learner when it is needed. Rather than focus mainly on the teacher as the central figure for instructional delivery, most network models emphasize peer discussion and interaction and access to online resources.

2.1.1 Mentorship

Mentorship is a traditional teaching method that for centuries has been used to teach intellectual and physical skills. When this apprenticeship learning model is applied to learning networks, the learner is called a teleapprentice who learns using various medium-appropriate approaches (Levin 1990). The online apprentice reads the messages, asks questions, obtains clarification, reflects on the theme, responds to questions, and further explores the topic in order to master the learning task. He or she may be asked to teach a topic or to provide summaries of group discussion. In the process of teaching, the apprentice develops metacognitive strategies, such as the ability to generalize and apply a particular concept to a variety of contexts. Network learners often refer to their learning projects as real-world situations or real problem-solving situations, noting that CMC brings the real world into the classroom. When provided with systematic design and guided coaching, online apprentices can develop active learning practices and achieve improved learning outcomes.

2.1.2   Access to Experts

In learning networks, students send messages with specific questions to experts in a given area. The "quick access to difficult information" and "the positive feedback of getting the question answered," explained one teacher, are the main benefits of this model. One difficulty with this activity has been occasional slow responses from experts, which could cause students to lose interest.

Various networks have a version of an "ask-an-expert" conference, with students engaging in short question-and-answer interactions with experts (Dr. Tree, Dr. Fish, Dr. Spider, etc.) who are available online to answer any questions in their area.

2.1.3   Access to Key Information

The use of online services, databases (commercial and noncommercial), and libraries to access information on specialized topics is a valuable resource on learning networks. The learner does an online search on a topic, accesses the information, and saves it to a file for later use.

Access to databases is important for supplementing libraries with current information and resources. One elementary networker librarian noted: "The school libraries are not up-to-date, and they can't be anyway. There is so much new information that a library cannot keep up and access to databases through telecommunications is needed. I think that in the near future all libraries will have to have access to information technologies."

The Internet provides thousands of free access databases that students can use to access information in particular fields. The AskERIC Service is one such tool. Sponsored by the Educational Resources Information Center (ERIC), a federally funded national information system that provides access to an extensive body of education-related resources, Clearinghouse on Information Resources (ERIC/IR), AskERIC is designed to develop and study Internet-based education information services, systems, and resources that best meet the needs of end users from kindergarten to grade 12. It provides a question-and-answer service for elementary school teachers, library media specialists, and administrators. AskERIC staff will respond to an email message with an answer within forty-eight working hours drawing on the extensive resources of the ERIC system. Questions about K-to-12 education, learning, teaching, information technology, and educational administration can be sent to: askeric@ericir.syr.edu. (Other free-of-charge databases that can be accessed through Internet are listed in Appendix A.)

2.1.4   Collaborative Projects

In the collaborative model, each student has a particular role in the learning project, and various groups work over the network to implemented shared projects.

The Writers' Link illustrates online peer collaboration to support writing skills enhancement for grade 4 and 5 students. Students submit their short stories to peer editors, who receive the story over the network, read and evaluate it, and provide feedback on the submission. The peer editors are three to four students in a single classroom who meet face to face to discuss the submission and write the feedback. The expressed purpose of the program is to provide real audiences for student work; it also reinforces editing skills learned in the process writing portion of the language arts curriculum. Here is an example of peer editor feedback, written by grade 4 students:

To Katrina

Story's name: The Blanket

We like the ending of your story because you said you like your blanket that is warm and cuddly. We think you could take out some of the "we, this, and the's" so it will sound a little better. And also have a more descriptive beginning sentence and another sentence. We also think you should write more because we can't see the whole picture in the paragraph you wrote. It was kind of descriptive: we can see the kitten on the blanket and the blanket on the bed.

Your editors,

Melanie, Lisa, and Wayne—Kidston Elementary

Other forms of collaborative learning used on networks are role plays and simulations. In an environmental course, one group of students played the role of defending the interests of a logging company while another group played the environmentalists in an ongoing debate. Students worked in their own electronic space to produce class presentations, which they then submitted to the entire class for debate and responded to the arguments. The exercise served to deepen understanding of the impact of forestry practices on the environment and the economy.

2.2   Networked Classrooms

There are various learning networks for kindergarten to grade 12, some commercial and others free, funded through public support or governmental funds. Here we illustrate the networked classroom approach with case examples.

2.2.1   The AT&T Learning Network

The AT&T Learning Network (formerly the AT&T Long Distance Learning Network) is a commercial service that supports curricular activities of grades 3 to 12 in many different countries. It is owned by the AT&T Corporation and uses proprietary electronic mail software. The network is based on AT&T mail and offers an easy-to-use interface that downloads all new messages to the school computer. The software has a built-in database where the messages are placed and can be retrieved at any time. Students respond to the messages offline, and the software automatically uploads the messages and sends them along the network to the addresses. The uploading and downloading features of the interface are easy to use and reduce the time online, thereby also reducing telecommunications charges. This interface facilitates the use of a local word processor for writing.

The educational design of the network is based on the Learning Circle, a structured activity used in teaching curriculum areas such as geography, history, and English (table 2.1). Each circle is composed of six to eight classrooms working on a common curricular topic. These classrooms are in different locations (even different countries). Typically, interested teachers or schools commit their classrooms to the project by contacting the sponsoring organization. In one example, a learning circle was made up of classrooms from Alaska, California, Texas, Florida, Illinois, and New York, plus Canada and Germany. A school pays approximately $190 per classroom to participate in one six- to fifteen-week program.

Table 2.1
Activities on the AT&T Learning Network, 1993

Learning circle choices	Curriculum area	Grade level	Length (weeks)
Classroom connections	Cross-curricular	E M H	6
Mind works	Whole language creative and expository writing	E M H	11 or 15
Computer chronicles	Journalism Language arts Cross-curricular writing	E M H	11 or 15
Places and perspectives	History Geography Culture Government	E M H	11 or 15
Energy and the environment	Science Social studies Current issues	E M H	11 or 15
Society's problems	Social studies	M H	11 or 15
Global issues	Current issues Social studies Science Economics	H	11 or 15

Note: E = elementary school; M = middle school; H = high school

In the Mind Works unit, students hone their writing skills by collaboratively composing, revising, and editing their compositions. At the end of fifteen weeks of sharing their work, they download and print a creative writing journal, with contributions from all schools in the circle. Under Global Issues they discussed the Gulf War and U.S. elections. In Places and Perspectives, students discuss environmental issues of concern to the whole planet with participants from different countries.

One classroom teacher serves as learning circle coordinator. The coordinator sends "welcome messages" by email to the circle members to facilitate the interaction among teachers and students, to provide guidance, and to monitor the progress of participants. Coordinators receive no fee for the work but are given special privileges on the network and participate in an online group for coordinators only.

Teachers who join a circle select a curriculum area and then receive a package containing software and instructions on how to access the network, the curriculum guide, detailed instructions on how to collaborate with their online peers, and sometimes photographs of participating schools, teachers, and students. Once they get online, participating members introduce themselves and begin planning the interaction and launch the curriculum activities. The coordinator ensures that every classroom is actively participating and that the discussion relates to the subject area. The final product is a report produced by participants, which is exchanged with all the other members. Once activities are concluded, that circle is closed.

The AT&T Learning Network uses a structured group activity approach to learning, with emphasis on integration with the curriculum. Students can also establish penpal activities through the network, but the messages exchanged are public, not private. Another advantage of this network is the global reach, enabling participants to interact with people elsewhere. One teacher noted, "We had access to children from a number of exotic places through the AT&T Network and just because of that the students became quite excited. But after a while they realized that the most important aspect of the program was the exchange of ideas and the fact that they were dealing with kids who were very much like them."

2.2.2 Southern Interior Telecommunications Project (SITP)

A consortium of schools in the southern interior of British Columbia, Canada, organized to pilot-test educational computer networking in 1990. Approximately 3,000 students and 300 teachers and librarians, from over 100 primary and secondary schools, are involved. The project is a public network and has the support of a provincial education technology center, several corporate partners, a university, and the provincial Ministry of Education. Many other Canadian provinces, U.S. states, and other regional educational systems are installing or planning similar learning networks. Thus, the SITP can serve as a model for such networks for kindergarten to grade 12.

The objective of the SITP project is to provide teachers and students with information and telecommunication technologies to assist the teaching-learning process. Long-term goals include the use of information technology to assist teacher training, the support of educational administration, and the use of the technology to service the needs of teachers and students, and the local community. Three curricular areas received particular attention in the first two years: English, environmental studies, and law. Teachers also use the network for professional development activities such as exchanging lesson plans, discussing joint educational projects, and accessing information relevant to teaching.

The SITP project provides a wide variety of online resources to teachers and learners, including a computer conferencing system, email, bulletin board services, various commercial services, online databases, and access to the Internet (figure 2.1). Two types of computer network accounts were given in the first year of the project: teacher accounts and school accounts. Students used school accounts. In the second year, selected students were given personal accounts. Online participants can find expertise, penpals, colleagues, peers, programs, and a multitude of information resources.

The project uses a combination of mentorship, ask-an-expert, access to relevant information, simulation and role playing, and collaborative work to support student learning. To facilitate online interaction, mod-

---

**Welcome to the Southern Interior
Telecommunications Project:**

1.	PARTI	Participate Conferences
2.	DIALOG	Dialog Classmate Database
3.	FREENET	Cleveland Community Services
4.	NASA	NASA Spacelink
5.	SOUTHAM	Southam Infomart Online
6.	TIX	Technical Information Exchange
7.	WEB	Environment Network
8.	XCHANGE	Simon Fraser University Exchange
9.	UNIXMAIL	E-Mail Services

Figure 2.1
SIPT online menu

erators and mentors are hired to work with teachers and students in the network environment.

Students have access to a variety of experts, such as scientists (Dr. Fish, Dr. Spider), academics, lawyers (the Legal Beagles support students taking a law course), and professional writers. Students taking English courses, for example, can submit their essays and poems to professional writers in conferences such as the Writers in Electronic Residence or the Online Mentor. Students receive feedback, advice, and encouragement from writing experts as well as suggestions from other students on how to improve their writing. Collaborative work is part of the project. In the science project Salmonids Online, students follow a schedule to do water quality analysis, to exchange the results via the network, and to discuss better options for increasing the health and numbers of salmon.

Simulations, games, and role playing are also often used in network learning. For example, students in Law-12 in British Columbia use mock trials, "a simulation version of a criminal or civil case that ends up in court for settlement. All of the major characters found in a real trial are assumed by 'actors'—defense lawyers, Crown prosecutors, the judge, the accused, the witnesses, the court clerk, the court reporter, the sheriff, and the jury (if required)" (Kissner and Joanne 1990). Some of the activities are conducted online and others face-to-face in individual classrooms. The SITP project implemented various mock trials on learning networks to support the provincial Law-12 curriculum.

The Treasures of the Southern Interior program is an online game designed to allow students to analyze interesting items of information about other communities in the southern interior region of the province. The program is designed to "allow students to discover how to initiate and observe changes in their local environments using electronic communication systems as vehicles for accurate research and for communicating with resource persons, students, and teachers involved in similar activities in the region and across the province" (Teles and Duxbury 1992).

Training is provided to teachers, students, and staff participating in the SITP to teach them how to use this medium to organize classroom-based activities. SITP teachers and students are now conversant with the technology, and its potential and limits. The project benefited from an initial core group of committed teachers, librarians, and principals who were willing to introduce the technology to schools and to survive the technical difficulties as the technology was implemented.

One of the main reasons attributed to high-level activity in such conferences as Wired-Writers, Law-Forum, and Ask-an-Expert was the quality of online moderation. When moderators were actively involved—responding regularly, posting new material, encouraging activities and discussions—students responded with enthusiasm and regular participation. Another important factor is the link with the curriculum: students were most active in conferences dealing with topics in which they found a strong personal interest or relationship to their curriculum.

Teachers have also been active in using technology for professional development. Approximately 60 percent of the teachers involved in the project had access to a computer and modem at home, either through computer equipment borrowed from school or their own personal computers. Data collected in the first year of the project showed that the online system was used twenty-four hours a day (figure 2.2).

The SITP project is based on teacher initiative to generate online projects, an approach that has been successful. In the second year (1991–

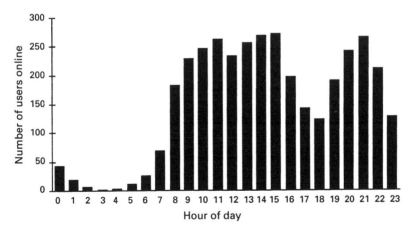

Figure 2.2
SIPT usage by hour of day (November 28, 1990–June 30, 1991)

1992) approximately fourteen projects were generated by teachers, including Salmonids Online, a waste management conference dedicated to recycling, a business simulation program with online discussions, and the Writers' Link.

One of the major lessons of the project is the importance of instructional design to coordinate online and classroom curriculum activities. Learning networks are successful when there are links to curricular activities and classroom management models, plus political and administrative willingness to integrate these learning environments. Commitment by the school administration significantly eases the introduction of learning networks into the curriculum.

Teachers are central to the process of implementation. As learning networks are increasingly adopted as part of the learning process, teachers will need corresponding support to integrate these new tools into their teaching and professional development activities.

2.2.3   The National Geographic Kids Network

In 1986, the National Geographic Society, the National Science Foundation, and the Technical Education Research Center (TERC) in the United States launched the National Geographic Kids Network, or KIDSNet, an international network designed to support science, social studies, and geography curriculum for K to 12 students. This network aims to foster the spirit of discovery and to encourage students to investigate new ideas by allowing them to conduct original research into topics of scientific, geographic, and social significance. Topics such as acid rain, water quality, garbage, and others are studied over a period of six weeks.

In a Hello! curriculum unit students are introduced to scientific research methods, telecommunications, and the computer tools used in science and business today. In What's in Our Water? students learn about the source of their school tapwater, examine the water, and look for pollutants. Other units are Solar Energy, What Are We Eating? Acid Rain, and Too Much Trash?

KIDSNet uses computer networking to combine group learning in communications, geography, weather, and the environment with local hands-on activity and supports the implementation of collaborative experiments among schools from all over the world. The results of the local experiments are sent to a central computer, where the data are processed and compared with results of other schools. The processed data from all schools are sent back to the students, who then compare all of the results. When they examine network data, "students discover how human activity affects the environment and how the environment affects human activity. With the help of a professional scientist, students investigate and try to explain reasons for geographic variations in the data" (National Geographic Kids Network 1992).

KIDSNet uses a combination of easy-to-use software (developed by TERC) and links to curriculum units. The managing editor for software of the National Geographic Society attributes Kids Network success to a blend of "curricular ingredients that had long been favored by educational researchers but that had failed to win acceptance in typical classrooms: reliance on hands-on experiments and discussion rather than on textbooks; interdisciplinary connections and extensions; students working in small collaborative groups; depth of thinking rather than breadth of facts; emphasis on science process skills, particularly building and testing hypotheses and analyzing data" (Brasher 1992).

Each KIDSNet account provides access to an eight-week period on the network (toll free in the United States) and 120 minutes of telecommunications time, a period that should accommodate thirty students and their data. Students are assigned to a team for conducting an experiment. The resultant data are analyzed by a scientist and results discussed with students.

The KIDSNet programs involve students in word processing skills, collaborative learning, report preparation, and communication and analytical skills. Approximately 250,000 students have used KIDSNet since its inception in 1986. Teachers and librarians also use the network to communicate and to exchange information. KIDSNet is available to educators all over the world.

2.2.4 Writers in Electronic Residence

The Writers in Electronic Residence (WIER) program links writing and language arts students in Canada with writers, teachers, and one another in an exchange of original writing and commentary. The writers, well-known authors in Canada, join students and their teachers in a computer conferencing environment. They read and consider the student works, offer reactions and ideas, and guide discussions between the students.

WIER was created in the 1987–1988 school year at the Riverdale Collegiate Institute, an inner-city secondary school in Toronto, Ontario. The program began after successful trials involving mail-based exchanges between writers and students, undertaken on SwiftCurrent, a Canadian electronic literary magazine used by writers in Canada in the 1980s. The WIER project was established at and supported through its first five years by the faculty of education at Simon Fraser University (SFU) and in 1993 was assumed by the faculty of education at York University (Owen 1993a).

WIER is now a national program in Canada and operates in some seventy schools with thirteen writers. There are programs for elementary school (Canadian grades 1–6), middle school (grades 7–9), and secondary school students (grades 10–12) and some postsecondary involvement through the community college system, as well as in teacher education programs in a form of "virtual practicum" (Owen 1989).

Students compose their original writing and responses to the writing of others before connecting to WIER, which runs on a host computer at York University, Toronto. Schools are able to connect with a local area call, via commercial data networks in Canada or via the Internet. Most of the original writing is poetry and short fiction, and students are encouraged to submit works they consider to be in draft stages rather than finished works in order to sustain the value of their interactions with writers and others on the system. Another reason is that issues regularly emerge that encourage writing in other forms, often in response to particular issues or concerns expressed in one or more of the submissions. Not surprisingly, textual discussions develop online in which students explore their ideas with one another.

In each of its projects WIER embraces telecommunications in general, and computer conferencing in particular, as a textual medium capable of promoting considered response through written expression and interaction to build a reflective community, both online and in the classroom. Throughout its existence, this goal has been guided by three primary learning objectives for students:

1. To be in control of the media before them and to utilize these media to broaden the shape and scope of the classroom experience.

2. To consider the value of revision in the writing process and the role that they may play in this—both for themselves and for others—using language to interpret and understand as well as to be understood.

3. To revisit their thoughts in the light of the ideas they receive and to respond in the textual environment that online computer conferencing systems offer them.

On any given day, students attending schools from Baffin Island in Canada's high Arctic, to urban centers in the south, and from Newfoundland in the east to British Columbia in the west, offer their own work for reading and comment by the writers and other participants in the program. The student writing reveals that Canadian identity is at least partly the result of where each person is from, illustrated, for instance, by how Inuit students from Baffin Island express notions about survival. Their ideas are quite different from those expressed by students who may identify themselves as Canadian-born Chinese from Toronto schools. And they are quite different from Vietnamese students who write about war, the boats, and escape and betrayal yet also search for ways to express fond memories of family and home, the value of trust, and the details of life in Hanoi. Still others consider equity and gender, race, freedom of expression, and other issues of importance to young people (Owen 1991).

Owen notes that the idea of the electronic residency was rooted in the nature of interaction as he had seen it on SwiftCurrent rather more than in an embrace of the technology that sustained it. "I saw the electronic residency as a forum of interaction in which the experience and expertise of all participants engaged them in a common task. This distinguished it from other online programs, like the 'ask-an-expert' model, which I saw as an imaginative use of what was essentially a technological notion— that distance and time could be overcome by technology" (1993b).

The electronic residency frames mentorship activity by task and interaction. In it, the role of the writer is to serve as a kind of first among equals in a field of interested participants. Not surprisingly, the role of the student is neither accurately nor usefully described as novice. Rather, students are asked to bring their "expertise"—or experience—to the online forum.

Email-based interactions tend to accept notes in the same ways that face-to-face interactions accept conversation, without too much concern for grammatical structure, or spelling/typos, and so on. However, computer conferencing is distinguished from mail in its ability to sustain opportunities for many-to-many communication. There is a greater opportunity to engage in what Owen has called "considered response" or what might now also be thought of as reflection through writing.

2.2.5 SchoolNet: Creating a Learning Network Nation in Canada

SchoolNet, an educational networking project launched by the federal government of Canada in August 1993, is designed to enhance educational opportunities and achievements in elementary and secondary schools across Canada by electronically linking them and by making national and international resources available to teachers and students. The aim is to network all 18,000 schools in Canada within a few years. (By the end of 1993, 646 schools were already participating.) Anyone with Internet access can make use of SchoolNet resources and services, which are provided on a Gopher server.

SchoolNet offers the following services and resources:

• A guide to the one hundred best Internet science- and technology-related resources.

• Over four hundred scientists, engineers, and other advisers from around the world who are available through the Electronic Innovators program. They serve as school advisers (advising teachers and students on areas of curriculum and project development), discussion leaders (monitoring subject-specific USENET news groups and answering questions posted by students and teachers), and in-class visitors (actually visiting classrooms).

• Online network training through SchoolNet/Internet Scavenger Hunts and a SchoolNet Navigator.

• Career selection guide.

• Subject-specific USENET news groups for teachers and students.

• Electronic classroom edition of the *Globe and Mail* and electronic National Press newsfeeds from Southam News.

• Access to institutional and university online library catalogs from across Canada and around the world.

• Access to databases from around the world.

• Innovative teacher-designed networking projects.
• Online technical support.

2.2.6   Computer Supported Intentional Learning Environment (CSILE)
The Computer Supported Intentional Learning Environment (CSILE), developed at the Ontario Institute for Studies in Education (OISE), is described by its designers, Marlene Scardamalia and Carl Bereiter, as a discourse medium (Scardamalia and Bereiter 1994). CSILE runs on networked computers, usually eight to a classroom, providing a single, communal database into which students enter various kinds of text and graphic notes. They can retrieve notes by others and comment on them (with authors being notified of comments), link notes to one another, or create group discussion notes. CSILE-mediated discourse can be carried on in any academic area.

CSILE is being used in about a dozen schools, with sites as widely distributed as Baffin Island, North West Territories; Toronto, Ontario; Cedar Rapids, Iowa; Oakland, California; and Eanes, Texas, and encompassing students ranging from substantially below to substantially above grade levels in performance on standardized achievement tests. CSILE has been used in a variety of curricular areas, from art to mathematics.

The teacher in CSILE discourse functions mainly as a participant, not obligated to respond to everything that is said. The teacher does, however, usually set the broad topic and the general nature of what is to be accomplished in the curricular unit forming the basis of a discourse. Although CSILE is designed for communication within and across classrooms, and outward to other places, it differs fundamentally from email in that it is not a person-to-person medium. Notes entered into the communal database are not notes to anyone; they are contributions to collective knowledge-building efforts. The only way to communicate directly with a specific person is by writing a comment on his or her note, and this comment itself becomes a part of the community database, available for comment by others. Thus, instead of addressing the teacher, as in conventional class discussion, or other students, as in email, students are encouraged to address issues, problems, and arguments.

In CSILE's communal database, collective knowledge—as opposed to school exercises, activities, or individual interests—is the center of attention. Specialized note writing environments are designed to engage students in conjecture, theory building, explication of confusion, and analysis rather than regurgitation of information. The students are viewed as legitimate partners in knowledge building, placed in the front of the knowledge-creation process as authors of databases, not simply reviewers of databases created by others (Scardamalia and Bereiter 1994).

The researchers provide the following as an illustration of the progressive character of knowledge building that CSILE is designed to support. In a biology class, a student noted that sponges had three ways of reproducing, a fact that caught the fancy of other students and spurred a series of twelve notes and comments on why sponges had such an array of options. In the course of the discussion, one student kept raising the question that if three ways of reproducing are better than one, why don't other animals have them as well? Scardamalia and Bereiter (1994) cite this as "an illustration of progressive problem solving in the construction of knowledge.... The answer that was finally proposed to the second question drew upon an idea that has figured prominently in evolutionary theory of recent decades: structural constraints on evolutionary possibilities."

Evaluations of CSILE indicate that CSILE students greatly surpass students in ordinary classrooms on measures of depth of learning and reflection, awareness of what they have learned or need to learn, and in understanding of learning itself. They also do better on standardized tests in reading, language, and vocabulary (Scardamalia et al. 1992). "What most impresses teachers and observers alike, however, is what the students are able to do collectively ... they seem to be functioning beyond their years, tackling problems and constructing knowledge at levels that one simply does not find in ordinary schools, regardless of the caliber of students they enroll" (Scardamalia and Bereiter 1994).

CSILE was initially based on LANs (local area networks) but is increasingly being networked into wide area networks, linking students with expertise and resources at museums, science centers, on the Internet, and to large databases. Now, the researchers note, "the challenge we see for the educational technology is to preserve a central role for the students themselves, lest they be reduced to passivity by the overwhelming amounts of authoritative external information available. The surest way to keep the students in the central role, it would seem, is to ensure that contacts with outside sources grow out of the local knowledge-building discourse and that the obtained information is brought back in ways consistent with the goals and plans of the local group" (Scardamalia and Bereiter 1994).

2.2.7 The MicroMuse at MIT

MUDs and MUSEs are real-time text-based imaginary worlds in computer databases on the Internet. Rheingold (1993, 45) defines MUDs as "Multi-User Dungeons—imaginary worlds in computer detabases where people use words and programming languages to improvise melodramas, build worlds and all the objects in them, solve puzzles, invent amusements and tools." MUSEs are later variations of MUDs. "MUSE is a Multi-User Simulation Environment, one of a variety of MUDs in which all players, not just wizards, are granted powers to shape the environment itself; MUSEcode also conveys the ability to build automata, computer simulations that can model real phenomena" (ibid., 155).

MUSEs are being adopted as educational media that are both used and created by educators. While students often join a MUSE as individuals, increasingly teachers view these virtual spaces as opportunities for networked classrooms, whereby children from different schools work together in a collaborative simulation and role play. The MicroMuse developed at and operated from MIT is an excellent example of students' creating new activities and worlds, interactively, online. (See appendix F for an example of a notice from MicroMuse at the Massachusett Institute of Technology, that was sent onto the Internet.)

According to Kort (1993), although MUSEs derive from popular text-based adventure games such as Adventure and Zork, they support real-time interaction among many participants who collaborate to build their own world and thus "support the constructivist model of learning, in the spirit of Dewey and Montessori. More than just multi-user programming environments, MUSEs foster a strong sense of community among participants."

MicroMuse, a multiuser simulation environment based at MIT's Artificial Intelligence Lab, features explorations, adventures, and puzzles with an engaging mix of social, cultural, recreational, and educational content. For example, the MicroMuse Science Center offers an Exploratorium and Mathematica Exhibit complete with interactive exhibits drawn from experience with science museums around the country. Kort notes that the highlight of the Mathematica Exhibit is Professor Griffin's Logic Quest, based on Raymond Smullyan's classical puzzles about knights and knaves. The Narnia Adventure embeds challenging puzzles within a familiar children's classic. Keeping with the spirit of cooperation and collaboration, a party of four is needed to solve the initial puzzle in Narnia. The Mission to Mars includes an elaborate tour of the red planet with accurate descriptions rivaling those found in *National Geographic*. The planets are reached by piloting sophisticated spacecraft, which operate according to Newtonian mechanics. Astro-navigation turns out to be a challenging team exercise, lest the crew find themselves lost in deep space enroute to Andromeda. Even very young participants can contribute interesting and sophisticated microworlds. An eight-year-old student designed and built an Oz adventure based on a movie version of that classic children's story, and a nine-year-old contributor returned from his family's summer vacation and created a working model of Yellowstone National Park, complete with erupting geysers and a wandering moose.

The first student to earn a grade for a Muse project, says Kort (1993), "was Erica Cleary, a graduate student in Environmental Studies at Boston University, who built the Amazon Rain Forest on MicroMuse as her term project. Since then she has expanded her work to include a Mayan Temple, complete with working astronomical calendar. Elsewhere, one can find a sailing cruise to the Virgin Islands which recreates the real-life adventure of the player who created it. Inspired by the success of MicroMuse, several other schools have begun to experiment with MUSEs in the classroom. Notable among these is MariMuse at Maricopa Community College District in Phoenix, where fourth and fifth grade students from the Longview Elementary School attended a highly successful Summer Muse Camp."

For younger participants, text-based virtual realities foster literacy skills (reading, writing, and composition) and technical skills (keyboarding and spelling). For adolescent students, social interaction skills, interpersonal skills, and personality development emerge as primary activities. College students who are not computer science majors enjoy the opportunity to gain some computer literacy and try their hand at creating their own contributions to the cyberspace worlds, usually with the helpful guidance of users with more experience.

The MicroMuse project seeks to expand its membership and explore the educational potential of network-based virtual realities, especially with respect to building computer literacy, cognitive skills, and scientific awareness through consciously crafted content geared toward informal science education, creative writing, and multicultural activities.

2.3   Other Notable Networks

2.3.1   Virginia's Public Education Network (Virginia's Pen)

Virginia's Pen is a network to advance and promote innovation and excellence in public education in Virginia. The network assists in the collaboration and exchange of information between and among schools, school offices, the Virginia Department of Education, and other state and educational entities. The primary purpose of Virginia's Pen is public school professional staff use.

2.3.2   Texas Education Network (TENET)

TENET is an educational network that provides email and bulletin boards to approximately 650 school districts in Texas. It uses computers to support curriculum enhancement, resource sharing, and access to databases via the Internet, to improve K-to-12 education, and to help pilot the high-speed data networks of the NSFNet.

2.3.3   People Sharing Information Network (PSInet)

PSInet is a telecommunications network for science educators built and made available through IBM. It is organized by subject area into conferences. One application of the PSInet system is CSSS Network, started by the Council of State Science Supervisors, which operates out of Ames, Iowa, and links all fifty states. Six intrastate networks link with the hub in Ames: California, North Carolina, Florida, Montana, Minnesota, and Iowa.

2.3.4   AppleLink

AppleLink is the official online information resource of the Apple Computer Community, with access to the service available for users with Apple computers. AppleLink offers a variety of online services: product information, news services (weather information, Reuters wires, *USA Today*), education, multimedia, and many others. There are many subtopics for education. A particularly active and resourceful subtopic is the K-to-12 Education Area, with conference schedules, research information, and lesson plans shared by teachers.

2.3.5   Free Educational Mail Network (FrEdMail)

The FrEdMail Network is an informal telecommunications network that helps teachers and students exchange information freely and simply. With over 200 nodes, it lets teachers share experiences with student assignments, distribute teaching materials and curriculum ideas, promote the development of effective reading and writing skills, and obtain information about workshops, job opportunities, legislation affecting education, and new nodes on the growing network. It aims as well to motivate students to become better learners and writers.

The network consists of a number of electronic bulletin boards, each representing a node in the network. The bulletin boards are operated by individuals and institutions.

2.3.6   Florida Information Resource Network (FIRN)

The FIRN network connects universities, community colleges, and public schools in Florida. More than 3,000 teachers and administrators in the state have free accounts for email on FIRN, as well as access to databases and library catalogs throughout Florida. To aid teachers in instructional planning, FIRN posts curriculum guides for using resources such as CNN, *Newsweek*, and the Discovery Channel in the classroom.

2.4   Community-based Learning Networks

Some learning networks support activities within a broader framework, offering community services and access to a number of resources and information sources, some targeted for schoolchildren and others to a broader population.

2.4.1   Buddy System Project

The Buddy System Project, introduced in Indiana, uses networks to integrate the school with the home. In 1987, in an attempt to "better prepare young people to live in the so-called information age, and also help adults improve their skills and knowledge," the state introduced a pilot project to test the idea of giving every student a computer in the school and a "buddy" computer at home (Hansen 1992). The intention was that both students and parents would benefit. Parents were considered important to the project because 30 percent of adults in Indiana had not graduated high school. Indiana considered adult literacy and training to be as important as student education. Further, equipping the computers with modems would permit linking homes, schools, and public and private information services providing both means of communication and access to databases. This concept became the Buddy System Project, integrating the home and school through networking.

Funding from endowments and a public-private sector partnership provided the project management, expertise, and equipment for five pilot schools, grades 4 and 5. By the fifth year 2,000 students and their families at twenty school sites were actively participating. The ultimate goal is a personal computer in the home of every student from grades 4 to 12 (Hansen 1992).

Test results indicate that students participating in this project produce longer and better work, do more homework, and acquire computer skills. Teachers have incorporated the computers and networking into schoolwork, involving students' telecommunicating on assignments, parents' telecommunicating with teachers, online summer school learning, and the development and use of databases on projects.

Significant parental involvement has resulted. Before each term, parents and students attend a training session to discuss the goals and purpose of the Buddy System Project, with children teaching parents how to use the computer. During the term, a survey indicated that three-quarters of the mothers and half the fathers used computers at least three hours per week.

Before a school can enter the Buddy System Project, it "must demonstrate a strong interest in using technology to extend learning in the home. The district must facilitate teacher input during the planning process and provide appropriate staff development to help create strategies for the home-school connection and to ensure effective curriculum integration" (Hansen 1992). The district must also commit to provide about 40 percent of the cost. The selection of hardware and software is left to the individual schools.

Future plans involve parents' paying a portion of the computer costs, where possible. Tax credits will be given to families buying computers and state grants to families unable to lease or buy.

The success of the project is attributed to the financial support of the state and endowment funds from the private sector, the requirement for parental involvement, the requirement for school district commitment in funding and teacher training, the use of the technology by the teachers in selecting interesting and useful projects for the students, and, most important, true need.

2.4.2   Big Sky Telegraph (BST)

The Big Sky Telegraph (BST) went online in 1988. Based at Western Montana College, BST is a rural educational, business, and individual telecommunications support service. Rural residents share their knowledge, information, and ideas through the online services offered by the BST. The system serves rural schools, providing modems, training on how to use them, and the development of online resources for the local community. Rural teachers take active part in online activities; to facilitate information sharing and learning in rural communities they can serve as Circuit Riders, Community Telegraphers, and Teletutors.

Big Sky Telegraph offers online courses, teacher in-service training for recertification, online databases, and access to the Internet. There are approximately 100 community sites (schools, libraries, chambers of commerce, women's centers, hospitals, etc.) connected to the network. The community users provide students with many options as they can access various services.

Among the programs and activities for schoolchildren are model corporation projects, with students from various schools modeling hypothetical corporation activities. Each group of students takes on a particular task in the modeling learning game; one designs the product, another manufactures it, and a third one markets the product. There is as well international student exchange of messages, particularly for language learning. Students in this program exchange homemade videos in the initial stage and then begin to exchange electronic messages. Awards are given to students who have demonstrated the most innovative ideas in using the network to provide community benefits.

Teachers and students benefit because the network provides access to information sources and experts. Students can also interact with teachers and professors anywhere in the world. High school students, for example, used the BST to access a course in chaos theory at the Massachusetts Institute of Technology.

2.4.4 National Public Telecomputing Network, Cleveland Free-Net

The Cleveland Free-Net was established in 1986 as a community computer system offering services in health, education, technology, government, arts, recreation, and the law. Individuals, community centers, and other organizations can participate free of charge. Since the network uses volunteers, participants are asked to contribute time, effort, and expertise. Thus, the menu of the system offers dozens of services, each operated by a particular group or individual. The menu is built around a metaphor of a community with an administration building, a public square, a library, and a university circle (figure 2.3).

The Free-Net has the following objectives:

• To assist in the development of free, open-access community computer systems in the United States and abroad
• To provide local and international email services through Internet to all members
• To provide "cybercasting" to all participants (dissemination of information on various areas, including education, business, science and technology, law, and government)
• To provide members with an independent news services through a weekly interactive electronic newspaper

By 1993, Cleveland Free-Net provided more than 250 computerized information and communication services to more than 3,500 users a

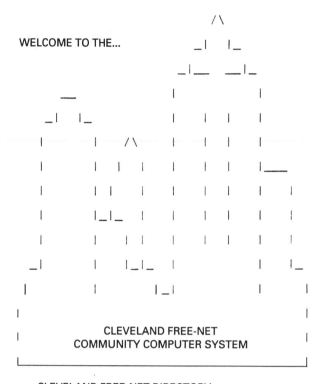

WELCOME TO THE...

CLEVELAND FREE-NET
COMMUNITY COMPUTER SYSTEM

<<<CLEVELAND FREE-NET DIRECTORY>>>
1   The Administration Building
2   The Post Office
3   Public Square
4   The Courthouse & Government Center
5   The Arts Building
6   Science and Technology Center
7   The Medical Arts Building
8   The Schoolhouse (Academy One)
9   The Community Center & Recreation Area
10 The Business and Industrial Park
11 The Library
12 University Circle
13 The Teleport
14 The Communications Center
15 NPTN/USA TODAY HEADLINE NEWS
16 <<<SPECIAL FEATURES>>>

Figure 2.3
The Cleveland Free-Net

day, including a number of learning networks for schoolchildren and teachers. One of them is the Teleolympics, one of two competitions for K-to-12 schools all over the world to compete in academic, analytic, and physical fitness skills. Students are given a scenario problem for which they have to discuss solutions, select the best approach to resolve it, and produce an essay explaining and defending their solution. In the NPTN Student News Network, participants send editions of their local school newspapers, which are edited to a manageable size (two pages approximately) and distributed across the network to all participants of the network. The Space Colonization Simulation is a third example. Although the title is futuristic, the program is actually an exploration of early American history. Students participate in a simulation of colonization of new planets. Once they arrive on the planet, they declare it independent from Earth. The most challenging part of the program begins once independence is declared. This is when students look at early American history to learn from and apply the lessons to the colonization of the new planet.

The Cleveland Free-Net also offers real-time communication, with a staff person online available to respond to questions. Schools can make arrangements with the administration and set up specific times to talk real-time with the staff person or any other user on the network. (See Appendix D.)

2.5 Multimedia Network Enhancements

A number of networks have begun to experiment with multimedia networking in the classroom. The examples here describe the use of audiographic teleconferencing networks, an interactive technology that offers the capability of simultaneously sharing voice and data images. Audiographic teleconferencing requires special equipment that enables full two-way audio (speaker telephones) and graphic transmission, allowing an instructor at one location to serve small groups of students simultaneously at several remote locations. Unlike a collaborative learning model, education by audiographic networks is typically a lecture-style presentation, with the instructor speaking over the audio system and using the graphics system as an electronic blackboard. Students can ask questions, respond to questions from the teacher, or solve a problem at the "board" by using a digitizing table to do a task presented by the instructor. All activities are transmitted real time among all participating sites. Assignments and tests are typically sent by mail or by courier.

Audiographic networks are dedicated systems and not computer networks in the sense that we have been using this term throughout the book; nonetheless, their experiences provide suggestions for the use of multimedia computer networking as these facilities become increasingly available.

2.5.1 Audiographic Networks: Electronic Site Tours

McGreal (1993) describes a number of exemplary programs in Canada based on computer or audiographic networks for secondary school students. For example, Electronic Site Tours promotes the delivery of electronic "site tours" of museums and art galleries to students in over 100 secondary schools in northern Ontario. Tours have been conducted by the Art Gallery of Ontario, the Royal Canadian Mint, the Currency Museum, the Royal Ontario Museum, the Museum of Civilization, the McMichael Canadian Art Collection and the Thunder Bay Art Gallery.

In these site tours, a representative of a museum or gallery takes the students on a "tour" by showing audiographic slides while students remain in their home community. The tour leader annotates on the slide while interacting with the students through audio teleconferencing. Students participate by making comments, asking and answering questions, and writing and pointing on the tablets at their respective sites. The tours are given in both English and French and reach students in the most remote regions, including participants from Young Offender Units.

In spring 1993, the Royal Ontario Museum delivered a series of tours directly related to the high school curriculum on various themes such as ancient Greece, Mayan civilization, and evolution. Teachers have also been involved in special training and information sessions. For example, the Art Gallery of Ontario gave a special information teleconference showing examples of their collection, using them to explain to teachers what materials are available and how to access them.

2.5.2 Music and Computers

Another interesting experiment in distance education is demonstrated by a grade 11 music and computers course. Using a PC-based audiographics network and adding Macintosh computers to participating sites, a teacher based in Thunder Bay, Ontario, Canada, delivers a course to four schools separated by more than a thousand kilometers. Each site is equipped with a Macintosh computer and software as well as a musical instrument digital interface (MIDI) and Roland D-5 keyboard synthesizer.

The course is designed to engage the students in creating, synthesizing, and composing original works using microelectrical devices such as the microcomputer and synthesizer. Some of the topics covered include operating the synthesizer, understanding the MIDI, operating the sequencer, and audio techniques. According to McGreal (1993) this course is having a major impact on the attitudes of residents of isolated communities of the north, whose students now have access to a sophisticated course that is not readily available in even the larger centers of the province. In addition, the teacher is using the course to train music teachers in the participating schools.

2.6 National Science Foundation and the CANARIE Learning Networks

As the technology that supports learning networks evolves into broadband networks for high speed and high volume of data transfer, new options are made available to network learners. In addition to text-based interactions, network learners will be able to access audio, video, and graphics capabilities over wide area networks.

2.6.1 National Science Foundation Projects

The National Science Foundation (NSF) is funding a variety of consortium and individual projects to explore the capabilities of high-speed data networks.

Common Knowledge

This project aims to implement major changes in the teaching environment of the Pittsburgh public schools through the installation of an electronic data network that will ultimately be available to all students and teachers in the school district. The Common Knowledge network is novel in its distributed architecture and distributed administrative structure. Teachers and students use the network to access information and people outside their classrooms. These new resources will be incorporated into the curriculum, and the network will be used as a tool for the development, implementation, evaluation, and dissemination of new curriculum components.

The project will develop a set of network-based activities and provide a framework in which such activities can be implemented throughout the local school system, tested, evaluated, and made available to other school districts around the nation. The project seeks also to establish mechanisms to institutionalize the use and maintenance of network technology in the Pittsburgh public schools. The model that is developed will be readily applicable to other urban school systems, and materials generated in the course of the project will be immediately available for the use of other school districts via the district's connection to the Internet. The project thus offers a test of the educational utility of wide area networks for the national K-to-12 community.

Common Knowledge is a joint effort of the school district, the University of Pittsburgh, and the Pittsburgh Supercomputing Center, which was jointly founded by the University of Pittsburgh, Carnegie Mellon University, with support from Sun Microsystems and Digital Equipment Corporation. The activities are intended to build coalitions involving these groups and many others across the local community. Within the school district, the project involves cooperative activities among students, teachers, instructional specialists, administrators, and the Pittsburgh Federation of Teachers. The proposed network is the key element that will allow these groups to work together efficiently and smoothly. It is also the key to significant changes in the structure and quality of education in the Pittsburgh public schools and, by extension, other school districts across the country.

The National School Network
The National School Network, a pilot project to test a potential national school network, links classrooms into online communities and provides

access to remote peers. Network computer servers called Copernicus will be installed, and the project will support email, computer conferencing, real-time interaction, simulation and interactive video, distributed databases, and multiuser simulations.

The project also conducts research to determine whether technology can bring educational benefits sufficient to attract large-scale investment by local, state, and federal agencies, as well as industry; be implemented in a robust, supportable form with low entry-level costs; and influence the design of infrastructure being implemented for industry, defense, and home access applications.

According to Newman (1993), projects currently underway within the National School Network testbed include:

Community of Explorers high school science teachers collaborate in developing approaches to the use of computer simulations of phenomena such as gravity, relativity, photosynthesis, and population ecology. The distribution of the simulations facilitates teachers' and students' sharing the output of their investigations.

InternNet a network of teacher interns and their university-based supervisors that allows rich communication among the interns concerning curriculum development and teaching, especially involving the use of Internet resources.

MicroMuse investigates the use of multiuser, text-based virtual reality in an informal, after-school setting. Middle school students construct rooms for others to explore.

Urban Math Collaboratives a national network of math teachers participates in the testbed to understand the incremental advantage of Internet connections over standard dial-up bulletin boards.

Empowering Teachers and Alternative Assessment two groups of practitioners work with researchers to develop new approaches to teaching and assessment.

Shadows a project to facilitate sense-making discussions within and between elementary classrooms. Participating classrooms collect sun shadows and other data as evidence for their developing theories of the relationship between the earth and sun.

Alice Collaborative Infrastructure

Building on TERC's model for learning and teaching of science—the collaborative inquiry model—the goal of the Alice project is to explore the impact of telecommunications technology on teaching and learning. The project aims to help establish communities of learners as well as working with existing communities. Each community, consisting of classrooms geographically distant from each other, is created around a common purpose and agrees on standards for gathering, reporting, and sharing data and findings.

The key to sharing data and findings is the Alice Network Software, which has been designed to facilitate collaborative inquiry. The software is an easy-to-use, integrated suite of software tools: a word processor, data table, graphing and mapping utilities, and telecommunications. Phase I prototype software running on both Macintosh and IBM platforms is in use in multiple testbeds, including TERC's Global Lab and Kids Network Middle Grades projects, establishing collaboration between the state education agencies of California, Connecticut, Nebraska, Texas, and Virginia.

In addition to testing the impact of simplified telecommunications on classroom learning, these communities are designed to guide national educational policymakers in shaping the future of educational telecommunications. Specific questions addressed include how to support teachers in the use of this technology and how to stimulate a commercial market to provide resources to teachers and students through telecommunications.

Learning Through Collaborative Visualization Project (CoVis)

CoVis provides an opportunity to rethink science education in the light of new pedagogy and emerging technologies. Traditionally, K-to-12 science education has consisted of teaching well-established facts, an approach that bears little or no resemblance to the question-centered, collaborative practice of actual scientists. Through the use of advanced technologies, the CoVis Project is attempting to transform science teaching to resemble the authentic practice of science.

In one of the first educational uses of wideband ISDN networks, CoVis aims to enable high school students to join with other students at remote locations in collaborative work groups. Through these networks, students also communicate with university researchers and other scientific experts.

Participating students will study atmospheric and environmental sciences, including topics in meteorology and climatology, through project-based activities. Using state-of-the-art scientific visualization software for specially modified learning environments, students will have access to the same research tools and data sets used by leading-edge scientists.

The CoVis Project will provide students with a collaboratory workbench that includes desktop video teleconferencing; shared software environments for remote, real-time collaboration; access to the resources of the Internet; a multimedia scientist's "notebook"; and scientific visualization software. The project works closely with teachers at the participating schools to develop new curricula and pedagogical approaches that take advantage of project-based science learning.

Collaborative visualization thus refers to development of scientific understanding mediated by scientific visualization tools in a collaborative context. The CoVis Project seeks to understand how science education could take broad advantage of these capabilities, providing motivating experiences for students and teachers with contemporary science tools and topics.

The next decade will bring widespread, networked multimedia interpersonal computing. The CoVis Project will be a blueprint to inform educators, researchers, and policymakers on the effective use of interpersonal, collaborative media in science education.

Individual NSF-Supported Projects

The goal of the Geometry Forum project is to develop secondary mathematics curriculum materials that integrate dynamic, interactive computer images and tools and simulations to support student experimentation. The Global Laboratory, implemented by TERC, will test collaborative science over high-speed data networks. The Weather Underground is based at the University of Michigan and provides students with access to atmospheric data for exploration. Community of Explorers supports physics and biology through simulations and communications in Canada and the University of California, San Diego. The Science and Mathematics Teaching Teleapprenticeship, based at the University of Illinois, uses apprenticeship approaches for network learning.

2.6.2   VIEW: An Example of a CANARIE Initiative

The Canadian Network for the Advancement of Research, Industry, and Education (CANARIE) is a not-for-profit organization building a broadband network across Canada that will also be connected with the U.S. information highway. CANARIE also supports the development of applications such as the Virtual Interactive Environment for Workgroups (VIEW) project, an open network of advanced education, training, and life-long learning resources.

VIEW is customizable, virtual workgroup environment intended primarily to support education, training, and professional development applications. VIEW provides four application modules: a course delivery module, called the Virtual University; a teletutoring system called open-VIEW; Science-VIEW, an electronic science magazine; and Resource-VIEW, a teacher resource database. VIEW provides both a teacher and a learner platform. In addition, a designer's toolkit assists in the development of new learning modules and applications.

The Virtual University, developed by Simon Fraser University, supports the design and online delivery of courses in a multimedia collaborative work environment based on the theoretical principles of active group learning and knowledge building. Open-VIEW, developed by the Open Learning Agency of British Columbia, delivers open learning courses to learning centers, workplaces, and homes. Science-VIEW, developed by Science World of British Columbia, is an electronic multimedia magazine enabling networking, communication, and group interaction related to science content for school, public, and home venues. The Resource-VIEW is an evolving database in which learning facilitators can retrieve information while developing course or project content and can add new information they find on a particular topic.

VIEW combines the capabilities of multimedia resource search, synchronous and asynchronous conferencing, collaborative work, and authoring tools with high- and medium-speed networking and broadcast facilities over local and wide area networks. The suite of tools provided by VIEW includes computer conferencing, video conferencing, image conferencing, email, video-on-demand, hypermedia, Internet connectivity and tools, and specific group organization and knowledge building facilities. The suite of tools is connected through hyperlinks, facilitating navigation, retrieval, organization, and structuring of information. In addition, a status bar provides ongoing feedback on user status. The program operates on Macintosh and IBM computers.

The VIEW system is being developed by a consortium or organizations, including educational institutions, industry partners, and government agencies.

2.7   Teacher Networks

Increasingly teachers are using networks for information exchange on lesson planning, educational computer programs, curriculum development, and pedagogical support and inspiration. Most teacher networks use the same connections as K-to-12 networks but have special places or conferences assigned for teachers only. These networks support teachers in a variety of ways, the most common being support for professional development.

Professional development and personal use of networks includes collegial communication and database use. Teachers find networks an ideal forum for sharing lesson plans, especially during times of curriculum change. Online exchanges help teachers adapt to and adopt innovations for their classroom activities. Peer communication via networks supports idea sharing and problem solving in all aspects of an educator's work.

K-to-12 teachers using learning networks found a number of educational and professional benefits (Teles and Duxbury 1992).

2.7.1   Increased Access to Information

Through learning networks teachers are exposed to a more current and broader range of information than school libraries can ever provide. Networking facilitates access to a vast array of information sources. Teachers connect to Internet sites to obtain information relevant to their activities. Learning networks such as KIDSNet enable information sharing with hundreds of teachers all over the world. Commercial and noncommercial databases are used by teachers for class projects, professional development, and personal interest. One teacher noted, "Telecommunications broadened my ways to communicate and get information for students ... [and] added a new dimension to doing research."

Teachers also access and share information with their own community. One teacher reported that his school access to learning networks helped to provide important information for his community newspaper: "I had a reporter from the local paper who came to me and asked me to help her with accessing information about incineration of hazardous wastes. The mayor was looking at a proposal for the town to create an incinerator. She was aware that our schools had access to electronic information because of articles in the paper about our school being connected to computer networks. I told her I was going to see what we could do to help her. I worked with my students and the next morning we had 75 pages of information for her on the laser printer. She wrote three articles out of that information. So, in terms of informing a real public about a real problem, our access to information has been really useful."

2.7.2   Help and Ideas from Colleagues

Sharing information and ideas with colleagues is a fundamental component of teachers' professional development, and computer networking has been a tremendous facilitator of teacher-peer networking. Ideas about curriculum activities, classroom management, program development, and many other topics are shared and discussed online. One teacher commented on the importance of peer input and idea sharing through learning networks: "With the computer, you've got a broader audience. When you put an inquiry into the network you may get an audience there that you weren't even counting on. There was a huge number of people who responded to my message and some of the comments I got I hadn't even thought of. I recall that early last fall we were trying to set up a teacher assistance purchase program for computers in our school. I just put a general inquiry out there in the net and I received all sorts of interesting suggestions that hadn't occurred to me. If one relies on the more conventional forms of mail then you have your mail directed only at particular persons. In the nets, just by the very nature of the medium you access that periphery out there that sometimes could mean a tremendous amount to what you are doing."

Peer communication and mutual support are especially valuable for those who are the lone teacher in a subject in their district or area. Through the network, teachers can obtain information about recent events and educational contests and can keep up-to-date with developments in the network area. Network teachers share a substantial amount of information about new educational resources, relevant issues to the profession, and new ideas for classroom improvement.

Teachers also use learning networks to share lesson plans, obtain new ideas for classroom projects, seek peer recommendations on classroom resources, and request support for particular classroom projects, such as linking two classrooms in different countries. Through networks teachers have access to a tremendous pool of new colleagues, local and international, and obtain help from a wide variety of sources.

2.7.3   Connecting the Classroom to the Outside World

Learning networks help to reduce the feeling of isolation of the school. A recurrent theme among network teachers refers to the benefits of learning networks in terms of their relevance to the real world. In the words of one teacher, "Networks expanded my thinking beyond school walls." Another noted that learning networks "provide a focus on themes that network the region together and make us become more aware of our neighbours."

The networks make people feel part of a larger community, as this teacher explains: "School is different from the rest of the world; it's not real life. I think that with telecommunications the fact that we can communicate outside of that classroom to people in the rest of the world has a lot more relevance than some of the things that they learn in the classroom and in that school."

This real-world linkage helps students to perceive themselves as active members of a larger community. They access expertise and resources beyond the school walls and can have an impact on the world outside. Online projects on topics such as acid rain, recycling, racism, or world hunger have prompted letter-writing campaigns and other real-world responses. A teacher on KIDSNet noted, "I think that telecommunications helps the students to appreciate that what they are doing is important, and has some relevance to what's going on in the world."

2.7.4   Increased Awareness of New Technologies

As new learning technologies become widely available, teachers recognize their need to find out more about the new options and the implications for the classroom. Learning networks provide teachers with exposure to a vast range of resources, ideas, and perspectives, helping them to become more aware of opportunities to change and improve classroom learning. Awareness of the opportunities and possibilities afforded by these networks also sparks enthusiasm and curiosity among teachers who use them.

Learning networks raise expectations about learning and having better access to information. As teachers navigate through the network and interact with peers, they become increasingly aware of the instructional value available in the network environment.

2.7.5   Changing Teachers' Role

Teachers report that the introduction of learning networks changes their role as educators. They become more of a facilitator or resource person, keep in better touch with current information, resources, and ideas, and expand their teaching role beyond school walls. Instead of teaching the same topic at the same time to all students, the teacher begins to work as a facilitator, helping individual students or groups with projects that employ online resources or are conducted online. This new role represents an important change to the dominant teacher-centered lecture model.

Change in teaching strategies requires a great deal of effort on the part of each teacher. One teacher explains: "In most other years with biology, I've said 'all right, we'll do this unit and this unit,' get some input from the kids in terms of their favorite, and go with it. This year [using the network] I threw it wide open. I said, 'pick anything you like. I don't care whether ten of you are doing the same one option or one or two of you are doing the same one.' They had free range of the entire six options and basically I became the facilitator. I went running all over the school—online, offline everywhere—trying to get materials for them. It was busy but I think it worked well. The level of commitment sure went up and I had several students who relied a number of times on things like Dialog to pull out information that they were having a lot of difficulty finding at the library or in the textbook. It worked well as they were able to access information to produce their essays."

The networks also expand the face-to-face, classroom role of the teacher. Many innovative teachers are now teaching in networked classrooms, sharing ideas and resources around the world.

Currently teachers are in a transitional phase, teaching the same curriculum to two completely different types of classrooms: the face-to-face mode and through learning networks, where the interaction is entirely online. Teaching online requires a different set of skills, those of a facilitator of a group discussion. While teachers also need knowledge in the subject area, this is not enough to cover the wide range of interdisciplinary questions raised by networkers. Increasingly teachers need skills to help students navigate networks, to foster learning interactions, and to moderate group work if they want to teach beyond the classroom walls.

2.7.6   A Teacher's Network: The Ontario Women Educators' Computer Conferencing Network

One experimental use of a computer conferencing network in Ontario, Canada, involved two sets of participants: graduate students of education, who took an online course for credit, and K-to-12 teachers, who took the same course for professional development. This activity, jointly facilitated by two instructors, demonstrates the possibilities of new forms of communication and knowledge production in the context of professional discourse (Harasim 1986).

The course focused on gender issues and computer use in education. A collaborative learning, group work approach was employed to enable teachers to bring their own experiential knowledge into play, share it with others, and be informed and stimulated by the introduction of materials from the professional literature (as well as each other). Online activities were designed to encourage active input and reflection. This method was open and inviting yet had sufficient structure to keep discussion focused.

The computer conferencing system, the medium for discussion, debate, and group work, was designed as a space for group interaction, organized topically and temporally into seminars and group projects. Participants communicated from cities, towns, and remote areas around the province of Ontario (and some from the Maritime provinces), using their computer, modem, and a telephone connection to the central computer conferencing system. There were two face-to-face meetings, one largely for training and to enable participants to meet the instructors and each other, and one at the end to follow up and celebrate.

The twelve weeks of the online course were organized into two parts. First was a sequence of weekly conferences or seminars on a topic. Each topic was introducted in a printed booklet, supplemented by one or two research reports or think pieces from academic sources. In the second part of the course, research groups of five to eight members were set up with the task of defining a research focus, conducting research, and developing a presentation for other participants. Those involved in the course/conference for credit were assigned major responsibility for research and report preparation for their group, but the process of defining the focus, specifying the research, and designing the report was the responsibility of the group as a whole. The groups worked together online and presented their final report to the rest of the class in this manner. Once the presentations were posted, the class read and responded to each one.

Efforts were made to avoid technical impediments to equal and open participation. The initial training session and subsequent ongoing support and advice were very much concerned with enabling participants to feel comfortable with the medium.

A subconference was set up whereby participants could talk over technical problems with one of the instructors and with each other. Participants took responsibility for helping one another. One participant noted that, beset with technical problems and being a computer novice, she had been tempted to give up: "I didn't understand the terminology and felt like giving up. When I admitted this on-line one morning at 6 A.M., I was overwhelmed by the response I received. The number of people who reached out with words of support and encouragement surprised me and helped to get me back on my feet."

To avoid the inhibitions many people have in relation to writing, the instructors emphasized (and modeled) writing casually, without correcting, straight on to the monitor. Spontaneity was stressed. Participants were told not to be overly concerned about spelling or grammar. These technical and social supports were effective. Participants became familiar with computer conferencing rapidly and overcame difficulties in both the technical and social aspects of communicating by computer. Undoubtedly this was as much due to their initiative and motivation as it was to the facilitative measures.

All participants were very active. Over 3,132 conference messages and approximately 4,500 email messages were written by the forty participants during the twelve weeks online. This is in marked contrast to some others' experience. Humphrey (1985) reported that his discussions with other moderators as well as his own experiences indicated that "achieving an active membership appears to be one of the most difficult tasks confronting the conference organizer" (1985, 14; see also Umpleby 1986) and noted that "the most commonly discussed problem in on-line courses is how to keep students current with the discussion and active on-line." The learning network opened up opportunities for communication that had been denied participants by the hierarchies of gender and educational institutions.

Learning networks have special relevance in the educational context. Teaching as a profession has a front-line kind of work organization. Although the training of teachers may be more or less standardized, teachers work in vastly different classrooms. The regional cultures may vary greatly; the wealth and educational policies of school boards create great differences in work contexts. Teachers are often quite isolated; their opportunities for professional discussion is not great; professional development days are important but are not designed to facilitate the exchange and refinement of experiential knowledge. Schools are often like little islands connected upward to school boards that may be equally cut off from one another. Educational change is generally conceived as beginning elsewhere than with the classroom teacher, though the classroom teacher is recognized as an essential participant in making change (Fullan 1991). There is a paucity of devices that enable teachers to bring together their experiential knowledge in other than informal ways, or to begin themselves to design change processes that are firmly anchored in local and diverse professional experience. Learning networks are such a device.

The technology of conferencing software was found conducive to creating openness and to reducing hierarchical or status differences. The attributes of computer conferencing enable a conversation-in-writing form of communication and the reduction of authority.

The massive inequalities in participation among students in the classroom situation did not obtain here. The tight synchronous frame of the classroom or other face-to-face group setting shuts out much potential contribution to discussion. The sheer volume of online activity must be seen in relation to the asynchrony of computer conferencing. Though the opportunity to speak (or to write) is not itself motivation to do so, the normal synchronies of face-to-face groups silence a significant part of potential contributions. Furthermore, analysis of the online activities demonstrated considerable equity in the distribution of messages among participants. All forty participants were active, and the rate and volume of participation online was relatively evenly spread among all participants. There was some variation—a few participated somewhat more and a few participated less—but overall most users contributed a similar volume of messages each week. On average, each participant sent approximately seven conference messages and nine personal messages to other participants weekly.

In the face-to-face situation, an instructor or group leader plays a central role in the control and management of communication. Often she is at the center of a starlike structure. Questions or comments are addressed to her, and she responds. In general, she assumes responsibility for managing communication, exercising control by devices such as breaking in, summarizing, regulating the allocation of talk to participants, and so forth. The sequencing of written entries to the conference excludes the devices normally used to regulate talk in face-to-face contexts. The instructor's or group leader's comments do not function to direct or redirect the course of talk. Her central role in the face-to-face group is undermined. Analysis of the online activities showed a high level of peer interactivity. Approximately 85 percent of the 3,000 messages sent were generated by participants, with 15 percent input by the instructors.

The asynchrony and written character of computer conferencing also meant that participants' contributions could be attended to more carefully and seriously than is possible in normal situations of talk. An entry could be reread; there was time to think about what had been said; response could be given thoughtfully. One participant remarked: "One of the unique features and values of this format is the ability to catch thoughts as they fly by." The opportunity to reflect before responding was credited with improving the quality of communication in the group discussions. Participants expressed an exhilaration with the power of the medium to make connections with peers and to discuss the subject matter. Within a few weeks into the activity, some participants already began to describe themselves as "addicted" to the medium and to the online community that came into being.

This combination of a dialogic procedure with simple orienting concepts appeared to be a successful strategy. Participants found that the course/conference bridged academic resources and their work environment. The common dichotomy between theory and practice was realigned. Rather than an instrument of top-down instruction from academy to working teacher, theory provided resources for the exploration of practical experience. Working teachers commented on the importance of this for their professional development. They contrasted this experience with the formalized professional development activities provided by the educational system of Ontario, which they saw as often too theoretical and removed from the reality of the classroom.

By contrast, the conferencing organization generated a dialogue between classroom and personal experience and the theoretical and research materials generated in the academy. This dialogue was enriched by the synergy of informational and resource interchange among participants, who rated the online connectivities as among the richest experiences of information sharing that they had experienced professionally.

3

Networks for Higher Education, Training, and Informal Learning: Exemplars and Experiences

Learning networks in universities and colleges, distance education institutions, and professional development and training agencies can be used to deliver formal educational applications, such as credit and noncredit courses and degrees, and informal learning and research activities.

The use of networks for postsecondary education shares certain common features with school-based networks, but there are differences as well. The predominant applications of school-based networks are based on curriculum enhancements; networks thus serve as a supplement or adjunct to regular instruction. This approach, referred to here as adjunct mode, is also the most common in university and distance education networking activities. However, two additional modes of networking are also widely used in postsecondary courses: mixed mode, in which a significant portion of a face-to-face or distance education class is conducted by email or computer conferencing, and totally online mode, in which the network serves as the primary environment for course discussions, assignments, and interactions. Mixed mode and totally online mode are less common in school-based applications, although online delivery of specialized courses for secondary students is being tried experimentally in rural and small schools in North America and Europe.

3.1 University Courses

Many universities, colleges, and distance education institutions use networks as part of their regular course delivery. We begin by illustrating the three modes in relation to learning network activities that are offered as part of the regular offerings by a university or distance education institution.

3.1.1   Adjunct Mode

Adjunct mode use of networks allows students to communicate with instructors and other students outside normal classroom or office hours for such purposes as extending opportunities for class discussion and debate, increasing access to instructors, submitting and/or exchanging class assignments, enabling group tasks among students in the same classroom or in a networked classroom approach, and expanding opportunities for informal group discussion and social interaction. In distance education courses, networking is used for better tutor-learner contact, educational support, information exchange, submitting assignments, and providing feedback. Networking also introduces opportunities for learner-learner interaction and collaborative learning approaches in distance education.

The use of networks in adjunct mode is typically an optional activity for students, although it may be formally integrated into the curriculum and form part of the grading process. Adjunct mode approaches can be a valuable enhancement to traditionally delivered courses and a good way for instructors to begin to explore the use of CMC. This approach is the most widespread form of networking in higher education, used by instructors around the world. It is also historically one of the first educational applications of computer networks at the university level. Email was first adopted for instructional activities in the late 1970s, to complement traditional face-to-face classroom interaction by expanding opportunities for class discussion (Quinn et al. 1983).

Adjunct mode is the most common use of learning networks in universities and colleges and provides several advantages: instructors and students can communicate when they want or need to; the provision of information in written form reduces misunderstanding and provides a record; and CMC improved the quality of the interaction. As one professor observed, "The most significant educational outcome of networks is more personal student-teacher time. When I'm in a good mood on a Saturday morning I can sit down and answer a bunch of student questions, rather than when I'm tired and busy on a Tuesday afternoon.

Computer networking lets us all talk to each other when we're feeling our best, and it allows teachers and students to speak freely without the restrictions of age and power differences that sometimes arise in an office."

Computer conferencing systems have been found valuable for such adjunct mode activities as electronic office hours. Many questions are of interest and relevance to the whole class, and the use of a conference for open class discussion avoids duplication of effort for the professor. Sometimes students assist one another, thus expanding the level of response to a question; students also use conferences to provide course-related information or tips for classmates. Private questions for the professor can be handled by email.

Instructors use email and computer conferencing for distributing class outlines, supplementary notes, handouts, instructions, assignments, test questions, and, sometimes, administering tests and quizzes. Professors use personal email messages to post grades and provide individual feedback on assignments. Many instructors allow, and some require, that students submit assignments over the network. Classroom management tools may be available on the network. The University of California, Los Angeles, provides software to assist faculty in grading assignments and in record keeping. Boston University faculty who have assignments submitted online can take advantage of a feature on the mailing system that tracks who has accomplished what assignment and when. Instructors are thus better able to keep track of who is at what level and to identify students who may be falling behind.

Use of the Internet is growing exponentially in universities around the world (Quarterman 1993). It is being integrated into course activities as well. Faculty and students use the Internet to access resources for their research (using FTP and Telnet), connect with peers and experts in various specializations (i.e., USENET, Netnews, distribution lists, and real-time chat lines), and remain current with their field through online journals and newsletters. Some professors require research assignments that use the Internet, in other cases it is voluntary. Participation on a network such as the Internet may be integrated as a formal part of the course curriculum or simply be encouraged in order that students learn about and learn to tap the resources on the Internet.

The Internet may also be used to link university courses on different campuses, even in different countries. In one example, students in two face-to-face undergraduate courses in communication, one offered at the University of California, San Diego, and the other at Simon Fraser University, British Columbia, were linked on the Internet to collaborate on an assignment: to develop and investigate a research question, using the Internet as the major source of data, and then present the final project report online to both classes at the end of the fieldwork. Students worked together in small groups. Each small group was locally based, but it is also possible for groups to be composed of geographically distributed individuals linked by the Internet. Mailing lists were created to link students researching related topic areas. Each group formulated a research question that was posed to the other class groups as well as to selected news groups, lists, and key informants on the Internet. Data were collected by administering interviews, surveys, through observation, and by searching archival resources, all online. Each group then assembled, analyzed, and synthesized the data into a research report, which was posted to plenary class mailing list. The entire process took about seven to eight weeks.

This adjunct mode approach was a variation of the networked classroom or learning circle approach used at primary and secondary levels. In the example, the two instructors planned the activities, provided hands-on training on how to navigate the Internet, and established the group mailing list facilities. The learning circle was launched with an introduction by each class: a letter that described the individual students in the class, the course, the university, the city, and the country.

3.1.2 Mixed Mode

In mixed mode delivery, networking is fully integrated into the curriculum. The networking activities constitute a regular part of the curriculum and part of the course grade. Networking in mixed mode forms one or more major assignments or activities in a traditional face-to-face or distance mode course, such as role plays, simulations, small group discussions or seminars, collaborative research, and group writing projects.

Mixed mode delivery has many variations. One approach is to use networks for role playing and simulation games related to the course curriculum. For example, some sections of a management course at NJIT conduct their management laboratory as a virtual laboratory, whereby students have the opportunity to apply the theories and techniques that they study to a simulation of the first fiscal year of a hypothetical corporation (Hsu 1992). Students play the roles of members of the management team in developing the management tools needed in a organization. Simulations using a computer conference have been used for the past seven years in urban planning at the University of Michigan. Participants are students in courses at the University of Michigan, between five and ten other universities, and staff in local planning agencies around the United States. The game covers about forty years of the development of an actual metropolitan community and runs for about eight weeks.

Email and computer conferencing have been used in management courses (undergraduates in business studies and M.B.A. programs) in the United Kingdom as well. A series of electronic case studies has been implemented at London's City University Business School, both to introduce students to the use of information technology within business and to teach group working skills (Rich 1992). The aim is to create an artificial business environment in which students can experience some of the pressures to which actual managers are subject. Email is the principal means of communication, but the university also provides access to a synchronous computer conferencing system and to background interviews on videotape. Several cases are presented, some running up to a complete academic term of ten weeks. In order to maintain dramatic tension in the longer case studies, various approaches are used, such as responding quickly to student material, incrementally adding new case material, and ensuring that students use the system by requiring two to three electronic mailings per week. The video interviews and synchronous conferencing are used to provide supplementary materials. Two paper documents (one giving some background on the company and the other providing instructions on computer skills) are also distributed to all students at the start of the term. The electronic case study approach was found very successful in raising student interest in strategic information technology issues. The level of success was mixed in encouraging student use of networking, "limited in places by the reliability of equipment, or by areas in which instructions are still unclear. The best acceptance of the value of networks comes when remote, particularly international, sites can be involved" (Rich 1992, 32).

The global nature of networks such as the Internet has been valuable not only for the resources and expertise but for the opportunity for intercultural communication and even linguistic learning. Courses teaching English, creative and technical writing, and foreign languages have introduced electronic penpal approaches to provide written communication opportunities. A professor in Mexico uses networking to enable his graduate students in biology to contact other biologists on the Internet. He notes that networking accomplishes three objectives: students improve their English by using it to communicate on a subject that is personally relevant, they are connected with scientific advances in their field, and the professors have the opportunity to intervene in the writing process.

Another approach is online peer review: students work together in dyads or in small groups, using email or computer conferencing, for peer review on the first draft of their course paper. The instructor provides a framework to guide peer critiques, and the grading assesses both the quality of the critique and the draft and final version of the paper. In some cases, students take on the role of both author and critic; in other examples, the roles are divided (a student is either an author or a critic).

Computer conferencing has been used at the University of Michigan to build an interactive reading log. Each week the professor provides a short comment on the assigned readings and requires each student to enter a response to the comments, reflecting their own reactions to the readings. This activity enables the professor to obtain a better idea of how the student understands the reading, and students discuss the readings with one another.

The use of online seminars in a face-to-face class is yet another illustration of mixed mode delivery. This approach has been used with undergraduate courses in communication at Simon Fraser University (Harasim 1993b). Six weeks of a thirteen-week course are conducted online as student-led seminars; the other seven weeks are held as face-to-face lectures and tutorials. Online, students participate in seminar groups of about fifteen people (there may be three or more such groups in a course). Six topics, one each week, are discussed by each seminar group. Students have two roles: as seminar leader for one week and as seminar discussant for five weeks. As seminar leaders, students work in small teams, with one to two peers, to prepare and present the topic, moderate the discussion for a week (synthesize, focus, and advance the interaction), and summarize that week's activities and key discussion issues. While face-to-face seminars are often restricted to small classes of very advanced students, the online approach has been valuable even with second-year students, encouraging active engagement in formulating and developing arguments and analyses. Online seminars enable all students to have a voice and participate, difficult in a face-to-face classroom, even with small numbers, and certainly impossible in large undergraduate classes.

In the online portion of the undergraduate courses, student interaction was high, quite different from the typical experience of traditional courses and fairly evenly distributed among most students (Table 3.1). Analysis of the number of conferencing messages sent to course conferences showed that students were active, exceeding the four messages per week set out as the course requirement. Overall, student messaging comprised approximately 90 percent of the undergraduate course

Table 3.1
Usage data from online undergraduate courses at SFU

Class	A	A	B	A	B	A
Year	1990W	1990F	1990F	1991W	1991W	1991f
Number of students	55	55	42	54	45	44
Number of conferences	27	45	27	38	28	31
Formal	18	35	17	22	16	19
Informal	9	10	10	16	12	12
Number of messages	1,675	2,314	1.587	1,646	1,437	1,656
Average number of messages per user	30.5	42	38	30.5	32	37.6
Average number of weekly messages per user	5	7	5.6	5	5.3	6.3

Key: W = winter semester; F = fall semester; A, B = different courses conference messages, and the instructor's input represents 10 percent of the messages sent. Analysis of a selected online undergraduate course indicates that 89.3 percent (1,002 messages) of the online seminar conferences came from the students; students also sent 85.5 percent of the messages in informal conferences (75 percent of the Help responses, 98.5 percent of the Virtual Cafe, and 52 percent of the messages in the conference, Teacher Talk).

Asynchronous discussions enable students to compose a response, refer to the textbook or other materials, and reflect on their response. Student assessment of online discussions is positive; weekly online seminars in which everyone must participate motivates students to keep up with the readings, while interaction with peers presents students with multiple perspectives on a topic and helps them think through the issues. It is the opportunity to lead a seminar, while the most difficult and even intimidating, that students typically rate as the most enjoyable and best learning opportunity. Such seminar-style presentations and discussions are examples of collaborative learning activities that are difficult or even impossible in traditional classrooms but that tend to work very well online, even in large classes of undergraduates. Mixed mode delivery is also employed in distance education.

3.1.3   Online Mode

Online courses use CMC as the primary environment for course discussion and interaction. Course activities—presentation of information, class interaction and discussion, group work—can be effectively undertaken online using a CMC system that provides some structuring of the communication activities (i.e., computer conferencing or bulletin board systems).

CMC is the primary environment in online courses but not the only medium used in the instructional activity. Online courses typically use textbooks and course readings in hard copy; other media may be integrated, such as use of audio- or videocassette, telephone calls, and audio- or videoconferencing. Face-to-face meetings may be offered for specific purposes, such as to launch the class and possibly during the course if the physical classroom is convenient. Face-to-face meetings are valuable for training on CMC, for introducing the curriculum, and for students to meet one another; they are not essential, however, and most online courses do not use them because of time constraints and travel costs. Like other forms of learning networks, online courses use a variety of activities based on collaborative learning. An online course may start and end with a set of plenary activities, to build the sense of group identity and community. Seminars, small group discussions, and small group assignments comprise the core curriculum, each lasting for one week or for a set number of weeks. Courses designed and offered in the mid- to late 1980s at the Ontario Institute for Studies in Education (OISE) illustrate this approach (Harasim 1993b). The courses were at the graduate level, with a limit of about twenty-five students to a course (some were considerably smaller and a few significantly larger). The first activities were plenary group discussions. Topics included conferences for self-introductions, setting personal and class learning objectives, and engaging in a "great debate." The courses employed seminars (plenary and small group), dyads, and project teams. The twelve-week course was organized into four weeks of seminar activity, followed by two weeks of a dyad assignment, four weeks of project work and class presentations, and two weeks of debates structured around dyad interaction. Between thirty-five and sixty computer conferences and subconferences were used to create the environment. The shape of the environment changed each week, as some topical conferences were closed and new ones opened.

The tasks and the groups changed, from plenaries to dyads to small group activities (see appendix G for sample course outline). The online course environment included perhaps ten conferences for core discussions (plenary and small group); ten for small work group presentations (with an equal number of work spaces); ten to fifteen conferences for dyad presentations (with an equal number of work spaces); ten to fifteen conferences for debating teams; and six to ten spaces for informal conferences.

Conference spaces were also defined by the size of learning group. The graduate courses employed a fairly complex instructional design. Plenary sessions were employed for group building, especially for initial and concluding core activities. The informal conferences were also designed as plenaries, to enable the entire course to "meet." In a large class (more than twenty students) or with distinct special interest or work groups, small group discussions helped manage the volume of online discussion. A conference for small group discussion typically had eight to fifteen students each; seminars might have eighteen to twenty-two students. Group assignments and tasks were organized around small groups, usually with two to four persons per group. Dyads or learning partnerships are another design for online group work. In this design, two students are partners for a specific task or assignment or for peer support.

System-generated usage statistics were gathered on the number of messages sent to conferences in online credit courses. Users were active in generating ideas and information; analysis of the online courses at OISE shows that graduate students averaged between five and ten conference messages per week per person (electronic mail notes were not tracked, but were prolific). As shown in table 3.2, thousands of messages were generated in the conferences over the twelve weeks online. This represents a large database of ideas and perspectives on various topics.

The online courses were distinguished by active peer-to-peer discussion and exchange. In the OISE online courses, students contributed 85 to 90 percent of messages, a level of student participation and interaction high even for face-to-face graduate seminars. The collaborative nature of the conferences is illustrated by the quality of the interaction as

Table 3.2
Usage data from online graduate courses at OISE

Class	W	W	X	Y	Y	Z
Year	1986W	1986F	1987W	1988F	1989F	1989W
Number of students	39	11	6	26	18	12
Number of conferences	58	35	19	58	36	39
Formal	53	30	14	53	31	34
Informal	5	5	5	5	5	5
Number of messages	2,670	1,320	542	3,177	2,016	1,484
Average number of messages per user	68.5	120	90	113.5	112	113
Average number of weekly messages per user	5.7	10	7.5	9.5	9.3	9.5

Key: W = winter semester; F = fall semester; W, X, Y, Z = different courses well. Analysis of selected contents of the online courses indicates that learners formulated positions and responded to their peers with active questioning, elaboration, and debate. Transcript analysis of online seminars and small group activities showed that students built on one another's ideas by posing and answering questions, clarifying ideas, and expanding on or debating points raised by others (Harasim 1991). Message map analysis of interaction patterns in selected online discussions demonstrated that students refer to the messages of others, adding on and building to the ideas posed (Winkelmans 1988). Peer interaction, in which students are exposed to multiple perspectives on a particular topic as well as to being challenged by a question or expansion of their own ideas, is a valuable opportunity for knowledge building and developing critical thinking skills (Webb 1989). Online activities facilitate such collegial exchange.

Online interaction displays fewer of the extremes typical of face-to-face class activity such as excessive or dominating input by a few and little or no participation by everyone else in the class. Educational computer conferencing does not entirely eliminate domination by a few participants, but it does ensure that dominance by a few does not exclude the ability of others to have their say.

3.1.4 The Virtual Classroom

The Virtual Classroom (VC) project was developed specifically for educational activities at the postsecondary level. *Virtual Classroom*™ is New Jersey Institute of Technology's (NJIT) name for a computer conferencing system enhanced with software tools to support collaborative learning and teaching. With major funding from the Corporation for Public Broadcasting and New Jersey's Department of Higher Education, the project had two focuses: the development of a sophisticated set of software tools to support the delivery of online courses and evaluation of how CMC changes the process and outcomes of college-level education as compared to the traditional classroom. Over a period of six years beginning in 1985, NJIT constructed prototypes and finally a marketed version of the software (EIES 2: Electronic Information Exchange System, version 2), offered many courses totally and partially online, and gathered qualitative and quantitative data on the impacts on educators and students. (For complete results see Hiltz 1988a, 1988b, 1993.)

The VC project undertook extensive evaluation to explore whether it is possible to use communication systems to improve access to and the effectiveness of postsecondary educational delivery (Hiltz 1990). The evaluation goals were to describe the nature of the educational experiences and outcomes in the VC, compare them to the traditional classroom, and determine those conditions associated with good or poor outcomes. To achieve these goals, it was necessary to observe a variety of courses, students, and implementation environments and to use a variety of evaluation methods.

The primary research design involved five matched sections of the same course taught either face to face or in the VC, using the same instructor, text and other printed materials, midterm, and final exams. At Upsala College, a small liberal arts college where students used a microcomputer laboratory for access, the matched courses were introductory sociology and a freshman-level required course in statistics. At NJIT, a technological university where all students are given personal computers for use in courses, matched courses for the evaluation research were introduction to computer science, an upper-level management practices course, and an upper-level statistics course with a calculus prerequisite. In addition, a large number of courses were included without matched sections. Some were totally online, and some used a mixed modes delivery consisting of a reduced number of face-to-face meetings in conjunction with the VC.

Data collection techniques included pre- and postcourse questionnaires, comparison of examination scores and course grades, participant observation in online conferences, computer monitoring of the amount and type of online activity, and personal interviews with some students.

The twin goals of the VC are to increase convenience of access to educational opportunities, and to improve the quality of the educational process. The results indicate that in the majority of cases, these goals were achieved.

All students participating in the VC were asked to compare their experiences to previous face-to-face courses. The majority (65 percent) felt that taking online courses was more convenient and that they had better access to their professors (58 percent). Most reported increased interest, involvement, and motivation and spending more time and working harder in online courses.

Interaction was found to be friendlier and more egalitarian than in the traditional classroom. The majority of comments in most conferences were contributed by the students. An informal tone with frequent use of humor was a dominant style of interaction. A side benefit of the VC was that the majority of students acquired improved attitudes toward the use of computers and increased computer skills.

In terms of overall quality of performance, the majority reported that they felt it was on the whole a "better" learning experience. However, there was no significant improvement in grades. In only one of five courses (computer science) were grades significantly better in the VC mode. Several possible explanations may account for this mismatch. One is that teachers may curve grades within a section and adjust grades so that there will be no difference between media. Some schools place an upper limit on the proportion of A's and B's that may be available. The management instructor reported that he did not want to penalize his students without the VC, so although the VC sections performed better, the traditional classroom section received the same overall pattern of grades. A second possible explanation stems from the number of students or "subjects": it takes a very large difference in performance to be statistically significant when the total number in each section is under thirty. When the management course was repeated several more times in both the traditional classroom and the VC modes, and student performance was assessed by a computer score, the VC scores were significantly better. Finally, there was a lot of variation in the extent to which students took advantage of the opportunity for greater connectivity offered by the medium. Students without PCs who had to travel to a laboratory for access tended toward procrastination, and students who lacked the self-discipline to set up a regular pattern of participation of at least three times a week tended to do less work and learn less than they would have in a traditional classroom.

In sum, Virtual Classroom proved a superior method for well-motivated and well-prepared students with adequate access to the necessary equipment who took advantage of the opportunities provided for increased interaction with their professor and other students. Outcomes varied considerably, however. Some instructors were able to design and implement group learning experiences online better than others, and some were much more available and responsive online.

The VC software tools allow instructors to create a rich and varied communication environment for an online course and to free them from some time-consuming tasks that can be automated. The Virtual Classroom can be thought of as emulating all of the communication modes or structures available in the traditional face-to-face classroom, plus providing some new capabilities (Table 3.3).

At the heart of the VC are class "conferences," typically several for each course, for different purposes—for example, a general discussion conference that lasts throughout the course, a student lounge or center for socializing, and conferences for each major course activity unit, such as a debate, student reports, or a seminar with a visiting expert. Having separate conference spaces helps to organize the online world. In the VC, anybody can open (or leave) a conference at any time. This is important for enabling students to form groups to work together. Whenever two or more students need a space to plan and write, they can open a conference. When their product is ready to show to others, the rest of the class can be admitted to their conference.

An "activity" in the VC context is any executable program and it can be attached to any conference comment. All of the activities were designed to support a group context for learning. For example, the Gradebook can be thought of as a spreadsheet with privileges. The instructor and any other designated privileged users can define the entries in the gradebook, designate their weight in the final average, and enter or modify individual grades. When a student asks to see grades, two types of data are displayed: the individual's grade and average at that point and also the class average on each assignment or exam, and overall. Thus, the student can see how he or she is doing in comparison to others. Activities are also designed to try to minimize work for the instructor. Because the program automatically computes weighted averages, the instructor needs only to choose to "send grades" after they are entered, and the system automatically notifies the students.

Table 3.3
Some communication structures in virtual and traditional classrooms

Virtual classroom software feature	Function	Traditional classroom equivalent
Conferences	Class discussion and lectures	Classroom
Messages	Private student-student and student-teacher discussions	Office hours "Hallway" conversations
Notebooks	Individual and working groups composition and storage of documents	Paper and ring-binders, word processor and diskette
Document read activity	Scan and read "published" material	Books and journals
"Personal TEIES"	Create, modify, and share diagrams	Blackboard
Exam	Timed student-teacher feedback with no other communication permitted during test taking	Exam
Gradebook	Teacher may record and change grades and averages; student may access only his or her grades	Gradebook (paper)
Pen names and anonymity	Encourage self-disclosure and experimentation	
Response activity	Force independent thinking and active participation	
Selection activity	Manage distribution of unique assignments	Circulate sign-up sheets
Directory	Self-supplied description of status and interests; telephone and mailing contact information; last time online; online groups to which one belongs	

A selection activity is a way of distributing unique assignments without having to engage in lengthy discussions and negotiations about who will do what. Suppose an instructor wants each student in the class to choose an article or topic for review or presentation to the rest of the class or a problem in math or science. Each selection has a short label and a longer description. After viewing the descriptions, each student makes a selection from the list, and his or her name goes up next to it. Nobody else can choose the same topic. Besides simplifying the process of distributing work among the group, this also provides motivation for students to sign on to get their choice.

The most frequently used activity is the Question/Response activity, which puts a software gate between the question, which appears in the body of the conference comment to which the activity is attached, and the responses. In Question activities, each member of the class must think through the issues and provide a response, before the responses of others become visible. This provides a balance between individual problem-solving work and the advantages of group discussion to develop a wide range of considerations. In setting up a Question activity, the instructor can decide whether all prior responses become viewable as soon as the student answers or keep them closed until a certain point. For instance, the instructor might want to add some initial reactions to and weaving of the student responses rather than having students see each other's raw (and possibly incorrect) responses.

Activities are an open-ended concept. Work is proceeding on developing a Questionnaire activity for constructing, administering, and viewing the results of online surveys and a Voting activity, which provides alternatives such as "Choose one alternative," "Rank-order the alternatives," or "Distribute a total of one hundred points among the alternatives to indicate relative preferences or acceptability."

A Binary file can be attached to any comment. It is a machine-readable file created by a PC-based program and can be used to pass around the results of using these programs, if all of the students have the same software on their PC. For example, in a management course, all the students might have the same spreadsheet program; in a writing course, they might all have the same word processing program; in a computer science course, a FORTRAN or Pascal compiler might be used. A PC-based program, Personal TEIES, was developed as part of the VC project to handle graphic material, such as equations and simple diagrams. The resulting graphic compositions could be attached to comments; students could download them and view or modify the diagrams on their PCs. Most courses do not need graphic communication, but when it is useful, it can be accommodated by putting the graphics software on PCs, and using the Binary File attachment capability to share the results.

In terms of tailorability, a developer's kit is also available for EIES 2. This enables organizations to change the interface. For example, a Spanish-language version of the system is being developed in Spain. It also allows existing features to be blocked out or changed or new features to be added.

3.1.5 Multimedia Modes

The Virtual Classroom Plus Video
After the initial funded phase of the VC project was completed, the use of the technology was integrated into the distance education program at NJIT, which offers a variety of courses via video, plus a number of courses that now integrate or combine the use of the VC with video media.

The video component comes in three or four forms. Some of the broadcast courses use standard public television courses, such as "Discovering Psychology," produced by PBS, in conjunction with VC for interaction among the dispersed class members. Others, such as a Computers and Society course, are filmed by NJIT in its "candid classroom" and subsequently broadcast on public television channels and/or distributed to remote students on videotape. The satellite-delivered courses are offered via the National Technological University (NTU). One section meets at NJIT, in the candid classroom, where it is being broadcast to students enrolled in a remote section, either through NTU, or carried to small groups of students on remote campuses of NJIT, through special lines. The on-campus and distance sections watch the real-time lecture at the same time. In all three video variations, the VC is used for all assignments and additional discussions, among the remote and on-campus students.

The same visuals are used in the on-campus lectures as in the video-tapes, and these are made available to the students in a workbook in an effort to standardize the course content and allow students viewing lectures via either medium to concentrate on the content rather than on copying the text of the visuals. The VC is used for both sections of each course, for all assignments. It allows the relatively few distance students to be integrated with the on-campus students, forming teams with them for some assignments.

For the past several years, Hiltz and Turoff have each offered a graduate course via distance education each semester, combining videotape distribution with the VC. Because enrollments have been small (about four to eight students per semester in the distance sections), there are too few students to generate statistical results. Nevertheless, there are qualitative observations.

About half of the students who enroll in the distance section live anywhere from one hundred miles away from campus to thousands of miles away. About half live within the traditional commuting distance of the campus but prefer the distance section. One student noted that the videotapes put the lecture pace more under individual control. The Pause button can be pressed to allow the studying and copying of a particularly puzzling or complex example; the tape can be rewound and replayed to aid in understanding difficult concepts or techniques. Fast Forward allows skipping of the material that was already understood, on a second viewing.

Having a large group of on-campus peers in addition to the other distance students in a common class conference allows distance students the opportunity for collaborative learning. As the first online activity, all the participants are asked to give an extensive self-introduction, describing personal interests, work responsibilities, and academic interests. The goal is to help students get to know each other and to start to feel that the class conference is a friendly conversation among peers.

All assignments are collaborative in nature, with students working and learning together. In one course, the first assignment uses a Response activity in which each student describes an example from his or her own experiences that illustrates one of the reasons for resistance to or failure of information systems, which are presented in the first set of readings.

The distance students are usually working in a high-technology organization and provide rich and relevant materials. The majority of the NJIT on-campus graduate students are international and provide a cross-cultural corrective to the often American-focused text materials. The next assignment requires groups of students to carry out a protocol analysis of a software system. The students form themselves into groups of three to eight members, many of them mixed between on-campus and distance students. Each student group sets up its own conference to plan and carry out its assignment. The third assignment is a controlled experiment on group decision support systems, which also mixes on-campus and distance students. These groups usually use special decision support activities, such as the List activity (ability for the group to build and edit a joint list) and a Vote activity (ability to apply any one of a number of alternative voting schemes to the items on a list).

In fall 1992, the students in the mixed video plus VC sections were asked to share their reactions by answering several questions, including the following: "What do you see as the advantages and disadvantages of the video plus Virtual Classroom/EIES 2 approach, as compared to just video?" and "What do you see as the advantages and disadvantages of the videotape plus Virtual Classroom approach, as compared to traveling to face-to-face classes at a university?" The following comments by one student, reflect responses provided by the others in terms of the advantages and disadvantages cited. This student has worked for five years as a software engineer and had a baby in the middle of her latest course:

An advantage of video in combination with EIES 2 is that one is able to watch the class and immediately ask any questions that occur to you. The response to the question usually will come within one day. One is also able to ask other students what they thought about a particular topic; this creates a less competitive atmosphere because one student does not know how well another is doing. I do not believe that students are intimidated by each other as they are sometimes in a traditional classroom setting.

One disadvantage is that the students who are taking the course from a "live" instructor are not necessarily hearing the same things that the distance learning students are hearing on a tape that was made a year or two ago. Sometimes the assignments are different and confusion can arise. Thus, the combination of EIES 2 and the video is essential.

Convenience is the greatest advantage of EIES 2 over the traditional classroom. I started taking the video courses so that I was able to be home with my son in the evenings, put him to bed, and then watch the course. I was not able to have that luxury and to be actually attending the course. I felt that having a child in day care during the day and not coming home in the evening was too much. Thus it was a choice between video and not taking any courses.

One must be very disciplined to take a video course. It is not very fun to sit and watch three tapes before an exam because you have let time slip away. However, it is great that the option is available.

Since there is one video classroom at NJIT, course tapes are being updated only about once every two years, probably the maximum length of time that should be allowed between updating lecture tapes in such areas as computer science, information systems, and management.

The Virtual University

The Virtual University is a customizable multimedia network learning environment developed at Simon Fraser University to support the design and delivery of courses and programs for all levels of post-secondary education, including university, corporate education, professional development, and workplace training (Harasim and Teles 1994). The Virtual University software supports the use of networking in adjunct mode and for totally online course delivery. It is the provision of tailorable educational environments and of special educational tools that distinguishes the Virtual University software from more generic networking systems such as computer conferencing or communication tools on the Internet.

The software enables teachers and learners to use simple point-and-click operations to communicate, create educational spaces and structures, develop and organize content, access and navigate around network resources and the Internet, and apply analytical and process supports available as embedded teacher and learner tools. Users obtain desktop access to a common set of basic communication media (computer conferencing, video conferencing, image conferencing, email, video mail, and the Internet), a variety of search and retrieval tools, and personal tools and workspaces. Most of the interaction occurs offline to reduce telecommunication costs and increase user convenience and control. The system combines the capabilities of multimedia communication, collaborative work, authoring tools, and resource access with high- and medium-speed networking over local and wide area networks. The system is designed for delivery on Macs and IBM compatibles and provides access to a customized suite of individual and workgroup tools.

Virtual space on a network, just as in physical space, requires structures and organization to become an educational environment. The Virtual University provides tools to easily create a variety of group spaces (instructional, research, and social) as well as personal workspaces. Participants have access to one of three platforms: teacher/moderator, learner/user, and developer's toolkit.

The teacher/moderator platform facilitates tailoring of virtual space into environments that support various learning approaches, including individual and collaborative group work. The platform offers tools to assist educators with activities such as designing courses and lessons, maintaining resources, structuring groups, organizing student activities, organizing administrative details such as class lists and grade books, and archiving course materials. It provides templates and resources such as

- Course design tools
- Multimedia authoring tools
- Group structuring tools
- Class management tools
- Assessment and evaluation tools
- Embedded teaching/facilitation tools
- Personal information managers.

Teachers and moderators can structure class interactions and discourse by time (asynchronous and synchronous), model (electures, seminars, dyads, labs), and medium (text, audio, video, or graphics). For example, a seminar might be designed as an asynchronous, many-to-many, text-based conference, enhanced with video clips. The tools embedded in the teacher/moderator platform offer value-added supports for educating the educators who adopt telelearning environments. Such tools function as prompts or cues to educators who are new to network learning, guiding them to a wider, richer and potentially more appropriate set of educational approaches and techniques for networked learning environments.

The learner/user platform provides special tools, including

• Embedded learner supports (i.e., strategies to facilitate problem solving, knowledge building, etc.)
• Embedded group support tools (i.e., strategies to assist in group decision-making)
• Personal tools and workspaces for idea structuring and information management
• Tools to visualize and analyze data.

The developer's toolkit is an authoring environment to assist in the development of new learning modules and applications.

The Virtual University software is designed to encourage active participation in group learning and knowledge building. Knowledge building is a learning theory based on a constructivist/social cognitive world view in which knowledge is constructed that reliably fits experience with the world. Understanding, in this view, grows out of interacting with information and ideas—for example, reconstructing ideas, setting ideas within frameworks, viewing multiple perspectives on ideas, questioning implications of ideas, and posing theories or hypotheses about ideas. A knowledge-building strategy is in contrast to more passive learning strategies in which knowledge is transmitted from expert or teacher (as intermediary) to learner. In the passive model the learner reproduces information and tells what she or he has learned without having transformed the knowledge. In contrast, a knowledge-building strategy treats the learner as an active participant, interacting with others in the group: the learner actively constructs knowledge by formulating ideas into words, and these ideas are built upon through reactions and responses of others to the formulation (Harasim 1990). Knowledge building benefits from tools and procedures that guide active learner engagement (Scardamalia and Bereiter 1993). In the SFU Virtual University system, special tools are provided to facilitate the organization, structuring, and visualization of information and idea linkages for individual and group knowledge building in order to help teachers and learners use networking for more than information exchange and retrieval.

Teletutoring and Telelearning in New Zealand

In 1989 audioconferencing and videoconferencing links were set up between Victoria University in New Zealand and Ohio State University for joint seminars in a course on international communications. Teachers and students had personal computers and a telephone headset, and they were provided with two telephone lines in addition to the one they already had in their homes. The idea was to emulate narrowband ISDN with its three channels. The students had access to BITNET so they could communicate with their colleagues at Ohio State, and the course had its own network that allowed for email and for teleconferencing with audio and data system for teletutorials.

However, in 1989 the public-switched telephone network was not up to the demands of such applications. According to Tiffin and Rajasingham (1993), "The biggest single problem—and it is one which continues and in varying degrees seems to be universal—was with the quality of the audio in teleconferencing. Added to this the BITNET connections were frustrating to use.... The networks set up for instructional purposes were used for gripes and became battlefields for flame wars."

The successful element was the teletutorial system, which linked three or four students and academics in their homes and offices. Each member of the tutorial would sit in front of their computer with a telephone headset on. A student would present an assignment, and everybody would be able to read the text simultaneously. The tutor could scroll through the text or highlight it with a cursor while everybody discussed what they were looking at, permitting a focused debate. The instructional process was reduced to basic elements; the text under discussion was directly in front of the eyes with no visual distraction, and the earphones cut out distracting sounds. Missing too, was the social self-consciousness that goes with face-to-face tutorials.

In 1991 and 1992, the Tri-Centre Project of New Zealand was introduced to link telelearning centers that were set up at a school, at a remote rural polytechnic, and at the Communications Department at Victoria University. This project was a response to a real problem of space and time: students in the remote centers could not make classes at the university, and the learning network enabled online courses.

The media combination used was email, fax, and audiographic tele-conferencing. From the lessons learned in the teletutoring project, fail-safe systems were built in. For example, all seminars at Victoria University were videotaped, and copies of the videos were distributed to the remote centers. Videos seemed to give the remote students a special advantage. Unlike the students who attended class conventionally at the university, students at remote centers used the videos for review and found by doing this they had better understanding of the issues raised in the seminar. Nonetheless, despite the best efforts of telecommunications engineers, the communications technology remained unreliable. Tiffin and Rajasingham (1993) note that "once again the biggest single problem was with the audio system."

By 1992 the system was working well, and an evaluation of the project established that the remote students were satisfied that the system was giving them an education that they would not otherwise have been able to have and that there was no significant difference between their learning and that of the conventional students. The project then linked the New Zealand network with the University of Hawaii for audiographic seminars for eight weeks. There were now two sets of students and teachers from different cultures plus authorities from around the world who would join in the teleseminars.

Student response was positive. Students spoke of a richness in the learning experience that came from looking at topics from many aspects. According to Tiffin and Rajasingham (1993), "This time the system worked. The players knew it and said so. What made the difference? From a technical point of view we had built in the kind of redundancy that exists in conventional classroom education. We used two lines, one for audio and one for graphics. If the audio signal was not clear it was still possible to follow the sense of what someone was saying from the way an argument was built up from diagrams and key words and bullets on the graphic system. In case the line carrying the graphics went down all pre-prepared graphics were faxed to the different centres before a seminar."

The international links worked because there was a heightened awareness of intercultural sensitivities. Initially, there seemed to be signs of a reemergence of problems in intercultural communication, and at one point, the link between New Zealand and Hawaii hovered on the edge of catastrophe. The New Zealand students were looking forward to debate with their Hawaiian counterparts; the idea horrified the mainly Asian students at Hawaii who wanted to know exactly what would be said so that they would be prepared. The New Zealand students could not see the point of conferencing if everything was predetermined. In the end one student representative from each group sat on a long-distance telephone call until they achieved a compromise. This proved successful, and the two sides began to see the value of each other's point of view. From then on relations between the two groups were excellent.

The success of this project prompted the Telecommunications Corporation of New Zealand to develop a national telelearning network that will be available for any instructional system, private or public, training or education, kindergarten or university. Another outcome has been the adoption of the system by the Maori of New Zealand to link rural Maori communities for education and access to information and to link with native peoples in other countries. Moreover, there are plans for research in educational virtual reality.

3.1.6 Global Classrooms

One pioneering global classroom made possible by learning networks is BESTNET, an acronym for the Binational English and Spanish Telecommunications Network (Bellman, Tindimubona, and Arias 1993). BESTNET, established in 1986 at San Diego State University, has now expanded to six additional California State University campuses, two University of California campuses, Arizona State University, University of New Mexico, Texas A&M, the University of Colorado, and Metropolitan State College (Denver) in the United States. The Spanish-speaking partners include a number of universities, university systems, and research institutes in Mexico, including the Instituto Tecnologico Mexicali and system, Universidad de Baja California, Centro de Enseñanza Tecnica y Superior, Centro de Investigación Científica y de Educación de Enseñada, and the Instituto Tecnologico de Monterey. BESTNET enables collaborative work in teaching and research between member institutions, with programs in border studies, social and economic development, agronomy, biology, anthropology, sociology, engineering, computer science, telecommunications management, and communications studies.

Faculty at each BESTNET institution teach online university credit courses at their local nodes. These course conferences are open to students enrolled at all participating institutions. In this manner students interact with each other and with participating faculty across institutions as a regular part of each class. Some courses are team taught by faculty working on different campuses, universities, or even countries. In addition, the faculty use the network for collaborative research projects.

Online courses on BESTNET have private spaces for specific course activities, but interaction between students in that class and other BEST-NET participants is also encouraged. For example, in many courses students participate in a course-specific conference and also in a series of topical conferences with students and faculty from other institutions on the network. The course-specific conference is for such activities as class business, online examinations, term papers, and the like; the topical conferences are collaboratively moderated by other faculty and involve exchanges on such topics as international conflict, intercultural medicine, international health, food systems, and ethnography. Some conferences are in Spanish and are hosted on Mexican nodes, some are in English, and some are bilingual. Another approach to online course activity in BESTNET involves integrating computer conferencing and videotapes. Students do not attend face-to-face classes (except for initial computer training) but watch a series of videotapes that they purchase at the bookstore (approximately $30 for fifteen hours) and then discuss the tapes and their readings in the conferences. The tapes are primarily documentaries related to the course curriculum. Guest lecturers occasionally participate in the online conferences from around the world.

BESTNET also uses adjunct mode and mixed mode delivery. Some courses involve online project groups and presentation of the final group paper online. Students are divided into project teams. Each group works in its own private conference and then puts its collaborative paper online in a main course conference for group input and discussion. In addition, the main conference is open to noncourse/seminar participants for input as long as discussion is relevant to the main theme. In other courses, students discuss projects in a computer conference, conduct research utilizing databases available on Internet via the BESTNET menu, and take exams online. In writing courses, students discuss script development with the instructor and fellow students, receive input from them, and discuss general writing issues in conferences. Students meet face to face only on occasion and do primary work online.

Yet another approach uses team teaching by instructors. For example, anthropology and ethnography courses from the University of California, Irvine, are collaboratively taught on the conferencing system with colleagues in Mexican universities. There is also a fieldwork component: students in each country visit the other, conduct ethnographic fieldwork, and then mutually discuss findings and post their reports online in conferences.

BESTNET is now expanding to Africa, in collaboration with the African Academy of Sciences, to establish an African Research and Information Network, AFRINet (Bellman, Tindimubona, and Arias 1993). An international computer communications network has been established in Africa for conducting international collaborative scientific work and teaching courses and seminars over the National Science Foundation Network.

3.2 Online Degree Programs

Several universities and colleges with on-campus programs also offer degree or diploma courses online. That is, students participate in online courses for credit leading toward a degree without the requirement of traveling to face-to-face classes or residence programs.

3.2.1 Connected Education

Connected Education™, or Connect Ed™, is one of the pioneers in learning networks, having been in operation since 1985. Founded and led by Paul Levinson and Tina Vozick, Connected Education offers several courses each term within an electronic campus that also includes a cafe, an online book order service, library, counseling information, and special campus events such as electures (electronic lectures) by visiting scholars. Connect Ed offers an online master's degree program in media studies, with a concentration in technology and society, as part of the graduate program of the New School of Social Research. Students may take individual courses in the program online or complete an entire master's program via Connect Ed. The tuition is the same as the regular tuition at the New School, which is about $1,360 a course. About one hundred to two hundred students are registered each term; terms start every two months. In addition, a number of not-for-credit courses, such as writing workshops, are offered at a lower fee. During summer vacation in July and August, the campus remains open for students to visit the cafe or library or work on independent study courses.

By 1991, several hundred students were enrolled in Connect Ed (Levinson 1989). Connect Ed is especially noteworthy for the international makeup of its students and faculty. Frequently students in a course dial in from North and South America, Europe and Asia; more recently, students and faculty from Russia have begun participating.

Connected Education does not engage in evaluation research itself but has made data from its students and courses available for analysis. Some of its courses were included in the Virtual Classroom project, for instance, and the course ratings and reactions of the students are positive. A transcript from an online writing workshop was made available to Beverly Rosenthal for her dissertation (Rosenthal 1991). This study describes how an experienced online teacher succeeded in implementing all of the precepts of collaborative writing in her course.

3.2.2   University of Phoenix Online

The University of Phoenix established its online campus in 1988, and by September 1989 the first students were enrolled: fourteen students in an M.B.A. program. At the time of writing, the program offerings had expanded to include courses leading to a bachelor of science in business administration, master of business administration, and master of arts in organizational management through its online delivery system. Completing these courses takes from two to three years. Several hundred students are enrolled in the online program today.

The Online Education programming is related to the university's mission of identifying and providing high-quality responsive educational programs to working professionals, regardless of location. The university operates on the tenets of adult learning, emphasizing the importance of collaborative and interactive environments for learning to facilitate the role of the adult learner as responsible for his or her own education. (The university offers on-campus programs and traditional distance education programs as well). The curriculum for the online courses and programs extends the university's instructional design strategy of viewing the adult learner as an active partner in the educational process. Computer conferencing has been found successful in providing an effective educational environment to meet the needs of these learners, regardless of their location and the time of day that they can participate.

The number of courses required for a degree, the sequencing of those courses, course prerequisites, and the content of each online-delivered course are the same as traditionally delivered University of Phoenix courses except that oral presentation skills have been eliminated as a program objective (Hedegaard 1992). The university believes that most working adults are fully socialized and have developed these skills through their professional pursuits. Students who require oral presentation skills are discouraged from enrolling in the online program.

Each online class comprises ten to fifteen working adults, who are typically geographically dispersed throughout the United States. To reduce the intensity of the material covered in the text-based networking system that places heavy emphasis on student participation, class size is kept small.

Online students enroll and complete the courses related to their degree program sequentially, one course at a time. As each class is formed, students are provided with instructions for accessing the computer conferencing system. Instruction consists of a formalized technical orientation provided online, complemented with telephone support if necessary. Before the start of each course, students are mailed textbooks and an annotated syllabus.

3.3   Distance and Open Education Applications

Distance education institutions integrate networking technologies into their programs. Different models of distance education institutions that involve computer conferencing are presented here.

3.3.1   The Electronic College: The Norwegian EKKO System

The NKI Electronic College in Norway was developed and implemented as an extension of the NKI College of Computer Science (owned by one of the largest nongovernmental educational institutions in Norway). The NKI Electronic College of Computer Science was developed for distance education delivery of a part-time program in information processing (programming and system analysis) as an alternative to the on-campus part-time program (the college also offers a full-time program). It is also used to supplement traditional forms of course delivery.

NKI chose to develop (rather than purchase) its own computer conferencing system. Dubbed EKKO, it was completed in August 1986 and first used as a teaching tool that fall as an optional adjunct to on-campus course activity. Conferences on EKKO are organized to serve different user groups: prospective students, current students, former students, teachers, and administrative staff. EKKO consists of four main modules: user directory, email, bulletin boards, and conferences. EKKO is now used as well by the College of Engineering as an adjunct to traditional lectures, as a mode of distance delivery, and for administrative communication.

The first experiment using EKKO for distance education was conducted in the fall of 1987. Since then the number of courses has been increased to a complete program in information processing, equal to a one-year full-time program. The program consists of ten course modules that may be taken as separate units, including examinations. NKI also trains its distance tutors through the EKKO conferencing system.

Everyone has free access to EKKO. NKI continuously announces how to access EKKO, to enable prospective students and hackers to become acquainted with the system. Registered students receive a password for logging on to EKKO through the public data network free of charge. The strategy of free access is considered to be EKKO's "most valuable marketing activity" (Paulsen and Rekkedal, 1990, 109).

Prospective students can use EKKO to seek information about the electronic college, the curriculum, and the conferencing system online. The college emphasizes the importance of ensuring that prospective students have sufficient information online to be able to decide whether to apply for a course, and if they do, to be able to apply and register online. To reduce labor-intensive counseling, prospective students are given access privileges to enable searching for information in such read-only conferences as the Curriculum board, the User Manual board, and the Published Articles board.

Administrative staff are responsible for distributing administrative information online. The Curriculum board, for example, is a carbon copy of the printed curriculum booklet. The User Manual board is an online version of the paperback manual. Published articles and papers describing the distance education projects are made available in electronic form on the Published Articles board. The Administrative board holds information on registration fees, application deadlines, and so forth. Selected examples of previous examinations are available on the Exam board.

Conferences are established to provide students with tutoring, administrative information, and social recreation. EKKO has specific course conferences and course boards for tutoring, the Cafe and a Presentation board for social activities, an Administrative board, and an Exam board. Each teacher has her or his own course board for distributing information to the class. The teacher also mentors a course conference, in which students have read/write privileges. Teachers are given access to one another's course boards and conferences, to facilitate sharing of pedagogic ideas and approaches to teaching online. The Faculty Club is available for discussing administrative and pedagogic issues.

Students may register for a course via electronic mail, by telephone, or by the postal service. A conference entitled The Admission Office is an administrative space in which the admission secretary informs the system operator and the teachers of new students who have registered for a course. Students are then assigned student privileges and registered in course conferences. Former students are also provided with access privileges if they wish to remain online. This enables them to learn about new course offerings as well as maintain contact with peers and instructors.

Correspondence courses, already developed, are used as the basis of instruction for the online classes. Students receive course textbooks and study guides. In some courses, the study guide and exercises are presented on EKKO as the course progresses.

Each of the courses offered online consists of three to six individual assignments, all of which must be completed for the student to be allowed to take the examination and receive course credit. Deadlines for submission of assignments are fixed at intervals of approximately fourteen days, in order to ensure that students in a class progress through the curriculum at a similar rate and to facilitate the work of the tutor and communication between students in the teaching-learning conference. The courses offered have different didactic structures. The majority of the courses are very structured (and also suitable for individual study), supplemented by social conferences; some courses rely heavily on group discussion. One course is organized as project work, with groups of two or three students completing a computer science project.

The experiences of the electronic college are considered successful, and the number of courses delivered online continues to grow. Experience indicates that there is a need to improve marketing to prospective students regarding what electronic study offers, the pros and cons, and the costs. Electronic distance education may attract a different student segment, one with learning needs and preferences distinct from the typical correspondence education student.

Lack of modems and of familiarity with the technology are considered the major barriers to recruitment to electronic distance studies at NKI. Research also indicates a need to simplify the system commands and procedures for novice users. In 1991, for example, NKI introduced local communication software, automatic commands, and signing-on procedures that lowered the user threshold considerably. Each student now receives a course package with Telix, a commercial communications front end, customized with built-in log-on commands.

Regarding online instruction, NKI teachers experience a need that is commonly voiced by online faculty at other institutions regarding the need for theoretical frameworks and methodological research to determine appropriate teaching methods and learning techniques for different subjects, learning objectives, content, and evaluation procedures. Research is needed to identify teaching approaches that can stimulate meaningful course-related and social communication. Educational designs that facilitate and encourage active student contribution are considered important. Another critical insight that echoes the experiences of others working in the field is that since teaching online is so demanding and time-consuming, there is a critical need to develop procedures that lead to cost-efficient teaching.

The NKI experiences indicated that an electronic college cannot be offered solely by computer conferencing; both computerized and manual utility systems are necessary to support many essential tasks. NKI reports suggest that future electronic college software integrate computer conferencing with necessary application software for accounting, grading, materials administration, and student software tools. They also note that "the greatest organizing challenge may be not to integrate the software, but the administrative staff" (Paulsen and Rekkedal 1990, 113).

3.3.2   The British Open University: A Mass Application
In 1988, the British Open University (OU) began using computer conferencing in adjunct mode as a small part of a multimedia course. This was the first use of computer conferencing for a mass distance education application. Thirteen hundred students were registered, each equipped with a computer, modem, printer, and software for logging on from their homes, throughout England, to the OU conferencing system. The undergraduate university course lasted nine months.

The use of computer conferencing in this course had several objectives: to provide hands-on experience in using new technology (the course was Introduction to Information Technology), to improve communication with tutors, and to enable peer networking (impossible in typical distance education courses). Approximately sixty-five tutors were involved, and each was given a closed conference for holding discussions with twenty-five assigned students. There was also a conference (entitled Forum) for socializing that was open to all students and tutors. Contrary to the initial expectations of course developers, this general socializing conference became the working space for almost everyone in the course who used the system and served as the main locus of activity, rather than the tutor conferences. The Forum conference developed several subconferences or topics, one for each block of the course, for assignments, for technical difficulties, and general course discussion (Mason 1990). The Forum conference generated active participation: by the end of the course, it held thousands of messages. Evaluation found that these discussions were dominated by about one hundred regular contributors (students and tutors) (Mason 1989).

Approximately one-third of the students in the course contributed one or more messages to the course conferences, another third were read-only members, and the final one-third took no part. Mason (1990) noted that although measures were taken to integrate the conferencing component into the course as a whole, "there is no doubt that many students regarded it as a marginal extra in an already overloaded course." Lack of time was cited by students as a major reason for not logging on.

Nonetheless, detailed assessment of student opinion indicated that students were positive about the value of computer conferencing for distance education. A major benefit was convenience. Students are generally reticent to use the telephone to contact tutors and found email and computer conferencing better alternatives. The OU experience also found that computer networking had a considerably equalizing effect on status and diminished hierarchies in the traditional communication structures. Mason (1990) cites the following lessons of the OU experience:

• For distance learners who take part, computer conferencing can be an exciting and satisfying way to increase interaction peer to peer and peer to tutor.

• Relegating computer communication to a very small part of a course (in the OU case, it was 5 percent) inevitably leads to marginalization and disuse.

• Cost can be a significant deterrent to use, particularly in the early stages of developing skills and confidence, if borne at the student's expense.

• With good user materials and available user support (human and computer), it is possible to teach large numbers of students the basic operations of computer conferencing at a distance.

• Extensive structuring of the conferences is necessary to achieve educational goals and enable students and teachers to make productive input.

• Conferencing can tap the invaluable resources of adult students' experience and expertise, to the benefit of all.

Important questions about how computer conferencing and networking can be applied to mass education remain. Peters (1983) has argued that the structure of distance teaching in the mass education model is determined to a considerable extent by the principles of industrialization (rationalization, division of labor, mass production). While the industrial model is challenged by the models of learning networks (Mason and Kaye 1990), issues of cost and economies of scale remain unresolved. As Bates (1991) notes "Third generation technologies (computer conferencing) are particularly valuable where relatively small numbers of students are concerned, since they avoid the high fixed production costs of the industrial model, but they do not however bring the economies of scale of the industrial model, unless the opportunities for interaction for an individual student are dramatically curtailed."

3.4 Training and Professional Development Models

The rapid pace of technological and social change has created a need for lifelong development in all professional and technical fields. Learning should be tied to production and organizational development in the workplace if it is to have an impact on updating and improving job performance. For this reason, educational programs that use CMC and other distance educational technologies to bring professional development into on-the-job training are generally more effective than purely classroom-based courses, which do not support the trainees in the application of new approaches to their work. Learners find that the flexibility of the asynchronous and place-independent CMC access offers a bridge between learning and its application, between theory and practice, between the "school" and the workplace. Not all such efforts are successful. If CMC is to be effective for professional development, attention must be paid to the same factors that influence the outcome of other types of online courses, including access, motivation, competitive pricing, and the critical mass to support positive group dynamics.

3.4.1 Executive Seminars

One of the first applications of computer conferencing to education was an executive seminar, launched about 1982 at Western Behavioral Sciences Institute (WBSI), headquartered in La Jolla, California (Feenberg 1993). The School of Strategic Management was conceptualized as an online alternative to residential graduate education for executives.

WBSI used conferences on the Electronic Information Exchange System (EIES) for the bulk of the program. Most participants were at the chief executive or vice president level in their companies. Tuition (initially about $20,000 a year, equivalent to Harvard's M.B.A. program) included the use of all computer equipment for the two-year program. Twice a year, week-long residential seminars were held in La Jolla for new and old students, faculty, and staff to meet one another and to introduce the themes and instructors for the next six-month period. The curriculum was organized around month-long seminars, taught by top experts in the field (for example, Jay Forrester of MIT, former chairman of the U.S. Federal Communications Commission Nick Johnson, and Paul Strassman, a former vice president of Xerox and author of *Information Payoff*). One or two seminars were offered each month, plus a variety of continuing general discussion conferences.

In addition to the formal activities, the participants decided that they wanted a more informal space for small group peer interaction and sharing. Thus, a number of online groups were formed, whereby the members could communicate about problems facing them in their organizations and receive advice from peers. After completing the program, many participants did not want to leave their online peer community, so the status of "fellow" was invented to allow them to continue online.

As enrollments and the costs of over two hundred accounts on EIES grew, WBSI acquired its own hardware and set up its own conferencing software. It also acquired its own building and a sizable staff. When the economic downturn of the late 1980s hit, the organization went bankrupt.

WBSI president, Richard Farson sees two main advantages of an online program for executives: it can provide a program of depth and intensity to executives without their having to take time off from the job for long periods of time, and it serves as the medium for the formation of a strong and supportive community of peers that can sustain its members even after the formal program ends.

3.4.2   Training for Health Professionals

For a number of years, a Danish consortium involving the Jutland Institute of Technology and Aarhus Technical College have used the COM computer conferencing system and other media to support on-the-job training tailored to the needs of specific organizations and professions in Denmark. One of these courses was based on the theme of food, environment, and new health strategies seen in relation to new production methods, changing socioeconomic conditions, and changes in the environment. The goal was to update the knowledge of community health workers, using an interdisciplinary, problem-oriented approach. (See Hiltz, Shapiro, and Ringsted 1990 for more details.)

The course began with a face-to-face weekend seminar used to explain the structure and main themes and give students hands-on practice with the system and experience in online debates. The course had an open curriculum structure, with projects and subthemes being defined by the participants in the initial phase, and the projects guided and supported by the instructors. The instructional team included experts from departments of home economics and food industries and educational technology experts from the Aarhus Center for Distance Education.

Each team spent two and a half months in conferences working on projects, which were actual attempts to introduce new practices or knowledge into the work of the participants. Each team had one main counselor (teacher), but all students could access all teachers for advice. All the faculty members could see the work taking place online in all of the conferences. The course was structured to create maximum synergy between a knowledge-acquisition approach and a learner-defined, experience-based approach. The learners themselves defined the themes or topics they wanted to discuss, formulated problems for their projects, and agreed on suitable methodologies and ways of presenting their results. At a final weekend seminar, the projects were presented and evaluated. This gave the learning groups a definite "product" to produce and a deadline by which their work had to be completed.

Evaluation questionnaires were distributed before, midway through, and after the course. Student responses indicated that the course (with its emphasis on computer-mediated peer group learning and exchange of experiences among a cross-section of professionals from the professional health services) was considered valuable. Participants felt that they gained a great deal of useful knowledge, insights, and new methodologies and approaches to local health care strategies and initiatives. Many pointed out that the online nature of the course had been crucial to enabling them to carry out their joint projects. It made it easier to access one another, comment on each other's drafts and ideas, and make use of the different specializations and qualifications within the project teams.

3.4.3   An Unsuccessful Attempt in the Health Field

By contrast, a project attempted in the mid-1980s for health professionals in the United States did not work out well. A hospital management organization requested a set of three professional development courses for about twenty employees. Management nominated the employees and requested the topics. The effort began with an on-site day-long training program, consisting of a nominal-group technique exercise on the future of health care, to try to build a team spirit and present an overview of the upcoming online courses.

The courses were presented in four modules, each a week long, that began with short electures, questions for discussion, and requests that the participants bring job-related situations into the conference discussion to which the techniques or principles could be applied.

Many of the students never signed on at all. Of those who did, most signed on infrequently and wrote little. Although the project did not have any budget to conduct an evaluation, some feedback was obtained by sending email messages to group members who signed on to inquire why they thought participation was so low. The respondents basically said that they had too little motivation, access, and time to participate. Most of them traveled to different hospitals a third to a half of the time, but they were not provided with portable computers to allow them to participate while on the road. At headquarters, they did not have computers in their offices, but had to go to a separate computer room to gain access. Between trips, they were too busy with scheduled meetings, paperwork, and telephone calls to make time to go to the computer room; moreover, they were not given any reduced work load to enable them to participate in the training. Also, they did not feel that the topics that had been chosen for them had any immediate payoff in terms of their job advancement.

Several other aspects of the implementation may have contributed to the low level of activity and apparent lack of success. The employees were spread around the three topic discussions, and with their low level of access, there were not enough active participants in any conference to change the dynamics away from a teacher-dominated presentation and toward a peer group learning situation. There were no forms of recognition or reward for successful completion of the courses such as grades or certificates. Finally, there were neither projects for groups to accomplish nor provision for any final meetings and group presentations that might have provided focus, task, and a deadline.

3.4.4 Training for Engineers

Professionals in all scientific and technical fields need to acquire skills in new specialty areas. The study examined here, of advanced training for engineers in the Reserve Officers of the U.S. Army, can serve as a model for training for technical personnel in nonmilitary, service-oriented organizations.

This project used a computer conferencing system called SMART (System for Managing Asynchronous Remote Training) to deliver a portion of the Engineer Officer Advanced Course. The course module corresponded to the material usually delivered in a two-week, full-time residential course on such topics as asphalt production, flexible pavements, bridge building, and airfield damage repair. The efficacy of the remote training course was compared to that of the resident program with regard to completion rate, performance, acceptability and cost (Hahn et al. 1990).

All students in this course were lieutenants and captains with at least some college education. They were engineering officers who needed to complete the course before they could be promoted to the rank of major. A variety of media were used for course delivery, including paper-based materials, CAI modules, videotapes, and synchronous and asynchronous discussions.

The online version of the course took thirty-one calendar weeks. Fourteen students began the course. Each was given a computer. The stated requirement was that each student spend a minimum of eight hours per week on the course. As is usual with military courses, it was team taught. A primary instructor was supported by four other instructors assigned roles at different times during the course. All instructors were given forty hours of training in using the SMART system for instruction prior to the course.

In phase 1, all activities were designed to be completed individually, with no group interaction, except for social interaction in the online Break Room. The students did communicate with the instructors to ask questions and receive feedback on their test and assignment performance. Students were permitted to work at their own pace as long as they conformed to the minimum work requirement of eight hours a week. All students had to complete the individual instruction modules before they could join in the small group activities. In phase 2, both individual and group activities were used. Student groups were given a deadline for the completion of the activities related to each topic. Phase 3 consisted of a culminating practical exercise: a team problem-solving activity (completing a construction plan) with online instructor-advisers to assist the students.

The 14 students in the experimental mode of delivery were compared to 331 students who completed the same course in the two-week, full-time residential program. The control group took the same exact course module, in terms of content, and had the same or similar tests, assignments, and culminating practical exercise, for which scores could be compared. In addition, questionnaires, observations, and interviews were used to compare the three phases of the course and to identify the strengths and weaknesses of the delivery mode.

Scores for the students on tests, homework, and the practical exercise were not significantly different; however, the number of students in the experimental treatment was so small that this is to be expected. Mean scores on exams for the SMART students were higher (92 versus 86 percent). One hundred percent of the SMART completers achieved passing scores on their criterion test on the first attempt; the comparable figure was 93 percent for the resident school. In terms of self-ratings of skill acquisition, SMART students reported perceiving a greater learning benefit than did resident school students; these differences were statistically significant.

Once students have actually traveled to a residential course, the dropout rate is very low (5 percent or less have an illness or family emergency that requires them to leave). In the SMART course, of the fourteen students who started phase 1, one dropped. In phase 2, two of the starters dropped. Another two students stayed in the course for phase 2 but failed to take all of the exams required for course completion. Thus, the overall completion rate was 64 percent of those who started the course. A relevant question might be, How many officers would like to take the course but are never able to clear two solid weeks for the residential version?

Costs for development and operation of the SMART course were lower than for operation of a comparable resident course. Travel, housing, food, and stipends for full-time residential students and faculty are very expensive, and lost time is another factor. In the SMART version, participants continued their full-time jobs and lived with their families while taking the course.

The formative evaluation identified the imposition of deadlines as the single most effective method of ensuring that students worked through the course at a desirable pace. The use of group activities also served effectively as a pacing aid. Timely feedback and the availability of support communications, including a free telephone hot line, were considered crucial. In addition, the requirement that the instructors respond to all student questions and assignments within twenty-four hours was considered to be important.

Students preferred phase 2 over phase 1 because of the group interaction opportunities. All of the students either agreed or strongly agreed that "working in teams motivated me to participate in the class." Many students also made spontaneous comments on the value of peer interaction, such as, "I'm enjoying the team exercises, and I'm learning faster and more thoroughly by being able to share everyone else's knowledge and expertise."

3.5 Informal Learning Networks

The models and examples presented to this point have illustrated the use of networking for formal educational activities; that is, the curriculum has been organized by a teacher or instructor. Yet there are ways to learn beyond the classroom. People of all ages and from all professions expand their knowledge and information through many means and media: libraries, television programs, museums, observing the work of an expert, and, especially, networking with peers and experts. The learning that occurs within informal networks—computer mediated and traditional forms—does not have certification or accreditation as its goal. "Rather they are groups of adults united by some common concern, some shared status, or some agreed-upon purpose that exchange information, ideas, skills, and knowledge among members and perform a number of functions having to do with problem solving and the creation of new modes of practice or new forms of knowledge" (Brookfield 1986, 151).

Traditional forms of learning networks have a long history within adult education, typified by free learning exchange, open to all, and based on equal rather than hierarchical relationships among members. Teaching and learning roles are fluid in the development of skills and knowledge. Traditionally, these networks have been face to face, but media have been used to facilitate local discussion groups, as in the Farm Forum experiment in Canada, which used radio broadcast to stimulate local listening and discussion groups (Kidd 1963; Faris 1975). Print media, in the form of journals and newsletters, have also been used to facilitate networking among professional and other groups.

Computer networks are a new and rapidly growing forum for informal learning activities. The Internet hosts tens of thousands of special interest groups, mailing lists, journals, and newsletters devoted to a tremendous range of topics. Commercial services such as CompuServe, Prodigy, America Online, and thousands of local bulletin boards provide similar opportunities and venues for personal, professional, and political learning.

Informal learning networks on the computer may take the form of special interest groups or informal courses. The role of the moderator varies from providing a forum for open exchange to facilitating a discussion or presenting a curriculum or electure. Special interest groups— clubs or associations—are a traditional and common forum for sharing information and knowledge, and the use of computer networks for them is a major communication application. Thousands of these groups exist on the various email, computer conferencing, bulletin board, and videotex services.

There are about two thousand distribution lists and news groups on topics related to educational issues on the Internet. Tens of thousands of distribution lists and news groups exist for other topics as well. An example is Comserve, an online association for researchers and academics in the communication field. Available free to users with Internet or BITNET accounts, Comserve is dedicated to the support of online education and scholarship in the field of communication. Comserve functions as an interactive, informal set of discussions or newsletters, called "hot lines", on a variety of topics. Most are public, although private hot lines are available for special projects or courses. In addition to discussions, Comserve provides information services about new publications, conferences, job postings and calls for papers in the communication field. By 1992, over five thousand individuals subscribed to at least one and usually several Comserve hot lines.

Community networks are another significant forum for informal learning. Free-Nets is a learning network dedicated to the general public, a form of community computing. The president of the National Public Telecomputing Network (NPTN), Thomas Grundner, says he cannot "imagine a 21st Century which does NOT have free public-access community computer systems, just as our century had the free public library" (NPTN, n.d.).

The Free-Net movement began in 1984 when Grundner, then of the Department of Family Medicine at Case Western Reserve University in Cleveland, Ohio, established a bulletin board service, St. Silicon's Hospital and Information Dispensary, to test the effectiveness of telecomputing as a means of delivering general health information to the public. The service had a single telephone line. People could call in using home, business, or school computers to leave medically related questions and receive responses by a board-certified physician within twenty-four hours. The experiment was so successful that it was expanded to become a community information resource in areas such as law, medicine, education, arts, sciences, and government and to provide free email services. From its beginnings as a single-line service, the Cleveland Free-Net now handles more than ten thousand calls per day, and Free-Nets have been introduced into cities around the United States and Canada. The economics of running a Free-Net are based on volunteer resources: the system is run by individuals and groups in the community who volunteer their time, effort, and expertise to place and operate the system.

Learning and self-help activities are available on commercial services as well. These may be in the form of special interest groups in which participants ask for advice or contact experts or can learn from tips posted by others on any range of topics from world travel to scuba diving as well as short courses. CompuServe, for example, offers three types of real-time conferences: roundtable, in which anyone can talk; moderated, in which a host moderates the discussion and controls who may speak; and lecture, in which a speaker stands at an "electronic podium" and addresses the crowd (Schepp and Schepp 1990, 137). Prodigy, another online service, offers a range of clubs in which members can exchange advice, opinions, and ideas with others. The clubs have resident experts who participate and give information and advice. Some of the experts on these services are paid by the service; others are "armchair experts" who enjoy sharing their knowledge. On the networks, as in other forums, however, it is important to remember that "the 'experts' sometimes aren't and that not all advice may be valid" (Kane 1991). It is always up to each user to decide whether to take the advice proffered.

Another forum for informal learning currently experiencing tremendous growth is that of online newsletters and journals for academic, professional, or special interest activities. DevelopNet News is an electronic newsletter published monthly by Volunteers in Technical Assistance (VITA), a private, nonprofit, international development organization located in Arlington, Virginia, and involved in long- and short-term projects in Africa, Asia, and Latin America. VITA specializes in information dissemination and communications technology, offering services related to sustainable agriculture, food processing, renewable energy applications, water sanitation and supply, small enterprise development, and information management. VITA's publications on a variety of practical subjects are designed to assist persons and organizations in developing countries, and it seeks articles from readers.

VITA also offers a free, public, online discussion forum, DEVEL-L, for the exchange of ideas and information on a wide range of issues and topics related to technology transfer in international development (e.g., technologies, communications in development, sustainable agriculture, women in development, the environment, small enterprise development, meetings, book reviews). Subscribers to DEVEL-L automatically receive the newsletter and can download documents free from an archive by using FTP or email messages.

Another example of not-for-degree-credit education is the Virtual Learning Community designed and operated since 1988 by Peter and Trudy Johnson-Lenz through their organization, Awakening Technology. This is a collaborative online community for self-enrichment learning. Some of the programs included have been a Right Livelihood Workshop, a twelve-week workshop for participants looking for more meaning and fulfillment in their work, and a Living on Purpose workshop, in which participants spend four weeks exploring their personal life purposes.

One unique feature of the software is an interaction space called "the circle." This involves an exchange of sequentially numbered text items called "rounds." In order to encourage an egalitarian, democratic learning atmosphere in the Virtual Circle structure, participants may enter only one response per round and may respond only to certain rounds of exchange at any given time. When entering the learning circle, a set of icons in a circle displays the name of each participant, giving the participants concrete imagery for the process being supported, which is likened to passing the "talking stick" around a circle in many native cultures (Johnson-Lenz and Johnson-Lenz 1991, 409).

II
The Guide

4
Designs for Learning Networks

Attention to instructional design is one of the most critical factors in successful learning networks, whether course activity is delivered totally or partially online or in adjunct mode. All education, on a network or in a face-to-face environment, involves intervention by an expert (the instructor) to organize the content, sequence the instructional activities, structure task and group interaction, and evaluate the process.

4.1 Learning Approaches

Seven models or learning approaches are common in educational computer networks. Electure, ask-an-expert, mentorship, and tutor support require online resource persons, such as instructors, mentors, and experts to support student work. Access to relevant information, peer interaction, and structured group activity are student centered. The choice of model depends on the content area and course design, but all approaches are most successful when structures and roles are well defined and the information accessed is relevant to a particular learning task.

4.1.1 Electures
Although "students seem likely to learn more by having to create an instructional module or a hypermedia presentation" (Schneiderman 1993), there often is a need to present some facts, approaches, or skills—in other words, to give an *electronic lecture*, or *electure*. Electures provide some crucial concept or technique that students need in order

to be able to apply it to a problem or discussion, especially when this information is missing from other available instructional materials.

Ideally, if long amounts of text material are to be presented, the available software will enable easy downloading for reading or printing from the PC. Even better is the availability of a hypertext or hypermedia capability embedded in the CMC system, to serve as a structure to allow students to weave their own path through a set of material. Among the fundamental elements of hypertext (Nelson 1965) are the establishment of linkages among text fragments, the conditional handling of the linkages among fragments, and the idea that the fragments may be active programs rather than just passive pieces of text. Usually portions of the screen, such as a word or phrase, are highlighted; clicking on this object with a mouse or similar device takes the reader along a link to learn more about the selected topic.

Hypermedia means that some of the objects may be digitized visuals, video clips, or audio elements, or programs that execute, rather than being confined to printed text. This can make an electure much more active, engaging, and tailored to the needs and interests of the individual student. Although few instructors have sophisticated hypermedia software available within a CMC, there are several elements that can guide the development of electures in general: small modules of text, with students given the choice to decide whether they want or need to see more on a topic after it has been introduced, relatively passive reading of text segments interspersed with more active involvement (taking a mastery quiz, answering a question, voting, or otherwise applying the information that has just been read), and audiovisuals that present or illustrate the subject matter under discussion.

4.1.2 Ask-an-Expert
This approach involves class interaction with a subject area expert who might present a lecture, respond to questions, and generate discussion about a particular topic. Teachers establish a list of experts willing to undertake this role and set up procedures for that activity, such as providing appropriate user accounts and agreeing to a level and frequency of participation on the part of the expert. This format is primarily a question-and-answer model but can be launched by a short lecture or

presentation by the expert. Students send questions to the expert and obtain responses within a few days. The quick access to current and relevant information and the positive feedback of receiving an answer are the main benefits of this model.

4.1.3   Mentorship

An online mentor is a professional in a particular subject area who provides ongoing feedback until the apprentice (student) masters the learning task. At that point the mentor fades away, and the apprentice engages in the exploration of expert practice. For example, a student submits a poem or a short story to an online mentor, who provides coaching in how to improve the writing. The student-mentor interaction may continue over several weeks or even months as the student submits and resubmits the work and obtains ongoing feedback from the mentor. Online mentorship is a technique that has been successfully used in the humanities and sciences, from elementary school to university and adult education.

4.1.4   Tutor Support

Tutoring complements face-to-face and online classes. In distance mode, online tutors may provide the primary source of instructional support and interaction. Tutor support is essentially a one-to-one approach between tutor and student, although the networks enable one-to-many and many-to-many form of interaction as well.

4.1.5   Access to Network Resources

Global networks such as the Internet provide access to online databases and archives (data files), libraries, and thousands of special interest forums on topics ranging from nuclear physics to environmental issues. For example, the World Wide Web, available on the Internet, offers a hypertext front end to locating and then entering databases and services on hundreds of computers. These resources could be integrated into the design of online activities to benefit the curriculum.

4.1.6   Informal Peer Interaction

Informal peer interaction may take various forms: electronic penpals, special interest group discussions, and social interaction, as in a "virtual cafe" or the Public Square on the Free-Nets set up for informal social-izing. Interactions initiated through such public spaces may then move on to the exchange of personal email messages, as learners find peers with similar interests. These forums are common to most learning networks.

4.1.7 Structured Group Activity

This is a curriculum-based approach designed to be implemented with deadlines for submissions and responses. There are many types of cur-riculum group activities—long or short, very structured or loosely struc-tured—and all are based on peer interaction and the guided coaching or facilitation of an instructor. Group learning structures that have been effectively reformulated for network environments include seminars, small group discussions, learning partnerships and dyads, small work groups, learning circles, simulations and role plays, and debating teams. In addition, such group spaces as a Cafe or Student Lounge and a Mutual Help space where students help one another with technical and other problems are valuable. In the next section, we examine these variations in detail.

4.2 Group Learning Structures and Resources

4.2.1 Seminars

An online seminar is similar in many ways to a face-to-face seminar: students prepare by reading the assigned materials and then discuss, debate, extrapolate upon, and critique key issues as they defend, refine, or modify their positions and understanding. Online they do this by log-ging on to a designated network space. A virtual seminar is an electronic equivalent of walking into a physical seminar room: students log on to the designated conference to type in comments and to read and respond to their peers and instructor.

An online seminar series may begin with the instructor acting as the seminar leader and modeling how to moderate a discussion, but it should soon move on to student-led discussions on topics. Student leaders, working individually or in groups of two to three, launch an online seminar by presenting a brief introduction to or review of the topic, perhaps with a summary of the reading, together with two or three questions to focus the class discussion. The other students in the seminar are discussants and begin by responding to the questions. Initially, discussants may interact primarily with the seminar leaders, but as the exploration and analysis of the topic develops, there is increased peer interaction. Seminar leaders should regularly weave the discussion threads, to synthesize and focus the discussion to date and move it to new ground. The instructor takes on the role of a facilitator, watching students teach one another, monitoring the group dynamics, and ensuring that discussions are on topic and that the information being exchanged is not incorrect or misleading.

4.2.2 Small Group Discussions

Small group discussions enable students interested in a special topic to work together with a small number of peers, from three or four to as many as twenty, to discuss and analyze a particular topic, usually under the guidance of a group leader or the instructor. This structure is particularly valuable for facilitating active discussion in a large-sized class or when there are special interest groups on a particular topic. As in a seminar, students prepare for the discussion by reading the assigned material or undertaking a related task, and then log on to enter comments and respond to messages already posted by others in the conference.

4.2.3 Learning Partnerships and Dyads

In a learning partnership or dyad, learners are grouped into pairs. One application of learning partners is to provide peer support. For example, dyads can be used early in an online class or networked classroom to serve as an icebreaker: the teacher assigns each student to a student partner (either intra- or interclass), providing a peer in what is otherwise a new environment.

Dyads are useful as well for group assignments and are especially valuable as a first experience in online collaborative work. A joint writing project is a common example. Each dyad is assigned to write a report or creative piece, review an article or research an issue, and then (electronically) present the final product to the class. Online, working in pairs is logistically easier than working in large-sized groups. Students need to coordinate only with one other person, and the work often proceeds more efficiently. In online course activities, a group assignment based on dyads is valuable as a first group assignment and provides an entree to small work groups. The dyad may use a conference as a work space or use the email facility to communicate. Having a conference work space for each dyad provides a record of the discussions and what has been produced; it also enables the teacher to participate and comment.

4.2.4 Student Work Groups and Learning Circles

Student work groups and learning circles involve student collaboration on an assigned task, such as undertaking a research project, producing a report, or solving a problem. Teamwork can be accomplished online even when members of the team live in different locations and are linked only by computer networking or conferencing. Effective online teamwork requires clearly defined tasks, principles for decision making, roles, labor distribution, and timelines, which should be established in advance by the students or the teacher, or both. Coordination is critical when timelines are involved and the work is interdependent. To facilitate the process, the teacher might assign the task, group roles, subtasks, and timelines, or any portion of the process. At minimum, suggesting a timeline for the various phases of the online project can be helpful. Coordinating group work is a complex but crucial aspect of collaboration online.

Group size is an important factor, with three to four students per group a manageable size. (Too many participants in a group may result in unwieldy decision-making processes, particularly if a deadline must be met.) A small-sized group is particularly critical in an asynchronous environment, where large numbers of people may stall the process of decision making if users log on irregularly or are unable to reach consensus.

Online group work can reflect different kinds of products and processes. The final product can be a composite of each member's input or the result of collective input, refinement, and completion. Learning circles are similar but may be used to enhance face-to-face classes or may be used in a networked classroom approach.

Among the benefits of the online environment for group work is the opportunity to work closely in defining the problem and sharing ideas for how to accomplish the task. Another benefit is the ease of presenting each report to the class. The working group needs a private space during the preparation of the final report and a public conference open to all class members for presenting the final paper. Allowing class members to read and ask questions or comment on each presentation contributes to expanding the learning of all participants on that topic.

4.2.5   Team Presentations and Teaching by the Learners

Research and practical experience indicate that the most effective learning comes from teaching others. Opportunities for students to teach portions of the class are readily available online. Students in online classes can assume roles typically associated with teaching, such as leading class discussions. Team presentations may necessitate researching, writing, and then posting (presenting) a report or paper online to a computer conference, where it is read by peers and the instructor for comment, or it may involve leading a topical discussion.

In one format, students work in teams of two to four persons to present, moderate, and synthesize a week-long seminar on a class topic to fifteen or twenty students. The task involves three components:

1. Preparing and presenting an introduction to the topic, and posing two or three key questions to stimulate and focus discussion (day 1 of the online week).
2. Moderating the week's online discussion (days 1 to 7).
3. Synthesizing the content and analyzing the usage statistics and group process (posted three days after the seminar).

Presenters introduce the topic based on assigned and additional readings. They then moderate the discussion to maintain the communication flows, encouraging students to deepen their analyses of the topic and stay on topic. Regular synthesizing or weaving of the discussion (every two days, for example) helps students see which points have been covered and what progress has been made. At the end of the online week, presenters write a brief report, describing and assessing the nature of the interaction in their seminar. Meanwhile, another group of presenters has launched discussion on a new topic.

4.2.6   Simulations or Role Plays

Simulations or role plays enable learners to apply their theoretical knowledge in a simulated environment. The online environment is particularly conducive for simulations and role plays, given the tools provided by networking for anonymity or pseudonyms and setting out hypothetical scenarios. Examples of role plays used successfully in online environments include an online Management Lab, in which students take on various roles in managing a hypothetical corporation; a Research Institute, in which learners assume the personas or perspectives of well-known scientists to debate scientific approaches and procedures; and Sam's Café, in which learners adopt the personas of characters in a bar to explore different philosophical perspectives and positions.

The instructor assigns the roles and establishes the task and the timelines. The outcome may be a product, such as a report, or it may be a process, such as an opportunity to deepen and pursue a discussion. Timelines might be short, such as a few days, or the role play may continue over an extended period, perhaps alongside other tasks.

Some contexts employ a synchronous communication environment, whereby a team enacts a particular scenario such as a budget crisis or an interview. Recent examples include the multiuser text-based virtual realities of MUDs (multiple user domains, multiple user dialogue), and MUSEs (multiuser simulation environments) accessible on the Internet. MUDs and MUSEs are computer programs that users can log into and explore in real time. Users can use commands to walk around the environment, interact with other characters, solve puzzles, play games, and explore or create new rooms or activities. Many MUDs and MUSEs are related to fantasy or combat games and role plays; others have expressly educational and social goals, such as simulating scientific labs and experiments in which students team up with actual scientists.

4.2.7   Debating Teams

The educational (and social) world is full of controversies. For many subjects of study, there are unresolved issues such as competing theories, interpretations of data, methodological approaches, value preferences, predictions, interests, or policies. These might vary from alternative theories of the origin of the universe to issues such as abortion. Students need to gain a deep understanding of the opposing facts, theories, and points of view. The worst way to do this is to give a lecture; the best way is a debate, especially one that continues over a period of time, enabling students to pursue and present additional information to support their positions. The understanding of controversy comes through participation. In the Hegelian process of thesis and antithesis, both argued and attacked vigorously, students can achieve their own synthesis and well-supported point of view.

Students should be instructed explicitly to debate ideas, not make personal attacks. The rules of a formal debate might be outlined to emphasize the importance of intellectual discourse, exchange, politeness, and focus on refuting ideas, not attacking people.

A debate can be organized around any issue or question with two or more sides. Debating teams allow learners an opportunity to deepen their analytical and communication skills by defending one position and critiquing counterpositions. An online debate can be unstructured, with students responding to a stated position (and defending their position), or it can be structured, as in a dyad or team format.

In a dyad format, the debate is structured around students working in teams of two, each with an assigned position (yea or nay) on a particular topic. Each team has its own conference space to present, argue, and defend its case. Other dyads may be allowed to read the debates of their peers, but they can write only to their own space.

One of the unique features of online activities is the full transcript of the proceedings that is automatically generated during the class discussion. This feature can be used for retrospective analysis or review, thus helping to develop critical and analytical thinking skills. For example, the rules of the debate might require that students gather their data and arguments from the class conferences. This approach encourages students to make multiple passes through the transcripts. Dyad debates are particularly valuable as an activity concluding a class or curricular segment, whereby students revisit, review, and rework the content of the class.

Experience with team debates indicates that the size of a team or side should be between five and fifteen persons. In a small class (twenty or fewer), students might choose which side to argue. If a large number of students is involved, an issue with three or more sides might be found, and students assigned to the positions in order to ensure a fairly even division. For example, a debate for management of information systems could have these four sides:

1. Information technology causes organizational centralization of authority.
2. Information technology causes decentralization of authority.
3. There is no technological influence on organizational authority.
4. Organizational authority structure influences the choice of information technology.

In the environmental area, to give another example, there could be an N-sided debate, with each team arguing the merits of alternative energy sources (solar, wind, nuclear, conservation, etc.).

When engaging in the debate, participants should be encouraged to research the issue before making a statement and to spend at least as much time rebutting the statements of the other side as in building their own case. By researching, carefully composing position statements, examining the statements of the opposition for weaknesses, and most of all, through the social dynamics of a contest of skill, the debate as a format for group learning is a very effective technique.

Typically, each student makes one conference entry stating an argument for his or her assigned position and then is required to make a minimum of one rebuttal. Most students make many contributions to the debate, unable to resist rebutting the rebuttal and engaging in several exchanges involving clarifications and refutations.

With small groups of students (six or fewer), the teams might be assigned to coordinate their arguments rather than have each person work and argue individually. This format would make for more comprehensive coverage of all possible points but adds approximately a week for preparation and organization to the debate process. In such cases each team would have a private conference to discuss and establish its position.

After setting up the issue, the sides, and the procedures, the instructor generally can sit back and enjoy the debate. The only other duty is to close the debate—a summary of the arguments on each side of the issue by the debaters or the instructor or some sort of judgment, by the instructor, or the students, on the best arguments.

Participation may continue after the debate is declared over. Because of the rich tapestry of positions and counterarguments, a debate needs a minimum of two weeks to play out online, and longer is sometimes better. The debate might be the central activity for that period and then continue while the class moves on to other activities. Even if a debate is over in terms of graded participation, if the topic was an important issue with many good points to be made on either side, students are likely to continue reading and responding.

A debate can be combined with role playing, with individuals or teams of students assigned to take the position of specific players (both individual and organizational) in debating the issue. For example, in a course on computers and society, an issue one semester was who should have access to hospital databases for analytical or other purposes. Students were assigned to play the roles of patients, doctors, hospital administrators, lawyers, insurance companies, the medical association, and the ethics committee of the computing professional society. The "doctors" were to argue for the status quo: only doctors and hospital administrators and researchers have access to the data. The other players were to propose and defend additional access rights by other parties.

Role playing might be done in an anthropology course by having some students play the role or interests of the natives and others the role of the settlers. In history, the issue of slavery might be debated by having some students represent the Confederacy and others the North.

Yet another variation on the debate is a trial, with lawyers for the prosecution and the defense, plus expert witnesses, judge (moderator), and jury. For example, in a course offered by Connect Ed on artificial intelligence, a human was put on trial for "murdering" an android, as a mechanism for playing out some of the social and ethical issues posed with the introduction of artificial beings. The concept of the scientific issues court can also be used to structure debates in such areas as environmental concerns. In a scientific court process every specific point in favor must be matched with a counterpoint, and the opposing points are individually rated by the jury. This is closer to the basic idea of a Hegelian process than a standard judicial court.

4.2.8   Peer Learning Groups

Peer learning groups can be based on dyads or small groups, with learners assisting one another on various tasks. For example, students may work together online to help one another improve their writing skills. Each student prepares and sends online a draft version of a paper to a peer for comment and critique. Based on the suggestions and input of the peer, the student revises the paper before submitting it to the teacher. Both the paper and the peer critique can be graded, or assistance may be encouraged primarily for mutual support networking.

If the task is conducted using dyads, the teacher has the choice of opening a conference for the activity or having students use email. The conference option is preferable when there is a need for a record of the interactions and/or for the teacher to participate easily.

4.2.9   Networked Classrooms

Entire classes or courses in different locations may be networked to engage in joint activities online. At the elementary school level, classes in different parts of the world are beginning to network online to learn about life in other communities. The class might jointly compose and send a letter to a sister class or school on a regular basis, such as once a week, or different classes may work together online on a joint newspaper. Other joint projects, such as investigating and exchanging information on environmental issues, have been used with great success.

At the high school level, students in similar courses in different schools have collaborated in various ways. For example, students in honors biology classes around New Jersey undertook to monitor, report, and jointly map and analyze the levels of acid rain and the quality of water in lakes and rivers around the state. By sharing the task of data collection, they could better see that these environmental problems needed both local and regional solutions. In addition, they held an online science fair, with the findings of group projects reported online and outside expert judges selecting the winners online.

At the college level, different sections of the same course have been networked to share some activities. For example, an NJIT graduate course on information systems is frequently offered at both the main campus and one or more branch campuses during a semester. One of the objectives of the course is for students to understand why information system implementations may fail, besides through poor design. Each student must find, analyze, and report the details of an actual case. A far richer set of cases is generated by the combined sections than would be possible by students in a single section of twenty-five or fewer students. In addition, the linking of sections online gives students the benefit of having two instructors who differ somewhat in disciplinary background and point of view.

Another possibility is to network classes that are studying the same topic but from different disciplinary perspectives. For example, one semester a section of Computers and Society taught by a sociologist at a liberal arts college was linked to a section taught by a computer scientist at an engineering school. This approach broadens the viewpoints and considerations to which students are exposed.

An increasingly adopted strategy is to use email networks to link students in similar courses at different universities. Such regional, national, or international networking is motivational and intellectually stimulating.

4.2.10 The Virtual Cafe

Social communication is an essential component of educational activity. Just as a face-to-face school or campus provides places for students to congregate socially, an online educational environment should provide a space, such as a virtual cafe, for informal discourse. The virtual cafe can contribute to creating a sense of community within the group. The forging of social bonds has important socioaffective and cognitive benefits for the learning activities.

The virtual cafe should be primarily a student space and not be directly tied to the curriculum. This is a space for students to talk about their interests, concerns, the weather, social plans, or even write an interactive group novel. The main point is that it should be a space moderated for and by the students, for socializing.

An electronic staff lounge has also been valuable in contexts where several teachers are on a network. It provides a space for teachers to share skills, exchange ideas, and provide professional peer support. It also helps to build community on the network.

4.2.11   Mutual Help

An online help conference based on mutual assistance is a valuable means for providing technical and system support. In a mutual assist conference, students can ask for and provide help about using the system and share tips on how to use it better. As a mutual help space, the questions and answers come primarily from the students. Student's helping one another encourages cooperation and social learning. The opportunity for students to share their discoveries in operating the system can also build confidence in using new communication and knowledge work tools.

4.3   Conceptualizing the Networked Learning Environment

The instructional models enumerated in this chapter do not by themselves create the learning network. They must be conceptualized within an educational environment. Moreover, approaches from the literature on collaborative learning in face-to-face classes need to be reconceptualized and reformulated for the online environment.

All education—face to face, distance mode, online—requires understanding the nature of the medium in order to conceptualize and design it as an educational environment. Online education is a new and unique domain. Although it is similar to face-to-face and distance mode education, the attributes of networking systems combine to offer both unprecedented opportunities and constraints for teaching and learning (Hiltz 1986; Harasim 1989). The characteristics of the medium shape the way in which educational tasks, timelines, and group processes can be implemented. Educators need to formulate instructional events based on the attributes offered by networking systems.

Five attributes distinguish communication that occurs on current forms of computer conferencing and bulletin board systems and provide a conceptual framework to guide design and implementation of learning networks (Harasim 1990a, 1993a).

• Many-to-many (group communication)
• Anyplace (place independence)
• Anytime (asynchronicity, time independence)

• Text-based (and increasingly multimedia)
• Computer-mediated messaging.

In enabling new teaching and learning options, these attributes offer opportunities for learning networks but introduce as well unique constraints for designing and managing the online educational environment.

Of the networking media available to teachers, systems that organize the virtual space into discrete spaces or conferences are the most amenable to instructional design. Computer conferences should be thought of as spaces that can be shaped by topical structuring and sequencing to form an educational environment. Shaping the features of the conferencing system into an environment for educational interaction requires significant work by the teacher in organizing the learning events according to topic, task, group, and timeline.

4.3.1   Turning a Conference into a Classroom

The instructor must make a computer conference feel and function like a classroom, turning the computer screen into a window on the world, so that students exchanging asynchronous messages feel and behave as if they are working together with a group of peers. Students who may never meet face to face must be able to function as a group using only computer messages to link them together. The instructor's challenge is to create appropriate conditions for a group learning environment using such limited tools as the ability to open and close conferences in various topical and temporal formats. A sense of group and community among electronically assembled individuals can be created by a combination of facilitation skills, team-building activities, and conferences for specific groups and tasks.

Computer conferencing, like face-to-face activities, supports group communication exchange if seminars, discussions, debates, and group projects are reconceptualized to fit within the attributes and constraints of the online environment. If we think of a typical group project, we generally assume certain givens, such as meeting somewhere—perhaps a series of meetings to plan and implement a task. An online group has different givens. For example, it is asynchronous, which means that members of the group do not meet at the same time. Online group communication can take place twenty-four hours a day, seven days a week. It is also place independent. These qualities increase access and expand opportunities for discussion, interaction, and reflection. Increased temporal and geographical access and the motivation of working with a group can stimulate active input by learners. Designs for online group work are needed to structure and organize the student input. But the asynchronous and place-independent characteristics also create problems of coordination. Some participants may lag behind others or disappear for a time. Text-based discussion can also be voluminous and soon overwhelm even an enthusiastic reader, so message organization and focus are important for managing the information flows and the curriculum. Managing group tasks among team members located in different cities or perhaps even countries is complex, especially using text-based asynchronous communication.

4.3.2 Metaphors

Metaphors of a campus, a schoolhouse, a classroom, or a community can provide a familiar concept or link to help new users become comfortable with the online space and be able to conceptualize this new environment and navigate around the various conferences. Using the example of the online campus, the teacher may compare each conference to a room, forming the setting for a specific activity or topical discussion. One conference may be designated as a seminar room for a particular topic; another conference may be a room for small group discussion; yet another conference might be designated as a virtual cafe, for informal socializing and drop in; a help desk is a conference for requesting or volunteering assistance. Each "room" is a conference. Users "move" from room to room by changing conferences. The metaphor helps users grasp the conferencing environment and not feel lost in the space. By knowing where to send comments or where to go to read discussions, users can feel comfortable and become productive.

4.3.3 Instructional Design

Intentional structuring of computer conferences—for example, defining individual, paired, and small group tasks and the definition of subgroup and whole group discussion—can create an organized environment for online educational activities. Designing an online educational environ-ment involves structuring conferences by type of task, size of group, duration of task, and scheduling of task.

For conference spaces distinguished according to the type of task, conferences are needed for course-related activities and for informal dis-cussions, such as virtual cafe and help line, which help build community online and support the socioaffective aspects of knowledge building.

Conferences may also be distinguished by group size. Some topics or tasks may require a full group or plenary group activity, while others benefit from small groups or dyads. If certain conferences are designated for small work groups, access to such spaces is limited to group mem-bers. An online class activity may involve students working in small groups or dyads to carry out an assignment and prepare a report for the full group. Each group needs its own online work space in which to discuss and draft its final report; only the group members and the teacher have access to this space. For the purpose of the class presenta-tion, the teacher opens a conference to which all class members are joined.

Duration is related to the length of time a conference is open or made available by the teachers for a particular topic or task. A small group may spend up to three or more weeks writing a joint report; other tasks, such as a small group discussion, may take only one week per topic. Activities and conferences such as the Cafe, the Library, or the Help conference should be open throughout the online course.

Scheduling tasks and conference spaces is important for sequencing learning and organizing the curriculum. Online courses benefit from schedules based on specified units of time, such as the concept of an online week, based on seven days (including weekends). Some tasks, such as a discussion, may utilize one online week per topic. Tasks with more extensive work may require several online weeks.

Structuring and sequencing the online activities can be accomplished by providing several conference spaces, each accommodating a specific task and topic for various durations. Topical and temporal structuring of conferences assists information management by organizing the mes-sages by topic and sequence. Providing a conference per topic, and spec-ifying the duration of each topical discussion or conference (such as a weekly topic or focus), can help organize the activities conceptually and procedurally for participants.

4.4 Integrating Other Media and Tools

One of the most frequent uses of CMC is in combination with face-to-face meetings. Many colleges and universities use learning networks in mixed-mode formats: the classes meet face to face, using lecture, for half of the usual contact hours, and online for the other half to conduct group assignments and most discussions. Another common format is to hold face-to-face meetings at the beginning of a course for training and orientation, and possibly even at the end for presentations or demonstrations of skill, with the bulk of the course activity occurring online.

Particularly for corporate training courses, the initial meeting may be several days in length, for example, a long weekend, and there may be other meetings of the course participants scheduled at intervals during a six-month to multiyear program. Keeping the trainees online between face-to-face meetings means that they can take the skills or perspectives they have been shown back to their jobs, try to apply them, and receive ongoing advice and feedback from peers and mentors during this process of application.

Learning networks might also be combined with field trips. For example, students in an art course might spend several days in museums together; those in a music course might attend concerts together. Although many distance education students cannot travel weekly to a class meeting, many might be able to set aside a single two- or three-day period during the course for intensive field trips. This format requires only one absence from work and home and only one expenditure of time and money for travel.

Alternatively, a face-to-face class may incorporate electronic field trips to a museum or online interviews with a music composer or orchestra conductor. Paper-based media are always used in conjunction with online courses. In thinking through the course objectives and the available media, the course designer can also consider integration of other telecommunication or computer-based media. For example, one secondary school project linking schools in Japan, Hawaii, and the U.S.

mainland holds periodic real-time audio conferences. Small group audio conferences or conference calls might also be scheduled.

Probably the most frequent media combination is the use of television broadcasts or videotapes with online communication. The visual medium is good for showing a science experiment, the derivation of an equation, or many other types of topics. Many high-quality video-based courses exist and can be licensed for use. CMC balances the one-way lecture delivery via video with an opportunity for active learner participation and multilogues. If this combination is chosen, the instructional designer must be careful to require CMC as an integral part of the course assignments. If it is made purely optional, without course recognition, to "ask the instructor questions if you have them," few students are likely to opt for the extra work of signing on.

Another variation is to incorporate periodic real-time (synchronous) audiographic conferencing, which links two locations with an audio line and a shared visual space. Sometimes the shared visual space is slow-scan television; sometimes it is an electronic blackboard; sometimes computer-controlled slide projectors that show the same image in both locations. In another version of audiographic conferencing, used at the University of the Virgin Islands, classrooms in two or more locations have an audio line plus shared projections of a computer screen, so that whatever is being displayed on the computer screen of the instructor at the hub of the network is also being shown on large screens at the front of the room in other locations. Control of the shared-screen computer projections can be passed by the moderator to another location, so that any student on any island can show possible solutions to a problem to the others. In this implementation, audiographic synchronous sessions to link up teachers and learners on several islands are combined with computer conferencing and electronic mail on a continuous basis.

Integration of various software packages and/or desktop communication packages is becoming increasingly possible in creating learning network environments. For example, PC-based software programs, varying from commercial tools such as graphics programs to course-specific CAI-type materials prepared by the instructor, can be integrated into a course. The availability of desktop multimedia communication software such as audio, image, and videoconferencing systems enables the integration of real-time multiple media with email and computer conferencing software.

Every medium that is added is a potential barrier to those who do not have the requisite equipment or funds needed to use it and another set of techniques or skills that students must master before they can concentrate on the substantive material being delivered via the medium. No course curriculum or activity should be overloaded with unnecessary media, which might overcomplicate or overwhelm the learning process.

4.5 Summary

An online course is like a garden in many ways, and one of the most fundamental similarities is the importance of design. The design of a garden refers to the shape of the beds and structures for the plants to grow in and on, and to the combinations of plant material, to produce both harmony and contrast. The design of an online course refers to the different types of structures created to hold and shape the interaction among participants, as well as the sequencing of these different forms of interaction. And just as a garden of all pink roses or all white baby's breath or all blue delphiniums would be boring, so is a single type of structure for class interaction unexciting; it is more effective to create a carefully planned mix of different forms or structures for interaction. On the other hand, to try to include a little bit of everything creates a lack of focus and cohesion.

5

Getting Started: The Implementation Process

As teachers begin to plan an online class activity or online course, they need to determine what kind of training students require, whether to ease slowly into group work or implement it quickly full-scale, and how to handle initial student uncertainty about group work online. This chapter considers these issues and provides a guide to getting started.

5.1 Individuals' Adoption of Learning Networks

When a learning network is introduced and implemented by an individual teacher or professor, the issues are somewhat different from those involved in organizational adoption. This section explores the activities that an individual should consider in contemplation of setting up a learning network.

5.1.1 Identifying the Need
The first step is to identify the educational activity that can benefit from online activity and determine what model or approach will be used: a networked classroom or an online course. Some educators start by integrating a networking component or activity into a traditional face-to-face classroom model. Others, with perhaps no greater expertise in networking, may decide that totally online delivery of a course is the way to get started. The latter approach requires more planning and preparation but is certainly feasible and is the way that some of the authors of this book started. The key starting point is an application that is appropriate and enhanced by the online mode. Student interest and support are also important, as is administrative recognition.

The impetus may be thought of as resulting from a push from an existing class that could benefit from networking, or from a pull from a potential market that is not currently being served. For example, in-class debates suffer from the inability of students to organize their materials and references and present their arguments effectively. In an anthropology course at Upsala College in the mid-1980s, this was the initial motivation for going online. The instructor found that online debate statements were much better than off-the-cuff oral statements made in a face-to-face debate about policies relating to Indian reservations in the United States. In addition, online debates provided a written transcript that could be reviewed and used as a resource rather than being forgotten as soon as the debate was over. With the desire to have an extensive online debate as the initial motivation, many other useful applications of computer conferencing were found for the course.

Alternatively, an unmet educational need may be identified, and networking may offer the solution to the marketing opportunity. For example, Northern Virginia Community College has combined computer conferencing with other asynchronous technologies such as video and voice mail to create entire degree programs for home-based learning. Hundreds of students per semester enroll, who because of work and family obligations and heavy traffic conditions, would find it impossible to attend regularly scheduled on-campus courses.

5.1.2   Ensuring Access to the Requisite Computer Resources and Systems

The second step is to ensure convenient and regular access to adequate and appropriate computer hardware, software, and telecommunication resources: a network system (computer conferencing, bulletin board system, or email) and computer network access for all students and teacher. A technical expert can advise on appropriate hardware and software.

If the instructional model is that of a networked classroom or adjunct mode use of networking, institutional resources, such as a computer lab with telecommunication linkages, are essential. For course delivery that is totally online, a critical prerequisite is that students have their own computer and modem (or have easy access, perhaps through their workplace or the educational institution).

The instructor should ensure that the network software system is appropriate for the application and available for the duration and extent required. Ongoing system support is also essential, to ensure that any technical problems will be fixed immediately and that new users can receive support as needed. Support for the instructor for such tasks as establishing new user IDs and creating conference spaces is also important. Finally, a related consideration is the "information highways" that the communications will travel. Long-distance telephone calls can be prohibitively expensive. The host computer for the software should be on the Internet or available to users thorough some other cut-rate digital highway, such as a community or state fiber-optic network, or a commercial service such as Sprintnet.

5.1.3 Obtaining Administrative Support

Obtaining top management recognition and support for implementing a learning network is important for ensuring the legitimacy of the activity as well as for ongoing support and organizational awareness, acceptance, and eventually adoption. The individual adopter is both a pioneer and a potential advocate for the organizational adoption of this new educational technology. Management support is critical since some resources will likely be needed to launch the application and, in some cases, to legitimize and explain learning networks to others.

5.1.4 Designing the Curriculum

This corresponds to developing a syllabus for the course or course segment. What are the educational goals in terms of the content area, knowledge, and skills that are to be gained? How does this translate into a series of topics, readings, and activities for imparting this knowledge? What are the goals of each of these modules or topics in the course? What assignments can be used to build and demonstrate the students' mastery of the knowledge and/or skills that are the goals of each module?

5.1.5 Developing or Locating Educational Materials

Having decided on a series of topics and a set of goals, the instructor must locate or develop appropriate curricular materials. Usually this process starts with identifying a textbook or set of books and articles or material published in other forms. Along with each set of readings or videotapes to watch or software to use, the instructor will need to develop a series of supplementary concepts or examples to be covered in lecture or electure, questions for discussion, and assignments or activities for students.

5.1.6   Designing the Online Environment
The decision on specific software structures and tools must be made in conjunction with the choice of one or more collaborative learning designs for the unit, such as seminar, debate, or role playing. (Alternative learning designs are described in detail in chapter 4.)

5.1.7   Organizing the Resources
Learning resources should be organized in advance of any online activity. Access to subject experts online needs to be arranged to ensure their availability for the activity. Course materials need to be prepared; if the course is entirely online, any textbooks or other paper-based materials need to be sent out well before the first day of online class. Online materials need to be organized appropriately, for access by students.

Those who are unfamiliar with the resources available through the Internet can consult *The Whole Internet User's Guide and Catalog* (Krol 1992), *The Internet Guide for New Users* (Dern 1994), or *The Internet Companion: A Beginner's Guide to Global Networking* (LaQuey 1993) and search out relevant news groups, databases, and information resources that can be accessed easily and free of charge, using an Internet Gopher. When relevant resources are located, the instructor documents how students can access them and then builds their use into the appropriate unit in the course.

5.1.8   Providing Training
Training should suit the level of experience of the user and be ongoing. That the teacher is adequately trained is essential and is assumed as a prerequisite to undertaking this entire process. The teacher requires skill and comfort in using the system at a higher level than is required for the students, since he or she will be expected to create conferences, provide

some user support, and perhaps even establish user IDs on the network system.

5.1.9   Attending to the Physical Environment

The physical environment—a school lab, the home, the work setting—needs to be planned as well, for enthusiasm with the new conceptual environment may be reduced by a poor physical environment, which can lead to the inability to concentrate, sore muscles, headaches, and other physical, stress-related symptoms.

Proper lighting and furniture are essential to reduce the incidence of physical stress. Computer equipment should be set up to correspond to the size of person using it. Chairs are optimally adjusted when elbows are flexed 90 to 110 degrees when the hands are on the keyboard. The computer screen should be just below eye level so that the eyes look down 10 to 15 degrees. Younger students in particular should be taught to remain a safe distance (eighteen inches) from the screen and should be monitored for signs of physical stress such as squinting or hunching over the keyboard. All users need to be reminded that ten-minute breaks must be taken away from the screen each hour and that not more than five hours daily should be spent doing computer work.

5.2   Organizational Adoption of Learning Networks

A small percentage of educators at any institution will take to this technology with no trouble, provided it is made available to them and to the students. This is the first and crucial step in the process, to be accomplished by those on the administrative side. Unfortunately, administrators may insist that a majority of the teaching group have to want something before resources will be spent on it. This is the catch-22 situation that has taken place at many institutions of higher education. The only solution is administrative support, based on a recognition of the opportunities provided and/or the negative consequences of not moving ahead in this area. Unfortunately, it is often the recognition of the disaster potential rather than the improvement potential that drives administrative innovation.

The presence of a small but enthusiastic group of educators and the needed resources will not ensure success unless the introduction is accompanied by policies that encourage utilization by other educators. The simplest way to introduce educators new to the technology is to provide the facilities as an adjunct resource to normal face-to-face courses and to encourage more experienced teachers to allow peers to browse in their courses in order to learn by observation some of the methods used to promote online learning.

The best introduction is accomplished on a departmental, program, or schoolwide basis, so that all the teachers and students in a department form a critical mass. After that start, other departmental functions (such as student advisement, senior projects, course scheduling, and so forth) can be introduced as a part of the functioning of the network.

The offering of remote courses through the network requires significant initial work on the part of the educators involved, in order to convert their material to electronic form and to rethink both the presentation and the assignments. Instructors benefit from some reasonable amount of course load reduction to design an online offering. This release time is a one-time-only requirement per course, and it is important in influencing whether the instructor will feel encouraged to make such electronic offerings.

Although most innovations are adopted because they have clear advantages over the previous ways tasks or operations were done, an array of factors can hinder the adoption process. The characteristics of the innovation (complexity, observability, etc.) and the types of individuals (innovators, early adopters, late adopters, laggards, and rejectors) play an important role in the introduction of any innovation (Teles 1988). These same factors affect the adoption of learning networks. Before the implementation stage, planners should thus give special attention to five factors in the adoption process.

5.2.1   Involvement in Planning

Once the institution decides to introduce learning networks, a key step is to involve as many participants as possible in the planning, both to co-opt potential resistors and consolidate the adoption decision. Many schools or other institutions that have introduced CMC without regard for this step have found that only a few individuals used the innovation, and it did not spread throughout the organization as originally assumed.

Ideally the institution wants to generate enthusiasm about learning networks so that people feel they have a stake in the innovation process. Meetings and demonstrations of learning networks, featuring individuals from other organizations that have already adopted CMC, are useful in this regard.

5.2.2 Easy-to-Use, Customized Software and Online Moderation

Ease of use is a major factor in the adoption of learning networks. When the software is not intuitive and requires the memorization of complex or numerous steps to log on and to write and retrieve notes, usage tends to decline. A typical nonuser-friendly software system has more than one password to log on, no visual aids to facilitate online navigation, and too many steps to accomplish a task. User-friendly software is customized to each individual, with logging on done through a single keystroke. The software might also display the logo of the school or educational institutional to provide familiarity. Visual aids with built-in macros should be made available to facilitate navigation and a number of standard online operations: log on to the net, download and uploading files, faxing from the net, moving from personal (email) to public areas (conferences, mailing lists), and so forth. Software that automates log-on procedures is becoming increasingly available and significantly simplifies network access.

Online moderators facilitate familiarity with the system. The moderator function may be provided by the course instructor or by additional tutors or teaching assistants assigned to small groups of students. A new user who asks a question and does not obtain a response within two days is likely to feel frustrated. Moderators should welcome new users, respond to all questions, and facilitate navigation through the system. In the initial stages, the moderator should use the telephone or face-to-face meetings to provide help to new users and to encourage potential adopters to join online activities.

5.2.3 Selecting a Core Group of Users

The implementation process should focus on including as many individuals as possible to initiate use of learning networks in the institution, but it is unlikely that everyone will adopt the innovation. Early adopters will be willing to experiment; potential adopters will find reasons to postpone its use; and others will reject it altogether. (This is true for adoption of innovation in general.) For this reason, initially there will be a fairly small core group of individuals who will use learning networks and serve as role models for others to observe and follow in the adoption as they see the advantages of accessing networks.

Support for the initial core group is critical to the success of the initiative. The role of the facilitator is to talk to each individual educator, assess his or her needs, and suggest online services to fit those particular needs. Everyone will come to learning networks in a different way—for example, one-to-one communication through email, participation in a particular service, or exploring the networks just for the fun of it. All are valuable ways to initiate individuals into this new domain and should be actively supported.

5.2.4   Inservice Training and Ongoing Help

Purchase of hardware and software is a critical cost factor but not the major issue in the implementation process. Rather, the most demanding part relates to the human factor: the training and the provision of ongoing support. The adoption of learning networks requires that individuals change their thinking about educational processes, roles, and opportunities to use and benefit from the networks.

After training, ongoing help can be provided in many ways, for example, one-to-one help in resolving specific problems, with the trainer coaching the learner through the steps of sending an email message or providing help over the telephone. Online help is also important, both asynchronous as well as synchronous help from the system operator. Finally, an especially important device is the creation of an online conference space for mutual help, in which students are encouraged to help one another. This approach builds on the use of group learning.

5.2.5   Provision of Full-Time Access to Learning Networks

Full-time access is recommended as the best option, with users accessing networks from anywhere at any time.

These considerations should facilitate the implementation process, but planners nevertheless should be prepared to encounter unexpected problems such as late delivery of software, the fact that potential adopters may not have available time at the initial stage of implementation, and so forth. Given this situation, planners should be prepared to spend double the time initially calculated to implement the innovation (Resta 1989).

5.3   Access and Resources

Access is a difficult and multi-faceted problem. The students and faculty who wish to use a learning network will see no distinction between the service on the host computers and the process of getting to those services via the workstations (e.g., personal computers), and the software they are using on those workstations. Unless they are fairly computer literate they will view everything that is required for access as part of one system. Yet a range of variations may exist in the process of access:

• Different operating systems on different types of workstations or personal computers

• Different communication packages on the personal computers (e.g., Procomm, Smartcom, Versaterm, etc.)

• Different digital network protocols requiring settings commands on different networks (e.g., Telenet, Uninet, Decnet, etc.)

• Different transmission protocols for the batch transfer of material between the workstation and the host (e.g., Kermit, Xmodem, etc.)

• Different offline editors the various users wish to use to prepare material locally for transmission

The various combinations of these facilities lead to problems; for example, the backspace or function keys may not work the same for each user. It is not unusual for people trying to help one another on the learning network to arrive at an impasse because they do not realize there are keyboard differences between them.

The students will first turn to the teacher for help, expecting him or her to know how to use these various tools of access, much as he or she knows how to use the tools of a normal classroom (e.g., blackboards, projectors).

The ideal situation is that the technology of the learning network is maintained and supported by a computer services department that cares about its users and supplies the required infrastructure and materials. The first requirement is a set of guides for users that takes a completely different approach from the reference manuals typically supplied with software packages. These manuals usually list every function and every option for every function in the software. They rarely have good illustrations of how a user sets and sequences these functions to accomplish a specific task. Therefore, it is essential to provide a set of one- or two-page starting guides that are designed around the specific tasks that the user needs to accomplish to gain access to the learning network. These should explain what to do and offer short explanations of what is happening and what the user should expect to see. For example, they could explain setting up and using the software, accessing Internet resources, uploading and downloading, using the local editor, and keyboard differences associated with different access methods. Clearly this task becomes easier when all the users have the same type of personal computer and use the same type of software. However, the real world is never so simple. If a computer services department is not supplying these guides, then those wishing to offer online education have to arrange to get them produced and reviewed for clarity and usability.

Another requirement for learning networks is to have one or more online user consultants, whom the users of the system can message any time they have a problem they cannot solve with respect to the mechanics of using the system or the resources they have for gaining access. Sometimes these user consultants also supply content knowledge, directing users to conferences or data resources on the system that might be of interest to them. A good user consultant is a kind of knowledge broker who matches users' needs and interests with resources available on the network.

One of the pragmatic characteristics of a learning network serving remote access is that it probably should support two different modes of access: the full-screen, full-duplex standard (VT100) and the line-by-line, half-duplex mode (TTY). Users coming in over a local area network or on a direct dial will find the full screen the more satisfying because it provides the same sort of interface flexibility they are used to on their workstations. However, many digital networks intermittently are very slow and cumbersome. When there are long delays between sending material to the host and then actually being able to see it appear on the screen, users become frustrated. In half-duplex mode, the input can be by a full line at a time, and the delays are much less bothersome. The problem of transmission delays can be very pronounced for international users and for use of some of the networks like Uninet where free academic use always seems to fill up available capacity. Considerations like this should be part of the guidance material supplied to the users.

Ideally, each user can access the learning network from home as well as from his or her place of work or study. With respect to planning a service of this type, instructors should be assured of the needed resources. The planning process should also include the possibility of students' being able to purchase machines and software at sizable discounts because of the large-scale orders that the network itself can support.

A large number of communication packages are available. Most accomplish the key functions that are needed and vary only in such considerations as ease of use and cost; some perform better with respect to incorporating error-checking routines for uploading and downloading. There is one key feature, however, that a communication package being used with a CMC system should have: the ability to review one's interaction while working online. That is, users can go back and review related comments made earlier while they are engaged in writing a response to an item.

It is impossible to be definitive about editors or word processing packages; the very best in the minds of most people is always the one they learned first. It is much harder for people to learn a new editor than to learn their first editor (it would be like asking a person to learn a new keyboard layout after having mastered typing). The only important functional requirement for an editor is that it allows conversion of the final text to a literal or pure ASCII version before uploading to the conference system. In this way, the internal hidden control characters that are usually used to format text will not foul up the presentation of the text material to those receiving it through the network.

A valuable new development is the offline reader, a communications program developed to save communication costs and to facilitate asynchronous transfer of messages (see appendix C). The system operates in a client-server model: personal and conference messages are uploaded to the server, and new incoming messages are downloaded and placed in the appropriate folders at the client or end user level. As a result of this operation, the time actually spent online is reduced, thereby reducing costs asociated with telecommunications and also facilitating ease of use, since the user is working in their familiar desktop environment.

A single learning network service can never control and smooth over all the problems that its users might have with respect to access and resources. (The exception is a company of sufficient size and with enough capital to provide the same network, host computers, workstations, and software to everyone.) As a result, most institutions that wish to offer a learning network should consider special seminars for students to provide a basic level of computer literacy for those who will be using the system. We know enough today to be able to design systems that are fairly easy to learn to use; however, even an easy-to-use system can be annoying and difficult when something is going wrong. Users need to know enough about the collection of systems they are using to be able to identify where the trouble is before they can find out what to do about it. This is a wise investment of resources.

5.4   Costs and Technology

Costs of implementing online learning communities can vary significantly. Whether the introduction of CMC technology for education is relatively cheap or expensive depends on the existing infrastructure for computer support in the learning community. If the prospective users already have access to PCs, it will cost relatively little to add the use of computer networks. Also, costs are relative to how basic or sophisticated the software system chosen is.

In addition, costs need to be considered relative to various indirect and substitution cost factors. For example, what is the cost that a student expends in travel to a physical classroom and how much time is lost in this process? What is the cost of using mailing lists rather than a conference system, in terms of the added time a student or educator must spend in organizing or tracking the material? (Most educational bureaucracies, however, do not consider the value of a student's or educator's time in various cost analyses).

Nevertheless, costs are no longer the major constraint to the introduction of this technology if the infrastructure exists. The most serious barrier is the human factor: introducing new approaches and new technology into a social system that may be resistant to change. The availability of personal computers for students and faculty is the second aspect of infrastructure.

The specific cost examples we use here are for 1992. In the future, they will not rise with respect to either hardware or software. Even corrected for inflation, they should decrease in the future.

5.4.1   The Personal Computer

According to some colleges and universities, providing a personal computer to every student is a cost saving relative to the size of the central computer plant that would be needed to support the level of computer capability otherwise required. At many institutions, machines are included in tuition costs, and thus paid for over the life of an undergraduate degree. The four to five years' obsolescence of existing equipment and the need to make huge capital outlays is thus no longer a major problem for the university. When analyzed on a life-cycle basis, it becomes readily acceptable to the most conservative of financial officers in university and college administrations.

A 1992 analysis for an American public school district determined that with an initial capital fund to support the introduction of personal computers for every student, a fee of $25 a month for every student would allow the same type of leasing to every public school student, with sufficient overhead to subsidize about 15 percent of the families that might find this cost a hardship. This was based on a five-year life for the personal computer systems. Children in kindergarten to fourth grade might have a simpler machine, traded in at the fifth grade. (Although some educators feel the beginning grades need powerful multimedia machines, that was not the belief of this particular school system and its administration.) Since there are legal limitations on funding for public school students in many areas of the United States, direct fees to the student for personal computers is a realistic approach. In any case, the option of a reasonable cost for parents (especially since multiple children in the same family could share one machine) offers one approach to providing a personal computer in the home of each student.

In suburban school districts in the United States, per-student annual costs range from $5,000 to $10,000. With the proper use of computers and software, some textbooks can be replaced, and teachers should be able to handle a few more students; thus the costs of about $250 a year per student are relatively small and also can be partially balanced out by some cost savings elsewhere. In poor districts or in less developed countries, where there is not enough money for textbooks or even the most basic supplies, costs are a far more serious barrier. Outside help in the form of government or private grants may be needed.

5.4.2 The Minimalist Approach to Learning Network Infrastructure

Suppose an instructor realizes that many students have their own personal computers and that others might obtain access through one or more computer laboratories at school and decides to network the students in order to improve their educational experience. The basic local network configuration begins with a reasonably powerful personal computer and simple, straightforward bulletin board software that might cost around $500 or might be available as a public domain package for far less. The instructor must make an investment in learning about the technology and the operating system as well as the management of files. It is also desirable to obtain an additional telephone line, so the computer has its own connection that does not interfere with regular calls.

Students in many high schools have set up their own personal bulletin boards for unofficial collaboration on homework. An instructor who wants to begin in this area might seek to join an existing student-run system.

The cost of computers is coming down and their power increasing manyfold each year, so setting up powerful microcomputers that support full conferencing-type capabilities and that allow multiple telephone lines into a single machine is reasonably inexpensive. The minimalist approach will allow students improved informal communications with students who already have access to a personal computer. It will give the instructor experience and sidestep bureaucratic constraints. However, this strategy will not provide equal access to all or support some of the more interesting learning approaches that can be taken. It also necessitates that the instructor becoming more of a technical whiz than is really necessary.

5.4.3   The Extended Laboratory

Most school systems have laboratories of personal computers, tied together in a local area network, with a larger machine as a database and file server. Usually the system supports a particular subject and is available only during school hours. At reasonable cost (a few thousand dollars at the most), a bank of modems can be added, and the server can be left running at night and on the weekends. Adding a bulletin board or simple conference package to this machine is a straightforward first step.

When the goal is to provide communications to hundreds or thousands of students, this add-on approach breaks down and a more centralized communications facility must be considered. However, this approach is the way for a school with an existing laboratory to set up a facility for a demonstration and feasibility trial. What is important is that the facility should be sized to support at least a hundred users, including the students, teachers, and family members. There is an inherent need for a critical mass of users in order to demonstrate any sort of group-oriented communications facility and its intended benefits.

5.4.4   The Electronic Mail Approach

Most minicomputers come with basic mail packages; that is, anyone who is given an account on the minicomputer can access the mail facilities to message others. Software is usually provided to interface that machine to other machines through a network connection, so that access to wide area message networks such as the Internet can be easily accomplished. Mail systems provide wide area coverage and the ability to handle large populations but do not provide for group-oriented communications facilities. Each individual must undertake to manage his or her communications. There are no automated procedures for organizing the communications for the group as a whole and for tracking changes to earlier communications. At most there might be a facility for a central database of all the past communication among a group, such as a class, similar to a primitive bulletin board system.

This approach requires a heavy information-handling load for both the instructor and the students. It may be adequate as a supplement to an existing face-to-face class but is little more than a faster method of sending correspondence.

For those who already have a minicomputer or even a powerful microcomputer, there are excellent group software packages for conferencing that begin at a few thousand dollars and range upward to the tens of thousands.

5.4.5   The Group Communication Approach

This is the point at which a careful technological decision has to be made about what package to purchase and the underlying hardware to support it. When volume involves hundreds to thousands of students, the capital cost per student probably ranges from $50 to $300, with lower per-student costs as the numbers of students increases. Furthermore, the technology has to be matched to an understanding of what is to be accomplished and of long-term educational goals.

Costs are a function of certain basic technological factors with respect to both software and hardware. The following technological issues have to be addressed:

• Is the system scalable? (This means that adding more users is merely a process of adding more hardware.)

• Can the system be fully distributed over several different servers (different computers in a network)? (Communication costs can be reduced by putting servers at different locations where there are concentrations of users and networking the servers with broader-band, more efficient communication lines.)

• Can other facilities be integrated? Can users use any word processor to create material? Can messages from other networks be automatically transferred into and out of the conference system?

• Can a group of people work together on creating and editing a single communications object or document?

• Does the instructor have special software facilities to control the membership and structure of the communication process for the class?

• Are there tracking facilities available to the instructor to be able to tell what various students have done and read?

• Are there facilities to allow much of the interaction to take place on the personal computer, in order to minimize communication costs?

• Does the system have an offline reader to reduce communication costs and improve user friendliness?

Some of these issues are a function of how powerful a personal computer the student has access to and the degree of windowing or multitasking that it can accomplish. A total system perspective is required for evaluating the technology and the associated costs. The greatest danger is buying into a technology that is limited and cannot be upgraded or extended to accommodate growth in function or use.

There is a fundamental trade-off in the technology between versatility (or flexibility) and concepts such as ease of use. For example, one can use a flexible communications package and communicate with any remote service, whether conferencing or databases. Anyone who is familiar with the operating system environment can move material among word processors, databases, and spreadsheets and upload and download material from a conferencing or message system. Another approach is a specialized communication package tailored to interface to a remote system and eliminating the need for the user to learn anything more to use the remote system. This approach is attractive to new users. A third alternative is to rely on the new generation of improved operating systems based on the graphics user interface. These systems are easy to use and incorporate general facilities for moving material between different applications. Those supplying the educational service can develop specific aids that integrate the different packages being used by that educational community. Once general multitasking becomes available at low cost, the local integration of tools for simultaneous utilization on the PC will be an obvious approach.

The most sizable cost of this technology is hidden in the communication costs associated with telephone line charges. Universities and colleges have connected to the Internet to reduce communication costs through large-scale sharing. In elementary school systems, most students are within local telephone call distances of their schools. Some teachers may not be in the school's calling zone, and the school system might have to subsidize their communication from home. Many states are implementing statewide networks for educational institutions, including elementary schools. Private schools have a more difficult problem; many of their students may live at considerable distances from the school. In the long run, we expect the Internet or an equivalent to extend to elementary schools.

5.5   Training Teachers

Teachers require a basic understanding of and comfort with the computer-mediated communication system to be used. Expertise in using the computer is not a prerequisite, but teachers must be able to manage the operating environment of the microcomputer in order to access and move around the CMC system and perform certain fundamental operations.

The skills necessary for operating a learning network environment are basically those that will allow the teacher to be able to design and manage an online educational activity or course and to help students navigate online. Instructors need to learn the mechanics of using the particular system, including the special tools or features that will make them "power users." In addition, they must be skilled in basic operations, such as how to do the following:

• Access and upload and download messages (in email, bulletin board systems, and/or computer conferencing)
• Read, write, delete, and forward conference and email messages
• Open, close, and delete conferences, etc.
• Join and remove conference participants
• Organize items for easy retrieval, either using PC-based files arranged by topic, or tools such as key words in the host system
• Navigate the Internet, using some basic Internet tools (Telnet, Gopher, Netscape, etc.)

Even more important than mechanics is the need to understand how to restructure a course to make its delivery effective in this medium and how to communicate positively and supportively so as to encourage participation by students. System skills and the theory of teaching online can be taught by a combination of print resources and a one- or two-day workshop or online, but the most effective way is through apprenticeship and an online peer network.

Ideally, a prospective teacher begins as a guest observer in an online course taught by a peer. After observing for a week or two, he or she may be called on to be a guest teacher for a small module of the course, planning the presentation and activities under the guidance of the experienced instructor. Alternatively, the neophyte instructor initially might use the medium in an adjunct mode with a current classroom-based course. A single online module might be prepared and delivered, followed by continuous use for communication about the course by the students for the remainder of the semester.

An online "teaching workshop" can be used for prospective instructors to plan and discuss ideas for future delivery of a course totally via CMC or mixed modes. Clarification of course objectives and discussion of optimal instructional designs to achieve these objectives should be among the topics of such workshops. Supported and advised by teachers who are experienced in the use of learning networks, plans and sample modules can be developed and critiqued within this environment.

The teaching workshop may be separate from or combined with an ongoing Faculty Lounge for peer support while teaching online. The Faculty Lounge conference should be a friendly and supportive place, where both serious and sociable communication takes place. One of the serious topics that it should support is the sharing of problems encountered while teaching online and possible solutions to these problems. Just as students gain from collaborative learning, faculty members also gain from group discussions of common problems and from joking and interacting with their peers.

5.6 Orienting and Advising Prospective Students

When networked learning is added to the modes used in a course, from kindergarten through grade 12, the introduction can be gradual, with students advised about the types of activities expected of them on an ongoing basis. In college-level courses offered via distance education, however, there may be a serious problem in adequately informing students about what will be required before they have registered and paid for a course, and it is too late to withdraw without penalty. Most course registration lists, for instance, allow a maximum of one additional line to explain any unusual aspects of a course. At best one may fit in here: "Offered via computer; contact instructor." Of course, most students will not contact the instructor unless it is required. Two types of letters or sets of materials may be prepared to advise and orient students before the course begins, to help them make the choice about whether learning networks are right for them.

The first letter, given to students when they express interest in the course, explains what will be involved. (An example is shown in appendix F). The letter is combined with the requirement that the student acquire departmental permission to register; each must visit the department and receive this and read it before permission is signed or call and have the flyer mailed before enrolling. This procedure does cut down prospective enrollees quite a bit, but it should decrease the incidence of expensive (for the student) withdrawals after the first week of class, when students discover that they are never going to "see" their instructor or do not have the necessary access to technology to sign online and participate regularly.

After registration, a packet of materials is mailed, including perhaps an ID and password for the CMC system, a training manual or training videotape for the system, and a detailed syllabus. The cover letter from the instructor that accompanies this initial mailing of material should explain expectations in some detail. (A sample letter of this type is shown in appendix F).

5.7 Training Students

Learning to navigate through learning networks is a little like learning to swim; reading a book or hearing a lecture about it is not very helpful. You have to put your face in the water and learn to float by trying it. In the beginning, a teacher may provide special supports and constant feedback, but the primary way to learn is to overcome fears and gain skill through experience. Thus, sessions to train students in networking should integrate information on using the system with hands-on practice and exercises. The teacher should begin by explaining the nature of the online activities, who will be involved, and what is expected of the students. Opportunities for questions and discussion are valuable. After being shown how to log on and find and read waiting messages, students should begin responding and participating immediately.

In university- or adult-level activities where students are not located in one place and travel to a training site is difficult or impossible, training may be successfully handled online (Mason 1990). Good manuals and some basic, easy-to-read one-page sheets illustrating a typical log-on session are adequate. A videotape of a demonstration session mailed to students might also be effective. Online and telephone help should be made available.

Face-to-face training, which may be offered if users live nearby, is an opportunity to build confidence in computer networking and a sense of community among the class members. Seating students two to three at a terminal is useful to initiate group work and group problem solving. Hands-on activities should introduce basic operations of computer conferencing and involve group tasks. To be handled adequately, this requires about a three-hour session or two shorter ones. Trying to fit training into too brief a period may produce confusion.

In launching online class activities Harasim (1987) generally allows for about four to six hours for training activities. Half of this time is used as an introduction to the course, the curriculum, the collaborative learning approach that is used, and what is expected of the student. Discussion about the use of computer networking for teaching and learning is also included. Once students have been introduced to the online curriculum and the concepts of online learning, they move to two to three hours of hands-on activities.

Launching the learning network should focus on some activity specific to the medium being used. For email networks, launching activities require seeding the network with two or three introductory messages addressed to the entire group. Learning networks based on computer conferencing and some bulletin board systems provide teachers with more tools to create an environment by setting up various conferences. Prior to the online segment, the instructor or trainer should have set up introductory email and conferencing activities so that this environment awaits students.

The first task for students is to log on and read the email message waiting in their Inbox. That message should be from the instructor or moderator welcoming them to the online class and asking a question, such as a request for their first impressions of online communication. Students respond to the message by sending a private message to the instructor. Their response enables the instructor to ensure that students have learned how to read and send a message and to understand their immediate feelings about computer conferencing. Students who do not respond or express discomfort will benefit from personal attention by the teacher at this early stage or a telephone call if the training is remote.

Teachers should acknowledge and respond to the first message from each student in a friendly and supportive manner. Beginners may feel that their entry has been lost unless they receive an explicit response. Thus, during the first week or so of online class activity, the moderator should ensure that each newcomer receives a timely response to her or his first online communication effort.

Having completed the task of reading and writing an email message, students go on to send and receive computer conferencing messages (or, in the case of systems based on email only, group messages on a specific designated topic that go to the entire class or classes participating). The first conferencing activities that students experience should be full group and based on something that they already know. Since students are confronted with new learning just in gaining mastery over the conferencing system, the subject matter should be familiar at the outset, beginning with the known and then moving to new curricular material. Harasim (1987, 1994) often begins with three conferences, all of which are plenary or full group:

• Self-introductions: A brief note by the student introducing himself or herself (focusing on such matters as interests or hobbies, where he or she lives, and so on).
• Our Objectives (for the course): The student's objectives for taking this course in terms of content and process.
• Great Debate: The student's position on an issue and an explanation for it.

The third conference, Great Debate, has been particularly useful and is quite different from formal debate. Whereas the debating teams described in chapter 4 occur toward the end of an online class and have formal structures and rules, the icebreaking Great Debate aims to initiate students to online discussion and debate. The goal is to engage students as soon and as much as possible, so that they feel that their computer has become a doorway into a world in which they will encounter new colleagues and activities. A particularly controversial statement related to the topic of the course is put forward in order to generate strong and different reactions. Students are asked to formulate their position and to defend it. Once students post their initial comments they become eager for responses to their comment, and also to read comments by others. Their curiosity and interest sets the tone for active engagement, and students begin to log on regularly. Soon after, within a few days of debating and self-introductions, the class moves into group activities based on the curriculum.

5.8 Evaluation Strategies

The introduction of new educational technologies, including computer networking, benefits from educational evaluation and assessment. Assessment includes both top-down accountability approaches (reporting of results for accountability purposes) and bottom-up instructional improvement (helping individual students gain most from instruction). Both perspectives share a common goal of improving education and are important at all stages of adopting technological innovations.

The strategies described in this section can be used in a classroom assessment model as well as for external research and evaluation purposes, and they can be integrated with traditional approaches to assessment such as writing assessment (analysis of content, organization, or sentence fluency using a process approach that examines prewriting, writing, responding, revising, editing, postwriting, and evaluating), portfolio assessment (a collection of student work exhibiting effort and progress of achievement in a given area), and teacher-based assessment (interviews, observation, analysis of representations of student learning, and quizzes). In keeping with a learner-centered approach, evaluation and assessment should be part of the learning-teaching process, embedded in class activities and in the interactions between learners and between learners and teachers. Evaluations should consider a multiplicity of evidence, such as participation by students in class discussions, project work, and individual and group interviews, in addition to assessment of written exercises and tests. Assessment of learning network activities as with traditional activities requires sound assessment practices, such as explicitly defined targets or student outcomes, assessment strategies that are congruent with both the curriculum content and process of instruction, student involvement through self-evaluation and reflection on the learning outcomes, and the integration of assessment with instruction.

Evaluation of online projects or classroom approaches in which learning is open-ended presents new challenges. Ehrmann (1988) argues that different students learn different things and their learning cannot be tested on discrete skill tests and quantified. He proposes that technology can assist the evaluation of open-ended learning in the following three ways. First, networks can help gather data. On the network, a verbatim transcript of all classroom discussion is produced, thus providing a permanent picture of each student's thought process and language production each day of the course, which can be studied later. Second, email allows researchers using networks at distant sites to talk with each other regularly about their work. Finally, combining email with hypertext allows discussions to be linked up with the sharing of actual data.

Evaluation of online courses should thus be planned in conjunction with the definition of course goals and instructional designs. There are two types of evaluation: formative and summative. Formative evaluation seeks to document what happens and to identify the sources of success and problems in order to suggest possible improvements in the future. In other words, the primary goal of the evaluation is to serve as feedback to the project participants. For this reason, the data should be collected and analyzed continuously and used to guide the instructor in making midcourse corrections, whenever possible.

Summative evaluation is generally conducted for the benefit of outsiders, perhaps funding agencies that want to know if their investment paid off or the research community, which wants to know what generalizable conclusions result from a project. Cost-benefit analysis is one possible component of summative evaluation.

Some data may be used for both purposes. One example of data that can be automatically collected on most systems is usage data. How frequently is each student logging on, and how many messages is each sending? This should be checked at least once a week during a course, to see if any students have disappeared and need to be personally contacted. At the end of the course, the weekly data show how the patterns of participation may change in different parts of the course, and the totals give one kind of picture of the amount of activity that took place. More sophisticated analyses would track the number of messages and conference comments written and their length, as well as time spent online. This can be shown for each individual student, to indicate degree of equality of participation, as well as for the class as a whole. Ideally, the system would automate such data collection and analysis; if it does not, the instructor may have to make hand counts each week. On some systems, only a running total of usage figures is kept, and if it is not printed out and stored each week or month, the possibility of knowing how activity patterns changed during the course will be lost forever.

Usage statistics are one form of unobtrusive measurement: the data are collected through a process that does not force participants to stop what they are doing in order to generate data for evaluation. Since education, and not research, is the primary goal of most learning networks, unobtrusive measurement should be used whenever possible. For example, a question on what kinds of problems students have with the use of the system and their feelings about it can be answered by examining students' Help messages if they are automatically stored in a file and can be read. Teacher access to these messages raises the issue of privacy and confidentiality. If Help messages are to be made available as data, users should be so informed.

Another unobtrusive measure is to collect and categorize spontaneous comments that are made about the course and the mode of teaching by the students. These might occur in substantive class conferences, in a special Learning Log or Meta-Discussion conference set up for questions and comments about the system or the way the course is conducted, or in private messages to the instructor. It is necessary to devise some categories to separate potentially relevant communications and file them as they arrive. On some systems, it is possible to add personal keys to items as they arrive, so that data classification and filing can occur automatically as one views an item that may be relevant to describing important aspects of student reactions to the course. On others, it will be necessary to download or print the items to classify and save them.

Questionnaires completed by students and personal interviews with some or all of the students and faculty involved in a learning network project are frequently used. A questionnaire distributed to all or a random sample of participants is the best technique to ensure a representative set of opinions. Personal interviews can be used to provide a deeper understanding of selected questions or issues. A set of pre- and post-course questionnaires, interview guides, and an outline for faculty course reports is included in the Virtual Classroom study (Hiltz 1993) and is available to other researchers to adapt (with permission of the author).

A test of hypotheses about differences among courses associated with medium of delivery or pedagogical strategy generally requires a fairly large number of cases to obtain statistically significant results. The design of experiments and quasi-experiments is treated in many research methodology texts and is beyond the scope of this book. An evaluation consultant to help ensure that procedures and conclusions are correct is helpful. In terms of planning for evaluation, however, an important consideration is that the more students and replications, the better. Thus, many different online classes should be joined into one overall evaluation design if summative evaluation is desirable or required.

5.9 Implementation: A Checklist for Action

• Locate a highly placed sponsor and fixer, such as a president, principal, or CEO, who is able to see the benefits of learning networks and who publicly gives the implementation plan for the organization her or his blessing.

• Promote user participation in planning from the very earliest stages; send out a newsletter to all faculty, for instance, about your plans; set up public meetings and orientation sessions. Talk about how learning networks might be used in your school or organization, and listen to the questions and reported problems and doubts that prospective online instructors have. Troubleshoot and overcome the serious problems (e.g., no telephone lines at school, no equipment available for faculty members) before proceeding further.

• Identify enthusiastic early adopters, and start your pilot with this core group of about four to ten instructors and courses. Once this group is established, they can become mentors to other faculty who wish to go online with their classes.

• Design and implement initial training programs for teachers. Organize continuing support, including online Teachers' Lounges for the discussion of pedagogical and technical issues.

• Rethink a course and invest significant time in redesigning it to take advantage of the opportunities for collaborative learning strategies online. In addition, carefully plan and support the first few weeks of online coursework for the students, to orient and train them to participate effectively and enjoyably.

• Providing for convenient access is a multifaceted problem: it involves hardware, communications software, communications networks, and the CMC system itself. Prepare short, simple, step-by-step guides to show participants how to get online using the configuration(s) they will have available.

• Costs are prohibitive if personal computers are acquired solely for this application. They should be seen as multipurpose learning tools that are used in many ways (e.g., CAI, text editing), of which one educational application is learning networks.

• Choose a CMC system that will be able to grow to support the learning network as it becomes larger and can support the needs of experienced users, not just novices.

• For elective or college-level courses, design a letter or other materials to recruit and explain to students what will be involved in taking an online course.

• Design and implement an orientation and training set of activities at the beginning of each course for the students.

• Integrate evaluation into the planning for online courses. Consider what online statistics can be collected and used by instructors to help them track activity levels. Also consider using a standard set of pre- and postcourse questionnaires or interviews, or both, for all online courses in the school or organization. Whatever types of evaluation data are collected, make sure that they are analyzed and reported back to faculty members promptly to help them improve their online teaching effectiveness.

6

Teaching Online

Computer-mediated communication offers educators unique opportunities and challenges. Teachers, trainers, and professors with years of
experience in classrooms report that computer networking encourages
the high-quality interaction and sharing that is at the heart of education.
There can be close and daily contact between the student and the teacher
and among all the students, regardless of their appearance, location, or
assertiveness.

Learning Networks provide the opportunity for a rich interchange of
information and ideas in which all students can participate actively,
learning from one another as well as from the teacher. Because personalities come through clearly in the written medium and because the
group shares a common world of knowledge that they collaboratively
build and is their unique experience, there often emerges a strong sense
of camaraderie. The fact that peers will view what they contribute provides students with a strong motivation to do work of which they will
be proud. Another factor that improves the quality of participation is
that students can spend a great deal of time reflecting before making
their contribution. These characteristics of online classes, along with
expanded, democratic access, generally result in students' contributing
material that is much better than something they would say off the top
of their heads in a face-to-face class. The teacher as well as the students
learns from the contributions made by the group. Teaching online is a
genuinely enjoyable intellectual experience.

On the other hand, unless the teacher facilitates the networking activities skillfully, serious problems may develop. A conference may turn
into a monologue of lecture-type material to which very few responses

are made. It may become a disorganized mountain of information that is confusing and overwhelming for the participants. It may even break down socially into name calling rather than building a sense of community.

This chapter explores techniques that can be used to improve the probability that using CMC will result in a rich and enjoyable intellectual and social experience for all the participants and to decrease the probability that problems will arise. These techniques apply to online teaching regardless of the course design that is chosen and regardless of the level or type of education.

6.1 Role of the Teacher

Delivery of education through computer networking alters the relationship of the instructor, the students, and the course content. Unlike traditional classroom activity, in which the teacher directs the instruction, leads the lessons, prompts responses, and paces the class, online group learning is student centered and requires a different role for the teacher, of facilitator rather than lecturer. The teacher plans the activities but then follows the flow of the conversation, offering guidance as needed rather than strictly adhering to the preplanned agenda or syllabus.

The teacher provides a set of group structures that enable students to work out a problem or undertake a task, search for strategies on their own, and evaluate their solutions. Though the teacher needs to be present, the network enables the teacher to play a facilitative, observant, but background role. The primary focus should be on the students' own thinking processes and on collaborative learning.

The many-to-many, asynchronous nature of the medium democratizes access and encourages student input. Generally the students should contribute the bulk of the material in the discussions. The ratio of teacher-to-student comments will usually be between one-to-ten and one-to-two. Those with the highest proportions of student contributions are often among the most successful.

The role of the teacher changes in several important ways in the online environment. A class taught entirely online requires additional planning because the full set of activities must be anticipated prior to the first day.

In this respect, the online class is similar to distance mode activity, for which the teacher or moderator must send all course materials to students in advance of the course. On the other hand, the interactive nature of online education provides a flexibility that in many ways resembles face-to-face classes. New information, perspectives, or changes to the course design can often be introduced and accommodated online. An existing curriculum can be expanded or modified by incorporating references to current events or including new information.

Schoolteachers have a unique role in online environments as they combine their face-to-face teaching with online activities. In this situation the networked classroom is an enhancement of school-based activities rather a substitute to them. For the teacher the logistics of online activities become an essential aspect to consider: How should routine classroom activities be linked with online tasks? Which online tasks can better support their curriculum? How should students be organized to participate in the networked classroom? The responses to these questions vary widely depending on the subject area and the instructional model used by the various networked classrooms. Before joining one of the many networked classrooms, teachers should obtain information about the variety of instructional models and approaches used to support their teaching. Once they have identified one that fits their needs, the next step is to contact that project and become involved in the networked classroom of their choice.

6.2 Setting the Stage

At the beginning of an online course activity or a project involving networked classrooms, students may feel confused and apprehensive, perhaps perceiving the computer as providing a very cold environment for human communication. They may worry about their ability to navigate around the system and to find out where they are supposed to go and what they are supposed to do there. The teacher's job is to create a warm, welcoming environment that will entice them to begin participating immediately and to reassure them by providing clear directions and support structures.

Each invited participant should be sent a personal message, welcoming them to the online classroom and congratulating them on having successfully signed online. The first message should invite a response, thereby encouraging interaction and providing a way for the teacher to monitor who has successfully accessed the system. A subsequent message might briefly describe the initial conference or topic and its purpose and include explicit directions on how to access the conference. (Never assume that anyone actually reads the user's manual or remembers what they were told in a face-to-face training session.)

The teacher should be clear in setting expectations for participation in the online activities and in giving directions to participants. The conference can begin with an opening comment that clearly states the subject of the conference, the agenda (syllabus or topics to be addressed), and expectations for student participation (volume, frequency, type of comments, etc.).

The second comment in a new conference might specify the activity for that week and include a simple request, such as, "Respond to this comment by introducing yourself and telling us what your hopes and expectations are for this course." The third comment may recap some important ideas from assigned readings or videotapes and ask for a response to a substantive question. Other designs are possible as well, such as launching the course with a debate.

One valuable type of question that can be asked near the beginning of a course (and throughout the course too) is a request for concrete examples of how the theories and concepts that are covered in readings or lecture have been observed in the students' own lives. These examples, when shared, help the students link theory with real examples and aid them in using the ideas they are learning to understand their environment.

From the outset, students should be encouraged to respond to each other as well as to the comments and questions contributed by the instructor. To help ensure that participants read and respond to one another's comments, the instructor can serve as a model. If there has been no response to a comment, he or she can make one, in a private message, by responding in the conference, or by mentioning the comment in a summarizing or weaving note.

By the end of the first week, all students should understand that they share the responsibility of responding to comments. The instructor can motivate active participation by recognizing the efforts by students to learn the system and to participate regularly, actively, and thoughtfully. Providing grades for student participation is a great motivator, and students will soon take the initiative to participate. A teacher who answers everything will decrease the opportunities for student participation, and the conference will become teacher centered rather than student centered. He or she should be patient in waiting for student responses and not rush to fill the silence. As the deadline set for responses nears, they will pour in.

6.3   Monitoring and Encouraging Participation

A late or poor start can negatively affect the student's progress in a course. Vigilance is essential, especially at the beginning of a course. The moderator should ensure that all students have been added to the conference and follow their status in the conference once or twice a week. Conferencing systems typically provide some sort of status list or monitoring facility to show how far each person has read in the conference. A student who is behind or has not contributed anything for a significant period of time can be sent a private message to encourage participation. If he or she does not respond to it, the teacher can try contact by telephone (or letter) to determine the problems, assist if there are any technical difficulties, and restate the expectations for active participation.

Active participation, encouraged by the atmosphere and course design and in other ways, is central to a successful online course. The following techniques have proved useful (Davie 1989; Feenberg 1993; Harbour et al. 1990; Johnson-Lenz and Johnson-Lenz 1990):

1. Create a casual, warm, welcoming, and supportive atmosphere. Many people have a fear of presenting something in writing that is not perfect. Be explicit that the conference is closed and that outside readers will be admitted only by unanimous class consensus. Establish a norm that contributions other than formal assignments are to be considered like "written conversations" rather than formal publications. Spelling and grammar do not have to be perfect. Consider having participants read

and electronically sign a sort of contract or covenant—for example: "To create a safe, supportive, and vital learning community together ... we agree to keep each other's items confidential, participate regularly, and inform our group when we are absent for whatever reason. We also agree ... to listen with care and compassion to each other" (Johnson-Lenz and Johnson-Lenz 1990, 312).

2. Make participation expectations clear. They may be stated in terms of both a minimal number of log-ons per week (two or three are common expectations) and a minimal number of items or "notes" that each student is to contribute each week (e.g., three to four messages per week are common numbers for minimal participation expectations). To show that participation is important, grade it.

3. Do not lecture. An elaborate, long, text-based presentation can produce silence. If an electure is used, keep it short and focused, and include open-ended remarks and interesting questions to stimulate discussion. A typical question might give a scenario or some facts related to the readings or briefly summarize some issue or theme treated in the readings, followed by two or three questions for discussion, which are interesting, perhaps controversial, and may have many different possible answers, examples, or points of view. The use of student-led discussions or seminars can be very effective.

4. Model responsiveness. Especially for the first assignment, each contribution should be acknowledged within twenty-four hours, perhaps as an individual response or a "weaving" (integrative) comment. Responsiveness, however, must be balanced by attention to setting the stage for equality of participation, for student-centered discussions. After the first week, wait a day or two before responding to any comments and encourage others to respond first. Contribute only every few days.

5. Encourage students to compliment or respond to one another. One means to do this is to redirect a question from one student to another, who is specified by name. For example, "John, your question is a very important one. Jane and Ed, what are your thoughts on this issue?" In either the group conference or private messages, ask individuals to respond to particular topics or items, based on knowledge of their interests and experiences.

6. Positively reinforce discussion contributions, and negatively reinforce silence. Especially in the early weeks, follow up on student contributions in the conference (e.g., "Jane, that is a very good point. I had not thought of that before") or send private messages commending especially good entries, suggesting references or other resources for following up on the ideas or information introduced, or suggesting how to develop the con-

tributions further. Send private messages to nonparticipants as well, noting that they have not contributed recently, and reminding them to take an active part.

7. Close a discussion with a synthesis or weaving of the topic (written either by the instructor or by students). Modify or clarify a question that is not working. If the discussion is not working, look closely at the transcript to try to determine the problem. Did the students misunderstand the question? Was it simply not of interest or too narrow in scope? A follow-up note clarifying or modifying the question or request for discussion might be in order. In general, it is better to have many assorted discussions than to try to get too much mileage out of a single discussion question. If the discussion seems to be finished, enter a summary or closing remark and move on to new topics.

8. Request meta-communication. Ask participants to tell how they feel about the course and the norms and procedures suggested, in the group discussion. Adjust these if the group feels it is advisable.

9. Use telephone, fax, or email to make sure that activities are well coordinated. There is not a single way to communicate, and all options should be explored.

6.4   Forming Groups

The size and composition of online groups varies for different activities. Groups or teams may work together for different periods of time, ranging from perhaps a week to a full semester. Groups may be networked locally or globally.

Group formation may be accomplished by the teacher or by the students, or both methods may be used. There is some merit in allowing students to choose their own group sometimes, but the process of self-selection online is often too complex. Email and conferencing systems do not yet provide tools to facilitate group formation, and the asynchronous nature of the media can create problems for the student trying to organize a group. Just the simple task of joining a group can be fraught with problems, especially if there is a deadline to the group work and a limit to the size of group. A student may not know whether a group is full and lose days trying to establish contact with someone in it, or a potential partner may have already agreed to join another group and then not log on for some time. The frustration and time lost in trying to establish a small group can imperil the real work of completing the task.

Assigning students to groups can avoid these kinds of management frustrations, particularly when the individuals do not meet face to face and when deadlines must be met. Groups may be organized according to various criteria, such as common interests or friendship or by principles of heterogeneity.

Another strategy to facilitate group formation is to announce group tasks and size a week or two prior to beginning the activities. Students can be invited to form their own groups and send a message to the instructor confirming the group membership before a deadline. Those who have not formed groups by then are assigned by the instructor.

Subgroup conferences or mailing lists are also valuable for discussion if the class size is "too large." Exactly what is too large depends on how many contributions are expected from each student each week. Conferences and discussion groups of about fifteen to twenty-five seem to work best in general, while teams of two to four people are effective in complex group projects. It is advisable to have one space for general announcements and separate spaces for discussion and assignments.

6.5   Assigning Role Responsibilities

Once groups have been formed, the teacher must decide whether to assign group roles and responsibilities. Assigning or encouraging group roles is often advisable for totally online classes, given the logistical difficulties that can occur. While group work is difficult in any context, the asynchronous text-based nature of networking can lead to difficulties of coordination. Students may lose time and energy identifying and assigning roles or not anticipate the need for roles at all. Teacher-assigned roles assist students to prepare for the tasks ahead and to spend their time more productively. When networking supplements face-to-face classes, students may form teams in the classroom.

Online group work can benefit from several kinds of roles. One generic role is the coordinator, who tracks task completion and ensures that the work is proceeding smoothly and in a timely manner. Another role is that of the editor, whose responsibility is to receive the various pieces of online work written by group members, edit them into a cohesive whole, and upload the final product to a specified conference space. Actual activities related to accomplishing the specific task need to be distributed among the various members, acknowledging the additional load on the coordinator and the editor.

If roles are assigned, the teacher might consider rotating the roles in different assignments to provide opportunities for students to experience different functions, learning leadership skills as well as technical skills.

6.6   Moderating and Facilitating Group Processes

The nature of networking systems (especially computer conferencing) is particularly conducive to a facilitative role for teachers. Once the course has been designed, the structure and procedures established, and students begin to engage in discussions or projects, the role of the teacher is to observe, monitor, facilitate, and provide information as appropriate. (See appendix G for annotated excerpts from an online course.) Monitoring involves responding to problematic situations, such as blocks in the discussion, student dropout, group dynamics issues, or misinformation that needs correction. For example, students may misunderstand or misquote a piece of information. A teacher who encourages critical thinking shows students how to get in the habit of pointing out to one another errors of fact or of reasoning. However, if a student does not point out misinformation fairly rapidly, it is up to the teacher to intervene and clarify or correct such statements. In addition, the instructor must ensure that the diverse ideas and information contributed to the discussion of a topic are integrated by the students and that there is a clear transition from one discussion or activity to another.

Online group learning is on opportunity to see what students have learned and how they understand and apply the concepts. Students in traditional classes typically have little opportunity to be active in discussions; students in online group activities must participate and articulate their ideas to be present. The presentation of ideas online enables the instructor to see how the material is being intellectually interpreted and integrated by each student. Monitoring of group activity should be unobtrusive so as not to undermine the group dynamics or the process of discovery and learning. Students may share some of the monitoring roles, but if help is needed or if an incorrect idea is not challenged, the teacher needs to intervene and clarify the information or the tasks.

6.6.1   Coordinating Interaction

In setting up guidelines and expectations for learning together, teachers need to sequence the tasks and activities and synchronize the interaction periodically. This means getting the group to start a module together, signaling when it is over, and getting the group to move on together to a new topic or activity. One valuable mechanism to accomplish this is to open and close (to further contributions) a separate conference for each module in the course. A few days before moving on, the instructor gives notice of this intention, so that participants have time to enter their last thoughts on the topic.

6.6.2   Pacing Interaction

The main approach to encourage pacing is to set time limits on how long a conference or online activity is open and accessible to students. Some options are online seminars that are open for one week and then closed to further input (Harasim 1989, 1993b), or scheduling readings and discussion questions that are accessible only during the first half of the week and an online quiz only available for the second half (Hiltz et al. 1990). Collaborative projects are another technique for pacing interaction since students have to work together to complete a task project by a specified deadline. System features may facilitate pacing by providing gating, whereby students can access material or an activity only once the prerequisites have been successfully completed. (See Johnson-Lenz and Johnson-Lenz 1990 for a description of gating in self-development education.)

6.6.3   Organizing the Interaction

Because time and place do not provide a natural center for online discussions, unless explicit cues are included, it may not be clear how a new comment is related to previous ones. In fact, sometimes it is not even clear what an item is about, unless its relationship to preceding notes is known. In addition, sometimes participants get confused about what belongs where and send their comments to an inappropriate conference.

Many systems provide tools that make the discussion thread clear. For example, there may be a Reply structure, whereby replies to an existing note are attached to it in the transcript (e.g., the first reply to note 8 in a conference may be numbered 8.1). In addition, there may be a question about whether a note is associated with or related to other notes; if the author enters this information, such discussion threads can be automatically retrieved. If such tools are available, the instructor/moderator should model their use and explicitly request students to use them also. If they are not available, the instructor should model explicit context-setting references at the beginning of each comment that is related to a previous one (e.g., "In reply to Genny's comment in item 8 ...").

Almost all systems provide a keyword and/or subject line feature. These are important in enabling students to review the transcript, retrieve notes they wish to read again, organize them, and pull together related items. Once again, the instructor should not only model the consistent use of keys and/or subject headers but explicitly request students to specify key words and references to previous notes.

Placing a comment in the wrong conference is a surprisingly common mistake. Sometimes students even put what was meant as a very private message into a class conference. When such mistakes occur, the note needs to be deleted from the inappropriate location and placed where it belongs. One way to do this, which works on all systems, is to copy the item and mail it to the author with an explanation of why this is being done; then delete the item. The author will have a copy to edit and send to the correct conference or recipient.

6.6.4 Meta-Communication

Conference moderators or facilitators play an important process role in initiating and encouraging meta-communication—communication about communication. This includes requesting clarification of an unclear remark, defusing hostile remarks, suggesting changes in the procedures of the conference, and so forth. Overall, meta-communication seeks to remedy problems in context, norms or agenda, clarity, irrelevance, impoliteness, and information overload (Feenberg 1989).

6.6.5   Weaving

When many comments and contributions have been made concerning a topic, the instructor needs to summarize them and focus the subsequent discussion. A good weaving message refers to specific ideas and information contributed in previous comments. It identifies points of agreement and disagreement, supplies a unifying overview by interpreting the discussion, and gives the group both a sense of accomplishment and a better sense of where they are going next. The comment may end with suggestions for further discussion of unresolved issues, or it may explicitly signal the end of that topic of discussion and call for moving on to a new topic. Weaving can be done by the teacher, a student moderator, or each student to synthesize their learning on that issue or topic.

6.6.6   Ending Conferences

When a discussion has lagged or attention has largely moved to other topics, it may be a good idea to close a conference. The moderator usually wraps up the conference and thanks participants. Members should be reminded by message that a conference is about to be ended; this sometimes results in a flurry of last-minute activity.

Because computer memory is a limited resource, closed conferences are usually purged, typically in three stages. First, the participants should be notified that the conference is about to end and that if weaving statements are to be submitted, a deadline has been set. Perhaps a week later, the moderator should make it into a read-only conference, and announce that it will be maintained in this condition for one or two additional weeks. This gives members the opportunity to download and save anything they want to keep. After a suitable time, the moderator can have the conference deleted from the system.

6.6.7   Socio-Emotional Issues

Most instructors encourage controversy and critical thinking, but students may feel insulted if their contributions are criticized. Students should be encouraged to say something positive about a contribution before presenting a critique. Moreover, if appropriate, critiques should suggest ways to improve. Other areas where there might be intense emotional reactions of participants include jokes or irony that is not understood as humorous in intent, because facial expression and tone of voice are missing, or anger when someone feels that there has been a remark that is insulting. Students may become very angry, and respond with a scathing counterattack. This may build up to an exchange of insults, called "flaming," if it is not managed and defused by the moderator or other participants.

Generally socio-emotional outbursts can be prevented or managed by making clear the rules of good netiquette—the etiquette of network communication and social interaction—and modeling considerate and polite behavior. Some systems have formalized such rules of acceptable online behavior, and participants can lose their access privileges if these rules are contravened. By actively enforcing netiquette the moderator fosters community among students.

Working online is a new experience and users can benefit from a set of guidelines to provide orientation on how to work with the conferencing process. The class netiquette should state the expectations and rules for student participation in relation to group dynamics and writing online.

6.7 Establishing Norms and Grading Performance

Motivational structures should be tied to the expectations or norms established by the instructor for the amount and quality of participation. Some students participate actively for the intrinsic enjoyment. However, many are more pragmatic: "Does this count?" or "Will this be graded?" are frequent questions. Generally the answer to such questions should be "yes." If participation in learning networks is offered as a completely voluntary, add-on, ungraded activity, pragmatic students will not participate at all. Grading formulas are seen as the ultimate statement of what is important in a course; if the teacher presents learning network activity as so tangential to the course that it is not graded at all, students will see it as unimportant too.

Participation expectations can be set in terms of frequency of sign-on, number and length of student contributions, and deadlines. Group learning is based on active student input and interaction, and passive reading should not be acceptable as the only form of participation. Thus, norms are usually set in terms of the minimum number and length of contributions expected. Norms are based on such factors as the nature of the activity, the grade level, and access to the computer. In the elementary classroom, for example, students may compose group messages once or twice a week. In an online credit course at the undergraduate or professional certification level, a frequent guideline is that each student is expected to make a minimum of two to four comments a week in the class conferences. Each comment should be one or two screens long; anything that is longer should be presented in a format that allows downloading for offline reading.

Another frequently used guideline is that students should participate at least three times a week (once to read any electures and determine the assignment or topic for the week, once to make their contribution or response, and at least once to respond to issues raised by peers). If the detailed syllabus and written materials for a course are distributed ahead of time and rigorously adhered to, reading these materials and using them to prepare the assignment can replace the first of these sessions. If participation is any less frequent than twice a week, the discussion can lag and participants become frustrated with the delay in receiving feedback and reactions from peers.

Required frequency of participation may vary with the course design and the design of a particular module. For instance, intensive group work assignments or debates may require daily participation in order to decrease the time spent waiting for responses or contributions, and thus to maximize success. Course designs that are built around tutorials may require logging in only once a week for a long session, to report progress to the tutor, and receive feedback on the previous week's report or submission.

Participation online should be recognized and rewarded by the teacher. Class participation can be tied to grading by making it an explicit proportion of the grade. We have seen variations from as little as 10 percent to as high as 50 percent of the course grade allocated for the quantity and quality of participation in online discussions. The mechanism for handling this may be a participation grade, given each week, or students may start with a class participation grade of 100, and points may be subtracted each week that their performance does not meet the minimum standards.

For completing specific assignments or activities, it is essential that deadlines be established at the outset of a networking activity. It is helpful to students in budgeting their time if there is a regularity to such deadlines; for example, the course may be organized in week-long modules, with the deadline for completion of each module Sunday at midnight. Late assignments or quizzes may not be accepted at all, or a penalty for lateness might be imposed.

Grading the quality of online work may be done in several ways. An alternative to using the judgment of the instructor as the sole criterion is peer grading. For example, if a student team makes a presentation, part of their grade may be determined by the number of questions and responses their presentation receives from other students. This is a measure of how interesting and relevant they make the material, and it also motivates students to help each other out by actively responding to one another's contributions. Another option is to give a group or team coordinator a total budget of points to allocate, and make it his or her responsibility to allocate the credit according to the value of the contributions of each of the team members to a final group product.

The greatest challenge may be in grading group or collaborative assignments, and the literature on face-to-face group work has many different approaches. The teacher must decide on a few basic issues. Do all members of the team receive the same grade, or is a grade assigned to individual team members, based on the amount and quality of contributions of the individual team members, as well as on the quality of the final team product? Students may feel that it is unfair if all team members receive the same grade if they did not contribute equally. There are several techniques that can be used to gauge the value of the contributions of the individual team members. One is that the instructor may be made an observer in the working conferences of the team. The level and quality of effort by each individual member of the team can then be directly observed by the instructor and used to decide if any of the group members should receive a higher or lower grade than that awarded for the team effort as a whole. Another is that the student groups may elect or choose some sort of leader, to determine partially the grades received by the members. For example, in the simulated organizations formed in Enrico Hsu's (1992) online management laboratory, the "chief executive officers" are allocated a budget not of dollars but of points, to use in motivating and rewarding the "employees." The evaluation of the student leader of the online group then forms a significant part of the total course grade. Finally, students should be encouraged to resolve problems internally and inform the teacher only if serious infractions have occurred. The participants in the group may assess a grade for each member, or they may collectively assign a grade to the person(s) who did not share the workload, based on the level of input.

Examinations need to be carefully handled to make sure that online students are graded under conditions similar to those created for on-campus exams. Distance education programs have generally devised practices for correspondence students that can be extended to CMC students. A practice that works well is the designated proctor. Each student is responsible for identifying a qualified person to supervise his or her exam—a staff person in the personnel department, a supervisor, or even a minister or rabbi. All exams are sent to the proctor, with instructions for the maximum time allowed, the period during which the examination is to be given, and any special considerations, such as whether the student may have a calculator or any notes. The proctor signs the exam to certify that it was taken under supervision, puts it in an envelope, signs the seal, and returns it to the instructor or to the distance education office. Proctors seem to take their responsibilities very seriously and this method, in combination with the use of essay questions that make it very hard to cheat, seems to serve well.

6.8 Moving from Teacher to Facilitator

Network learning enables students to assume much of the responsibility for their learning. Nonetheless, it requires regular (often daily) attention by the instructor, and thus mechanisms for sharing the load and reducing the potential time demands are crucial for online activities. The answer is to view the learning community as a genuine community of scholars. While the instructor is the chief guide and expert, he or she is really only the facilitator of the shared learning process. From early on in the course activity, students as individuals or as groups should take responsibility for researching topics and posting electures and questions for discussion. They may share moderating functions in guiding these discussions on student-initiated topics and even suggest sets of possible questions for examination based on the material they present. In addition, they may be assigned weaving or summarizing responsibilities on a rotating basis. These mechanisms save the teacher from feeling overwhelmed by the work of teaching online and are good pedagogical practices. One of the best ways for a student to understand a topic is to organize and simplify it in order to present it to others.

Visiting experts may share the work of presenting material in a course or leading discussions of some of the topics. Teachers may collaborate by regularly serving as "visiting lecturers" in one another's online courses, or experts from outside the school or university environment may be brought in. Graduate students or adjunct instructors may take on the role of "tutors" or "graders" for small groups of students, to relieve the instructor from this task, as is frequently done with traditional university classes.

Learning networks also provide a good mechanism for incorporating the volunteer efforts of course or school alumni or community members who would like to work with learners as mentors. Such mentors may establish an online relationship with individual students to counsel and assist them. Frequently students who have completed an online course have enjoyed it so much that they do not want to "leave." They may be assigned roles as assistants and helpers in subsequent semesters, in exchange for continued access to the system. For instance, they might be made judges for debates, advisers for online group projects, moderators for social spaces such as the Student Cafe, or technical advisers who answer messages addressed to Help.

For collaborative, student-centered learning to be effective, participants must learn to view their evolving discussion as a data resource. Items become a knowledge base of ideas and information on which to build rather than information to be read once and discarded.

To facilitate this view of the transcript, an early assignment should require students to review and reorganize the material presented thus far, perhaps as a small group assignment. The instructor might pick as many themes or topics as there are small groups, with each group assigned to review, reorganize, and briefly summarize the main contributions related to the topic, in the form of an outline with pointers to item number and authors. They then add "unsolved issues" that could benefit from further discussion. These reports should be entered in the class conference.

6.9   The Problem of Laboratories

For some subject matter, such as chemistry, biology, or physics, hands-on laboratory type exercises may be considered crucial to demonstrate basic concepts or phenomena; describing an experiment in words alone is an inadequate substitute. Among the alternatives that have been successfully used for this problem are computer-based simulations, videotapes, home experiment kits, and arrangements to use facilities in the locale of the student.

There are not many computer-based simulations of scientific laws. Cornell Medical School has developed computer-based simulations for the training of medical doctors that might be useful in undergraduate courses. One may virtually dissect a simulated rather than an actual frog, for instance. When planning a course that normally has laboratory components, the first thing to do is to investigate whether appropriate CAI materials exist that students can buy, just as they buy textbooks.

If presenting a demonstration is adequate for the course purposes, then laboratory exercises such as chemical reactions could be videotaped and distributed by mail to students. The tape might describe and demonstrate the reaction or phenomenon of interest; online, the students might be asked to explain why or how the phenomenon occurred.

If individual hands-on experience is considered necessary, one option is to design a home kit that is sold to and sent to the student along with the syllabus and other materials. The Open University in Great Britain has designed many such kits for use in courses of study such as electronics. The kits are typically used in several courses in the curriculum and may be returned for recycling and refurbishment when the student has completed his or her studies.

Another possible solution is to combine a residential component with a laboratory course. This is one of the strategies used by the Open University in Great Britain, where students typically spend one or two weeks during the summer in residence on a campus once or twice during their degree program. Intensive laboratory components may be one of the activities that are conducted during such residential segments. For a single course, there might be a "laboratory weekend" midway through a course, during which many laboratory assignments are completed.

If none of the above alternatives seems feasible or adequate, arrangements might be made to borrow or rent the use of laboratories in high schools or universities in locations reasonably close to each of the students enrolled in a course during any particular semester. This is the most labor-intensive alternative, since not only must detailed lists of instructions and supplies be compiled (as with home kits), but also the instructor will have to make personal contacts and rely on professional courtesy to arrange the loan of facilities with colleagues in other parts of the country or world. For a course with an international student body, the loan of laboratory facilities might be combined with the residential weekend idea, with the intensive laboratory segments occurring in different locations.

6.10   Facilitating Online Courses: A Checklist for Action

The key concept in network teaching is to facilitate collaborative learning, not to deliver a course in a fixed and rigid, one-way format.

• Do not lecture. An elaborate, logically coherent but long sequence of comments often produces silence. Use short comments that are open-ended and invite response.

• Be clear about expectations of the participants—for the course as a whole and for each module, assignment, or time period within it.

• Be flexible and patient. Guide the conversation, but do not dominate it.

• Be responsive. Especially at the beginning of an online course or activity, ensure that every comment is responded to. If no one else replies, respond by message or by mentioning the author's comment.

• Do not overload. Contribute no more than one long comment a day, or less if the students are actively contributing. Several short notes are more likely to be read and appreciated more than a single long entry.

• Monitor and prompt for participation. Read the status report offered by the system frequently. Send private messages to those who are falling behind or are reading but not writing. If they have not signed on for a week or more and do not reply to these messages, call them on the telephone and help them with their problems or suggest ways in which they might contribute.

• For assignments, set up small groups and assign tasks to them. If the class is too large to have a single discussion space without overloading participants, divide it into two or more discussion groups.

• Be a process facilitator. Make sure that participants understand and abide by good netiquette by not insulting each other or getting far off the course topic. Encourage meta-communication about the process, and make suggestions for improving the experience for all the participants.

• Write weaving comments every week or two, or assign individuals or groups of students to take on this task of summarizing and focusing the discussion.

• Organize the interaction. Electronic housekeeping includes moving or deleting items that do not belong in a particular conference and organizing and modeling the use of key words and explicit references and associations among items to show relationships.

• Set rules and standards for good netiquette, and encourage meta-communication about anything that is causing the experience to be less valuable or enjoyable for all than it might be.

• Establish clear norms for participation and procedures for grading online work that give credit for good participation.

• Assign individuals or small groups to play the role of teacher and of moderator for portions of the course.

• Close and purge moribund conferences in stages, giving members an opportunity to save whatever messages they wish to keep.

• Adopt a flexible approach toward curriculum integration on global networks. Curriculum areas will be affected by the diversity of opinions from different locations in the world. The best approach is to be open to changes and accept new views on various topics.

7

Learning Online

7.1 Learner Characteristics: Who Is Successful?

Participating early and often in online classes is the key to learner success. A related characteristic is a positive attitude. Think of an online course as a voyage of discovery through the world of knowledge. As with ocean voyages, one of the main attractions is the opportunity to interact with complete strangers who become one's fellow passengers.

For network neophytes, the biggest barrier is overcoming inhibitions about communicating via this medium. The discussions that are taking place may seem strange at first because the predominant writing style is different from the way that is usually taught to write assignments. Some users take to this medium quickly and apparently without any acclimation effort; others need time to get into the swing of it. Many newcomers to a network spend ten to twenty hours just reading the online discourse to see how others communicate before they will risk saying something. As humans, we have a natural propensity to be reluctant to change from modes of communication that we are familiar with. This means that newcomers will feel some discomfort and that the self-activating nature of the medium provides the opportunity to put off and delay the start-up effort. Those managing an online educational program should keep track of which students are first-time users and make instructors aware of such individuals. Care should be taken to track if they are following what is going on, and private messages might be needed to encourage their participation. Newcomers should not feel reluctant to ask for help and guidance on getting started. Knowing such things as the best conference space for informal socialization is crucial to getting comfortable with the medium.

One of the few studies of correlates of grades and subjective student evaluations of online learning found that just as in other modes of learning, the best-prepared students tend to excel (Hiltz 1993). The highest correlation was with the mathematics aptitude scores of students on the SAT (the standardized precollege examination that U.S. students take prior to entering college). However, even students with very low scores were able, on the average, to pass courses offered online over learning networks, and their subjective evaluations were actually more favorable than those of students with slightly higher aptitude scores. In short, although academic ability certainly helps in the online learning environment, as in any other learning environment, a user does not have to be a genius to enjoy it or to perform adequately.

Students report many benefits to learning networks. For example, they can review and reread what has taken place as often as is needed for understanding and retention. They can take as long as is needed to reflect on what they are reading and decide what questions to ask or comments to contribute to the discussion. No one in the class can observe how long it took or how much effort went into an individual student's response, a characteristic that provides the slow learner with a virtual equality that is not usually available in the face-to-face class. The freedom of self-activation, however, carries with it the responsibility for the timely investment of effort. It is far too easy, with this technology, to put off to tomorrow what should be done today. Some systems have features to remind students who have not been keeping up with assignments and discussions that they are falling behind. At the very least the instructor should have a tracking ability for detecting those who are not making the necessary investment in effort.

Previous computer experience, typing ability, and even whether the language used in the online course is the student's native language make no significant difference in outcomes for online courses (Hiltz 1993). The primary reason is that students may work at their own pace and take as long as necessary to read, compose, and edit a reply. For example, students participating in English-language-based courses, for whom English is not the native language, report specific advantages to online class activities. They read items several times in order to understand them, consult dictionaries, and then draft, edit, and upload replies. The result is that they are able to participate on a more equal level with English-speaking students in an online class as compared to a traditional classroom.

All students, regardless of ability, benefit from the opportunity to self-pace activities, whereby they can explore issues and insights about a topic of interest more deeply. This is why good students often report that they learn more in the online environment. One honors student sent a message at the end of the course saying that he had been so bored in previous courses that he had considered dropping out of school. The online learning community was the first experience he had in college to challenge and exhilarate him, making him realize that he did want to complete his degree.

The factors that make a difference in student success in online courses are access, attitudes, motivation, and the self-discipline to participate regularly. Practice of good network etiquette and communications style makes the experience much more enjoyable. A systematic method for retaining, organizing, and reviewing the text files as they accumulate is also necessary.

7.2. Access and Regular Use

Ideally each student should have a personal computer, modem, and printer for access at any time. This is especially true for adults but is also desirable for in-school learners. Students in online courses without the convenience of access from home will need to schedule times to use shared facilities, such as a computer lab at school or work.

In public schools, computers are often not accessible after school, when buildings are closed. Any community that decides to foster this technology for public school or adult learners must provide access elsewhere—perhaps at the public library. Twenty-four hour access is the ideal that those with home units can enjoy; however, for a large segment of our society that is still a too expensive solution.

Online interaction should be engaging and fun. No one can enjoy it or derive the benefits of interacting with peers if there is not enough time to read, think about, and enjoy what is on the screen. When fatigue sets in, a break—a brief walk or anything else to rest the eyes and mind—is in order. Though midsession breaks to avoid physiological strain can be beneficial, once a user chooses regular times to participate online, he or she must stick to them. Falling behind by not signing on for awhile is the one certain ticket to failure in an online learning network.

A case study of the use of the Caucus conferencing system at the management school of Lancaster University in England (Hardy et al. 1991) includes excerpts from interviews with students that emphasize this point. The two-year program uses CMC as the main vehicle for group and tutorial work between residential workshops that occur only three times a year. Most students had a PC at home and experienced no difficulty in finding appropriate times to participate. For those who relied on access from their place of work, regular participation and, ultimately, success with and satisfaction with the program, were more problematic. Consider the contrast between the experiences of two students. Maggie found that the system allowed her to keep in touch every day with the other members of her learning community: "I feel quite connected to the other people.... If I want I can read what they have put in there every day.... It can thread through my life to quite a large extent.... I don't have to sit and save something up. If I sit and have an idea I fairly immediately put it on. I can also quite immediately get a response." She was able to turn to a computer in her office and to make time to participate during the workday. However, another student, Jenny, found it much more difficult to use facilities at her place of work; she fell behind in the course and never did catch up. She relied on shared equipment that was in high demand during the workday and had to stay late in the evenings or go back on the weekend in order to find a free terminal: "I had got into a pattern once I realized I could access through the Information Technology Center; I started this business of going in on a Sunday morning and a Saturday morning because I couldn't fit it in with the time scales going in on weekdays.... I was using the Staff Student Research Room, which is quite small, and that meant that I was queuing, going through the day and thinking, I can't fit it into a working day."

7.3   Peer Interaction and Support

Learning networks emphasize peer learning and active participation. Following are the key actions for students:

• Get into the class conference or discussion and obtain any new (unread) material.

• Enter new comments and or/replies to existing comments. (In some systems this is two separate operations.)

• Edit or modify already written items.

• List the members of the class and determine their identification and their progress with respect to participation. (Some systems provide membership lists that indicate the location of the person in the discussion.)

• Send private messages to the instructor and other students.

• Find other conference or discussion activities related to the educational program and/or to socializing among the participants.

• Set up private discussions for a small working group.

Basic equipment for access is normally a PC, a modem, and a communications software package. In addition users normally have word processing software to prepare assignments and reports. In this environment, they have to learn the following sort of operations:

• Connecting to the network via the communications software and whatever telephone access is provided.

• Being able to download or capture text from the network into the files on a local PC. Most communication packages have a range of facilities and protocols to make this a relatively easy task. However, occasionally one has to know how to convert the internal format of the text on the network to the standard ASCII to eliminate hidden formatting (invisible control characters) that have no meaning on the PC or interfere with normal use on the PC.

• Being able to convert text produced on the word processor to the standard ASCII or some other standard format like RTF (Rich Text Format) for uploading to the network for presentation. Once again the uploading can be facilitated by the communications software.

Some networking systems might supply their own PC communication package for use on a personal computer, which will handle a lot of the operations. It may actually automate the downloading of all new items, to facilitate browsing through at the higher screen speeds possible on the local PC. There are a number of different standard protocols and data formats, and it is not important that the student try to understand them. It is important to discover which protocols and formats the network can deal with and to match communications software to the network. The operators of the network should provide the basic information. If they do not, service providers can supply the information.

In some technical courses there may be a need to upload and exchange binary files with others. Binary files are the raw data types that can hold executable programs and various types of graphics. Outputs from typical spreadsheet packages usually take the form of binary files. Most networks today support the transfer of full eight-bit binary files. The networking software should provide a place to store these files online so they can be downloaded.

Perhaps one of the most important aspects of the technology is to learn how information is stored in the system, to be able to search for and retrieve useful information, and to be able to store what is written and contributed in a manner that makes it easy for others. Most systems present users whatever is new as it occurs. As a conference grows in size to hundreds or even thousands of items, it becomes increasingly important to be able to go back and selectively find items from the past. Hopefully those running the educational program and the instructor will supply some guidance for this process. One typical approach is to supply a fixed set of keywords that should always be used to classify items.

Most remote learning systems (if not now, then certainly in the near future) provide access to the Internet and to a very large world of resources that can be used to support different educational programs. The result is that there are in essence three different technologies that both student and instructor must gradually master: the PC and its software, the group communication system, and the network software such as on Internet. The saving grace is that not all the available functionality has to be mastered at once. Those conducting an educational program should collect the minimum that has to be learned to get started in the learning process, and distribute that to the students.

7.4 The Internet: An International Community and Resource

The Internet network has a long history and many prior incarnations. Less than a decade ago the number of users was officially under 10,000 and was largely composed of computer experts. Today the network has increased several thousandfold, and it connects almost every major university and college in the Western world, as well as many research, nonprofit, and corporate organizations and public school systems. It is growing so rapidly that users have difficulty keeping their knowledge of the scope and resources of the network up to date.

An organization wishing to join the network pays a monthly fee based on its size and type of organization. It also rents a high-speed data line to the closest existing node in the network so that it may tie into the network. Furthermore, the institution uses its computers to provide a gateway from the Internet to whatever computers in the organization are going to be made available to the network. The backbone (long-distance high-speed data lines) of the network has been financed by the U.S. government, but that funding is gradually diminishing and the current organizations will have to make higher payments in order to cover those missing funds. While this change is unlikely to lessen the current momentum of growth, it may have some influence on the services provided.

Each member decides what services (e.g., databases) it wishes to make available to others on the network. To date there is a rich set of services that universities, colleges, and government agencies and laboratories have made available. There are literally thousands of alternative resources in terms of databases and various group communication oriented facilities. In addition to these public services it is also possible to use the network to reach any organization's computer that the user has an account on. This means that a user in a member organization in San Francisco could be using a database on a computer in England without any telephone charges. Even before the offering of public databases, it was typical of many college students in computer science to trade student accounts with their counterparts at different universities so they could experience systems not available at their own institution.

While the Internet offers tremendous potential benefits to users (students or faculty), there are certain problems. One is that there is no directory of individuals using the network, yet users need to know a network address to send a message or a file. A second problem is that the sending of a message or the attempt to access a system can fail when certain computers are down or taken offline for local maintenance. Letting a user know that a message did not succeed or having any information provided when a network access fails is a haphazard process. Most people exchanging messages with others are in the habit of sending a return message if for no other reason than to make sure the sender knows the message got through. Finally, changes in the resources offered may not be updated very quickly, and with the rapid growth taking place, knowing what is new and what has been removed from access is also somewhat haphazard. Some critics say that Internet users get what they pay for and that these problems are the natural consequence of a free system. Actually, this network is now the largest of this type ever to exist, and we are facing the classic information retrieval problem for a very large collection of resources that is changing so fast that it is difficult to maintain updated information.

Anyone using the Internet should view it as participating in a grand international experiment in the free flow of information and the sharing of computer resources. This outlook on the part of the user is necessary to overcome some of the learning effort and performance difficulties of using the Internet. To some extent it should be the burden of the educational service provider to smooth over the problems of using Internet by providing specific information and guidance on what is available for the specific course the student is taking. This approach can ease the problem of knowing what to seek and where.

In effect, the growth of Internet and the rich variety of databases is resulting in the creation of an international virtual library. Many institutions have put online the database of their own library holdings so that students can determine where certain journals and books can be found, before leaving home to seek them out. Following is a description of the primary facilities that exist on Internet that students should learn about.

7.4.1   Telnet

Telnet is the equivalent of a communications package on the network. When a user signs on to the network, he or she first signs on to a computer at the local institution. To use Internet to sign onto another computer somewhere else, a user executes the Telnet utility, which is on every machine that ties into the Internet network—for example, telnet eies.njit.edu. The "eies.njit.edu" is the address of the machine and/or software the user wishes to connect to. In this case, it is indicating the computer that operates the EIES (Electronic Information Exchange System) at the New Jersey Institute of Technology, which is located on the educational portion of Internet. A user crossing an international boundary would normally have to add the standard abbreviation for the designated country (e.g., .ca for Canada). Thus, a user needs to know the network address of the system that he or she will use. Unless it is a public facility he or she will need to have an account on that system, which usually is composed of a log-in ID and a confidential password.

There are other functions available as part of Telnet to enable switching back and forth between talking to the local and remote computers. Also the host computer will have established a special character to be able to escape from the Telnet connection.

7.4.2   File Transfer Protocol

File transfer protocol (FTP) is a utility that allows moving files from one computer on the network to another. In many cases, when a user requests a standard mail or group communication system to send something to a network address, that application package is triggering FTP to do that task. However, sometimes a user may encounter a file of text stored in the ASCII format, or a binary program or graphic stored in the binary format, and wish to bring it back to the host computer. Entering the command "ftp" triggers a program that allows commands to be executed for manipulating these files, such as:

ftp > get 'source file name' 'destination file name'
ftp > put 'source file name' 'destination file name'

This is similar to a Copy command in a single DOS machine. The commands listed are for getting a file from a remote machine to bring to a host machine or taking a file from a host machine and putting it on the remote machine. There are other commands within FTP, such as telling the system what type of file is being used or for going to the right directory where the file is located. A user terminates FTP with Quit.

When dealing with a text file and when the file is viewed on a screen (the FTP Get and Put functions do not display the file that is being moved around), a user can also use the Capture function in a good PC communications package to create a PC file of what is shown on the screen. Learning how to deal with files on a personal computer is probably the best way to learn FTP on the network.

7.4.3   Archie

Archie is a public service utility program available on a number of different computers by regions of country and the world. A user has to know the address of a computer that hosts Archie as a public service. Archie indexes available files on Internet that may be obtained by users because they are public. These files may be programs, diagrams, text, or something else. In 1993 there were well over a thousand computers and millions of files indexed by Archie.

A user would go to Archie and log in. If the system did not reject the user because of capacity limits, he or she is allowed to log in without a password, which is the definition of a public utility on Internet. The user then indicates to Archie what type of search match he or she wishes to do (e.g., exact string match, a UNIX expression match, or a match as a substring). Archie allows searching for a match on a file name or doing a "what is" search on a descriptive index, which is composed of keywords associated with files.

Since there are no rigorous standards on either keys or names of programs, any Archie search is likely to result in very poor precision of search. Because of this and the demand for Archie searches, it is possible to learn how to use email to send a search request to an Archie host and wait to receive the result of the search back as a message. This is probably the most efficient way to use Archie currently. Educational providers should give users specific relevant examples of how to use this facility.

7.4.4   Finding Others

A user who knows the name of the person he or she wishes to find and what machine is that person's home can use the facility called "finger" to find out the exact name (complete first name or a complete last name and the address of the host) used on the system. Many hosts do not activate "finger" because they are worried about external users seeking valid log-in names to which they may be able to achieve an unauthorized entry.

The "Who is" facility is an old attempt at developing a White Pages that dates back to the days when the system was the ARPANET. Today it is a list of the people who are working on Internet itself as a system and those doing related research.

The USENET User list contains the names and email addresses of all individuals who have contributed to entries in the USENET news groups. Anyone making use of material from some of these news groups can use this facility to find email addresses.

In the future we will see the introduction of the X.500 Directory Services, an international standard for a White Pages to handle all commercial electronic addressing. It has the form of: Country.Organization. location.person. Beyond this, it becomes fairly complex in specification, but for specific implementations, there may be more user-friendly implementations. X.500 will be impressive because of its scope of coverage; however, it will lack the fundamental utility of allowing people to be able to find one another by common interests and concerns.

This limitation and the lack of total coverage are serious bottlenecks to the exercise of personal communications. Anyone who wants to use email has to know the address of the receiver.

Studies of human networking have shown that increased feelings of productivity from the use of networks correlate with the number of new people whom users meet online. If people communicate only with those they already know, they do not feel the network is anywhere as productive as if they meet others whose views and ideas are of interest to them. Thus, the lack of adequate facilities for people to find and get to know one another is a serious limitation on the potential for Internet.

7.4.5   Electronic Mail on Internet

Probably the most widely used feature of any network today is the ability to send a message from one person to a set of other people. The host computer will support a specific implementation of mail-sending software and provide instructions on how to use that specific facility. The minimum functions a mail facility should provide are to receive and organize mail, to allow the user to view the list of new and old mail items and choose what to view, to allow the user to respond to individual messages and capture items, and remove unneeded items from the mail list.

A group communication facility for learning may have been interfaced to the local mail facility. This means that within the interface for the group communication facility, a learner can use the same edit and interface facility to create, review, and read communications for dealing with Internet mail as is used for the electronic classroom. This is the ideal approach.

Those providing an account on a host computer for the electronic classroom will specify the Internet address.

7.4.6   Network News

Some software is designed to aid in reading a specific news collection. Each news group is like a bulletin board, with everyone interested in the topic of that bulletin board included in the list of mailing addresses, so that they are always sent new entries for that group. Today this is the principal way of getting involved with a group of people who share interests. Service providers can provide a friendly interface or give carefully designed examples of how to tie into the relevant news groups.

News groups are formed as part of a naming hierarchy just like files. For example, rec.music.folk. might refer to a recreation-oriented group interested in discussing music, specifically folk music. The common top-level nodes today are:

comp	computer science
news	about the network news service
rec	recreation
sci	scientific discussions
soc	social issues (e.g., political)
alt	alternative issues

talk   things to argue about, controversial topics

misc   anything else (e.g., job advertisements)

There is a large and growing number of local news groups that are not an official part of the USENET hierarchy, many sponsored by professional groups such as biologists, public school teachers, and electrical engineers. These groups hold discussions and post draft articles for others who may be interested. Better-organized news groups have individuals who act as moderators or editors to weed out material that does not belong in the news group's activity.

The common pitfall for new users of these groups is the ease with which they can join hundreds of such groups and spend large amounts of time reading numerous new messages a day. Users should limit themselves to groups that reflect their needs and interests. Five or under is a good limit.

7.4.7   Gopher, WAIS, and WWW

Three systems have been designed to try to ease the problem of finding material of interest to the Internet user: Gopher, Wide Area Information Servers (WAIS), and the World Wide Web (WWW). Gopher is analogous to a card catalog system in a library, WAIS is a large-scale indexing system, and WWW is a hypertext approach to organizing available information. In addition other approaches are under development. Improving information retrieval systems on Internet will remain a major challenge for a long time to come.

Gopher started as a package at the University of Minnesota (home of the Golden Gophers). Its primary function is to "go for" things. It is a set of nested menus that can be quite large and have considerable depth. Once a user has made a set of choices that gets him or her to an item to retrieve, Gopher can often get it if it is a text file or tell how to reach it via Telnet. Learning the Gopher system that is available is a matter of deciding to invest a few hours to explore the menus. Service providers should provide some guidance on how to reach relevant material.

WAIS is an index, rather than menu, approach to allowing users to search for material. Once again, the provider has to tell where a WAIS service is located. It is largely oriented toward handling documents. Indexing approaches are harder to master than menu approaches, but once this approach to searching material is understood and the nature of the keys used in the index is perceived, a user has a far better chance of getting high recall of material. In the menu approach, in contrast, there is considerable chance that useful material might have occurred down a branch in menus that the user did not take. On the other hand, if menus are well designed, there is more chance of getting material on the subject being requested. Precision of the results can thus be higher in menu-type access.

The newest and most rapidly growing approach is the World Wide Web. This is a distributed approach in that the host usually has a WWW interface and one can use the local host to do the browsing. Each local host is responsible for making available through the WWW software whatever files and information it wishes to provide for public access. Everything is handled by hypertext links that can occur in the text of the material being examined. These links can point to material anywhere on the network. When a user starts out in WWW, he or she usually goes to a master index (alphabetical) provided by the local host or to one provided by CERN, which created the software that supports the WWW.

As a user chooses items in WWW, the material is sent from the location of the material to the host and interface. Someone who is requesting material from Europe or Asia might notice only that going to the next screen takes slightly more time than usual. A single screen of hypertext links could be spanning ten different countries. In fact, a lot of the services we mentioned above can be found somewhere in the WWW.

The WWW is the most flexible of the current approaches, but it suffers from the problem that has plagued most implementations of hypertext: getting lost in the hypertext web. When dealing with hypertext and the continual threading of links, one becomes lost among the trees because there is no effective way to view the forest as a whole. This is a very powerful and versatile approach, but it takes time to learn and use.

All these systems depend on other humans' putting in the material and linking it properly to the menus of Gopher, the indexes of WAIS, or the hypertext links of WWW. The vast majority of this work is not being done by professional reference librarians, who are trained to categorize information for others to use, but by technical people, who may do a relatively poor job of dealing with the classification of information outside their field. This problem is likely to get worse before it gets better. Ultimately, Internet will need a system that puts the information classification into the hands of the professionals in that field of knowledge and provides tools for the more active involvement of reference librarians. As a result, it is important for the students in a course to share their explorations of Internet facilities and to let others know which search approaches lead to productive and useful material and which lead to dead ends. Exploring Internet should be a cooperative effort, and the instructors should encourage it being done in this manner.

7.5   Peer Interaction and Support

Learning network students are responsible not only for managing their own learning but also for helping others with theirs. They should:

• Read and respond to comments by peers rather than pay attention only to what the instructor says.

• Focus on the issues raised. When reading something, think, "What do I know about that?" "What do I think of that point of view?" Then jot down notes about the item, look up additional relevant information if necessary, and reply to it.

• View all items received as a possible stimulus for a contribution to a conversation. Relate concepts from the readings or examples from practical experience to illustrate or substantiate points.

One of the greatest advantages of online learning networks is the opportunity they provide for students to work together. Collaborative learning means that learners will be exposed to a wide variety of points of view and that group members can improve one another's understanding by pointing out omissions or logical errors. Group learning and the obligations it entails may not be familiar or comfortable at first. Students may not be used to talking in class or may worry that their ideas will be ridiculed. They may be inexperienced or wary of working in groups, and it may seem difficult to have to cooperate with other students rather than work individually. A positive attitude and considerate behavior will generally help all students become productive group members in the online environment.

CMC provides a whole battery of electronic bridges to enable students to bypass some of the conventional blocks on participation; no powers of public oratory, interruption, or loquaciousness are necessary; rapid exits from unpleasant or threatening encounters are viable; and no physical presence is required (Grint 1989, 189). Despite these potential protections for the shy or unsure student, many are still afraid to make contributions, especially if they are beginners in a class with others who are more experienced with the medium. Nevertheless, students are usually very supportive of their peers. No one is expected to produce a finished, complete paper on a topic when contributing an item. The medium is generally more like a written conversation than a published piece of scholarship. Learners and teachers describe online conversations as "talking with your fingers."

On the other hand, all entries are read by many others, so each student must be explicit about what he or she means. A basic consideration is to be concise and to the point. Students who ramble on burden their readers.

In addition to class discussions, instructors usually set up groups of students to work together on various assignments in an online course— perhaps groups for collaborative writing, whereby students provide constructive criticism to one another on their draft compositions, or study groups for reviewing material before an exam. Individual students can also take the initiative to find partners and form a group (first checking with the instructor to make sure that this will be acceptable as a form of work).

In any small group, productivity or effectiveness is related to group cohesion, which is increased by pleasurable social interaction: to getting to know the group members, providing positive feedback, sprinkling communications liberally with light humor, and avoiding any comment or joke that could be insulting. The group that has fun working together ends up doing more and better work. Group members count on each other to do their part, and the whole group may fail if members do not do their share. If a group member "disappears" or does not contribute, good-humored messages and telephone calls may entice him or her back into the fold.

Hsu (1992) reports that the "CEO" of one of the online simulated organizations in his Virtual Management Laboratory simply disappeared. The other group members posted a "missing persons report" and conducted a humorous "detective game" to "find" him. The peer pressure, delivered in a humorous rather than insulting manner, eventually induced the missing leader to return to his online "company," and it subsequently performed very well. If this sort of strategy does not work, the group will have to reorganize itself to reassign the roles of the missing member. This information should be communicated to the instructor.

Learning networks give students more responsibility for their performance and that of peers. This may even extend to participation in the assignment of grades. In one approach to work groups, the student group is asked to elect a leader who will have the authority to make the final assignment of work among the members. Usually the instructor will assign the same grade to every member of the work group for the resulting group product. However, in this approach the student group leader is allowed to raise and lower grades for individual members of the group, as long as the average for the group as a whole is equal to the grade assigned by the instructor. An example is an assignment in which each member of the class was to find an important technical article and review it. Each class member then rank-ordered the reviews by their usefulness, and the instructor used the resulting average rank order to assign the grades. Such an approach requires a rank ordering voting tool in the conferencing software.

One result of seeing each others' work is to achieve some understanding of the grading process and the relative fairness of the instructor. Some of the problems that students have with grading and appreciation of the fairness derives from a lack of ability to compare their work with that of other students.

A student who is going to be traveling or otherwise unavailable online for a period should inform the instructor and other group members about the impending absence and expected return date to prevent others from wasting time waiting for an answer that will not come or trying to call to find out why he or she is absent from the online group. Sometimes students who are experiencing severe personal difficulties are not able to meet their responsibilities to their group members for a particular task or assignment. They should immediately alert the professor indicating that they are in no condition to contribute or take an active part in the group discussion for a specific period of time.

7.6   Netiquette

Netiquette (network etiquette) refers to the evolving rules for considerate behavior on the networks. Netiquette guidelines will often be posted at the beginning of an online course, or perhaps in the Cafe or Student Center where all students mingle. If they are not, the following guidelines are useful for building good relationships with others in the online world.

7.6.1   Netiquette and Group Dynamics

Netiquette related to group dynamics concerns issues of building and maintaining a sense of community online. Positive climate building can reduce anxiety about communicating online and contribute to a pleasant collegial environment. Climate building can be developed by:

• Using first names or nicknames by participants
• Responding promptly to messages
• Using reinforcement phrases (e.g., "Good idea!" or "Thanks for the suggestions")
• Personalizing remarks
• Avoiding hostile or curt comments and never using objectionable, sexist, or racist language
• Displaying humor
• Promoting cooperation by offering assistance and support to other participants and by sharing ideas

No student should ever make hostile or ridiculing remarks about another student's contribution. Critical responses can be couched in a context of recognizing something of value and then pointing out suggestions for improvement or areas of disagreement—for example, "Bob, I find your ideas on surrogate motherhood very interesting. However, have you considered the following argument, which would not support your conclusion . . ."

There are people who like to insult one another for the fun if it, and it is often a mutual game of one-upmanship. On some systems they will set up a private conference for the purpose of insulting one another, and everyone who likes to try their hand at being insulting can go to that private conference by choice. There is always a very fine line between what some people enjoy discussing and what is offensive to others. The operators of a network should not have to impose censorship when private discussion groups can be formed that are restricted to those truly interested in dealing with a particular topic. Recently a major commercial service censored a discussion by a group of people who believe that there never was a Holocaust. Some users found this discussion offensive. Others were equally offended by the service's response. In this sort of situation, no resolution will please all participants. The fundamental policy should be that the operator of any group communication facility should clarify its policies on censorship.

In the United States certain types of communication are illegal: sending threats or conveying information (e.g., credit card numbers) for criminal purposes. If there are complaints about these types of communications, the operator of the facility has every right and some obligation to report the problem to law enforcement authorities and to inhibit the use of the system by such individuals. It is not clear, however, whether operators may monitor communications of their users for such activities. Currently there are no laws, but operators should provide some clear policy on what they will and will not do in this regard. Some law enforcement agencies have been trying to claim that many group communication facilities (e.g., bulletin boards) are publishing operations and therefore responsible for any illegal communications that may occur. If this were true, such facilities would have to monitor every communication taking place. Ultimately this issue will be resolved in the courts.

The use of humor can be very tricky; sometimes it is seen as sarcasm or derision rather than as funny. One of the most widely used symbols online is the "sideways smiley face," to mean "Just kidding." Including symbols or parenthetic phrases (e.g., :-) or "ha! ha!") can help to convey emotional tone and help to prevent misunderstandings. However, careful consideration of message, tone, content, and concern for the sensibilities of the reader are essential to good netiquette.

All users need to be aware that unless there are some explicit cues, readers will have a hard time deciding when someone is joking or angry.

The very ease of responding immediately may cause a user to "write in haste, repent at leisure" in a manner that could upset others. Use of some of the developing netiquette conventions can help to clarify intentions and convey intended messages more accurately.

In discussions of course material, it is important for students to get across such feelings as how confident they are about a particular viewpoint. This is important information when different interpretations of concepts can occur. Paralinguistic cues—"I feel strongly about this," or "I am confused; what do you think is right?"—are helpful. All users must let other students know when they agree or disagree with what is said, since no one can see a nod of agreement. Voting can provide an overview of the reactions of the class to a concept that has alternative views. The explicit detection and exposure of disagreement is useful for guiding the instructor's facilitation process.

7.6.2. Netiquette and Message Organizing

Since all discussions, debates, and interactions in a computer conferencing system are text based, guidelines for writing messages can help the communication flows.

Comment Keywords

Users should categorize each message with one or more keywords, to act as an advance organizer for the message content. If responding to a previous note, the author should explicitly specify which note, so that the reader can refer to it if needed (e.g., "In response to Pat's note 14 about apples"). In some systems the creation of replies is automated and the associations automatically set up (e.g., comment 20.5 is the fifth reply to comment 20). Keywords and explicit associations help to create organizational order and conceptual links.

Comment Length

Current technology suffers from the "small window" problem. Most screens display only about twenty-five lines of text. In addition, most people do not own a screen with high resolution. As a result, it is tedious and eye-straining to read long items online that go on for screen after screen. Therefore, each message should have a maximum limit. For class discussion, one to two screens per note seems to be a good length. If an item is longer, the main entry should provide only an abstract or summary, and a method used to enable participants to view, download, or print the longer text, if and when they wish to read all of it.

Comment Title or Subject Line

Another useful mechanism for categorizing comments is to provide a title in such a manner that one can view a listing of all titles, so as to be able to pick out comments that look interesting. Titles attempt to establish the uniqueness of a given comment in a single phrase; keywords attempt to establish a relationship among a group of related comments. These two very different objectives should guide students and instructors in the use of both facilities.

Message Focus

A message should contain one point plus examples. This rule of thumb makes subsequent references clearer and easier to track. If there are two points, they should be two separate entries.

Visual Layout

Messages should be presented so as to be easy to read. For example, double spacing or using only uppercase is difficult to read. Including paragraph breaks is helpful to visual layout. So are indentations and outlining. If automatic "word wrap" is not provided by the system, participants should strive to preserve fairly even right-hand margins. Being able to see lists of comments in short form, such as viewing only the titles and keywords, aids browsing.

Message Tone and Typos

Online discussions may be viewed as talking with one's fingers rather than formal writing. Short, spontaneous messages sent to online discussions need not be inhibited by concern about formal grammar or typos. As long as messages are readable, it is the flow of ideas that should be important. Semantics always dominate over syntax. As long as the content is clear, minor grammar and typing problems can be ignored. However, assignments presented online should be well written, corrected, and formatted.

For longer items, students should be careful to use correct spelling, grammar, and formatting, so others will not have difficulty understanding. Although the medium is usually informal and a few typos are acceptable, long items full of grammatical problems or disjointed ideas pose a barrier to others. Peers cannot understand or learn from poorly articulated or disorganized messages.

For any comment longer than a screen or few paragraphs, it might be faster to compose on a personal computer, run it through the spelling checker, and look it over before uploading. In any case, the complete draft item should always be checked before adding it to the discussion to see if lines were inadvertently deleted or if more paragraphs or spelling corrections are necessary to improve clarity.

The introduction of hypertext-style linking of comments will allow more creativity on the construction of nonlinear documents that represent the collected views of a class working together to explore a certain knowledge area. Some instructors use the contributions of students in prior classes to expand the material they have available for the benefit of future classes. For example, one instructor maintains a file online of all reviews of professional articles done by students in prior classes so that they may be used by future classes to browse and find what they should be reading for special project topics. The addition of hypertext-like composition capabilities will add to the utility of such collections by allowing meaningful lateral paths (by topic and subtopic) to be constructed through very large files (thousands of paper reviews).

7.6.3 Beyond Netiquette: Dos and Don'ts

• Demonstrating courtesy online is fundamental. Moreover, many conference moderators and bulletin board system operators are providing advance warning regarding the use of any form of libelous or abusive comments in public spaces that would result in the loss of the user's account.

• To build community and trust in this new and somewhat foreign environment, user accounts with real names can be important. Pseudonyms and/or anonymity, if employed, should be restricted to specific tasks.

• Nonparticipants should not be given access to any of the conferences (either viewing on screen or in print) without the prior consent of all participants and conferees. Private messages should never be passed on or shown to others without permission from the author.

• The words or text of others should not be cited without proper acknowledgment of the source (if this was in a public space) or, if private (as in a conference), without the author's permission.

• If emotions are running high, waiting a day to reply may defuse the situation.

• "Crackers" (criminal hackers) try to break into accounts or systems in order to destroy or alter information. They can seriously hurt networks by deleting material that has taken people a long time to create. A user who observes any suspicious behavior online that may indicate a cracker should report it immediately to the persons or organization operating the system.

7.7   Managing Online

A group is collaboratively building a knowledge base about the topics being discussed. This information must be stored and organized if it is to be used in the future to study for an exam or work on an assignment. Trying to read through the whole set of accumulated material online the night before an examination is not likely to be an effective way of reviewing.

Active reading is valuable. While reading an item, users can think about whether there is information or ideas to review or reply to later. If so, they can take a print or download it. Each new item received is a piece of a growing information puzzle to retain, organize, remember, and understand.

One method for dealing with the wealth of new material is to establish topic-oriented files on the PC and add new items each day. Notes or key words might show the topics and items to which each new interesting item is linked. A boldface font can be used to highlight key terms for easy finding. If there is a hypertext system on the PC, it can be used to organize and link the items by topic and cross-references.

A user who does not have a hard disk may wish to store and organize the material on paper instead, leaving large margins for notes, using a highlighter to emphasize important ideas, and adding key words and cross-references by hand.

Some conference systems provide the ability to place personal keys on items, useful for classifying items while reading. Others provide a primitive marking facility, for calling up the marked list of items later. As yet few systems provide what they should with respect to how people actually read complex material. A user should be able to mark multiple sections of text in different colors; form personal hypertext links to relate the material to anything anywhere in the discussion; and make notations in the margins. Given these sorts of common things we do with paper, pencil, index cards, scissors, tape, and copy machines, we would be better able to accomplish serious reading at a screen. The lack of such functionality explains why many people still prefer to use a paper printout of a long discussion rather than read for comprehension at the screen.

7.8   Infrastructure for Learning Networks

7.8.1   Online Helpers and Telephone Hot Lines
Most systems have a Help mailbox for technical problems and a telephone number to call for users having trouble gaining access to the system. Users should jot down this number in a prominent place and keep other numbers handy for dialing into the system.

7.8.2   Administrative Support for Online Learners
Many systems provide a wide variety of supports and services for online learners, in addition to the class discussions connected with a specific course. There may be a Technical Corner conference where questions are asked and tips exchanged about how to use the system itself. If there is a Café or Student Center, dropping in for conversation is a sociable "online coffee break."

There may be online counseling about topics such as the degree program and its requirements, careers, or even personal problems, as well as online access to library materials and other databases.

Finally, it may be possible to participate in teleregistration. Many institutions with online programs have provided the administrative infrastructure to post lists of course offerings and allow students to complete the course registration process online.

7.8.3 Learner Tools

PC owners have many tools available to make work in an online course more productive; among them spelling checkers, grammar checkers, spreadsheets, and hypertext database systems for organizing downloaded information. Anyone purchasing a machine should make sure it has enough memory to accommodate the tools needed when taking many courses or an entire degree program online. Often informal conferences or message lists about technical topics are a good place to exchange information about software that is particularly helpful for students.

7.9 Checklist for Action

1. If you have not used CMC before, the learning curve can be steep. Before the course begins, become familiar with how to use a word processor and your communications package to upload and download.

2. Make sure that you have convenient access to the PC or terminal you will use, and make a plan for a regular schedule of signing on and participating several times a week.

3. Learning networks emphasize collaborative learning. Respond to the ideas and questions of other students, not just to the instructor.

4. Be polite, considerate, and friendly online. Make your entries short and to the point in class discussions. Take the time to socialize with others in conferences or forums set aside for this purpose.

5. Devise a systematic method for saving and organizing the material for later review. Most adult learners cherish both independence (self-determination) and cooperation with others.

6. Make sure you understand the instructor's expectations for online tasks. In a face-to-face class, students are expected to pay attention to the instructor's presentations and to ask for clarification when needed. In online environments this is also the case. Besides instructions for particular tasks or assignments, there may be general expectations stated about the minimum number of times students are expected to log on each week, how many messages are expected to be sent each week, how to form teams for group work, and so forth. Though the network

environment is generally more democratic and student centered than traditional environments, grades reflect the extent to which students meet the requirements stated by the instructor.

Specific tips include:

• Write down your access code and password in two places—a piece of paper to keep in your wallet and one at home—and never give it to anyone else. If you think it may have been compromised, change it. Some students think it is funny to play a practical joke by using others' accounts.

• Keep a pencil and paper handy to jot down the identifier of items to which you want to reply or to return later.

• Be open to new ideas and new perspectives.

• People who put in the earliest notes on a topic are the most likely to be responded to and referenced by others (and appreciated by the facilitator).

• Long messages are boring. Keep entries to one or two screens, on a single point or topic. Use separate, short entries for each idea or distinct response.

• Avoid one of the most common mistakes: hasty posting of an item to the wrong conference. Either your note will be out of context, or the moderator will delete it and send it back to you to deposit in the correct forum.

In sum, CMC, though it requires considerable time and effort, is a medium for education that can be a balance between these sometimes contradictory needs.

Students can become a "power learners" (Davie and Wells 1991), taking control of their own education and playing an active and meaningful role in courses. They need to master the skills, processes, and netiquette and work to build an online community of peers who work together to provide mutual support and challenge. Students become empowered as individuals by contributing to and learning from collaborative group efforts.

8
Problems in Paradise: Expect the Best, Prepare for the Worst

8.1 Technical Problems

The primary difficulties teachers and students report are related to technical problems, and yet most technical problems are a transitory phenomenon in learning networks. With each group or class that goes online, there is a flurry of concerns and problems at the outset. Participants need to learn how to set up their system, how to use their system as a communication environment, and how to access and use the network. These tasks can be complex, and some networking systems are easier to learn than others. However, all technical problems disappear over time.

The most common technical problems occur in setting up the modem/communication system, learning how to access the network system from home or work, becoming lost in the system, editing online, and uploading and downloading messages. All of these relate to the specifics of the communication software on the PC (and there are hundreds of different versions), the CMC system, or the interface between the two. Problem-solving strategies such as checking the manuals and trial and error will eventually help to sort it out. The availability of an expert, whether the software vendor, a technical support staff, or a knowledgeable friend, is often the most efficient and satisfying route.

There are various approaches to assisting new users. Establishing expectations at the outset and providing training and technical support are key and can be handled in several ways.

The first issue is the decision about delegating responsibility for technical support. In primary and secondary schools, technical support is often the responsibility of the teacher or a computer consultant. Post-secondary institutions typically have computing service providers. It is usually the responsibility of the postsecondary student to learn the basics, although some training by the instructor may be provided. A common approach to online courses at university and adult training levels is to inform students at the outset to set up their equipment and gain some familiarity with it before class actvity begins. Students who are purchasing new equipment should look for an easy-to-use modem and software and equipment that is supported by technical staff at the school or university or buy from a reputable dealer who will provide service. No one should obtain pirated copies of communications software; not only is this illegal and unethical, but the user will have no manual and no source of assistance.

Most educational programs provide some training to familiarize students with the system and with the curriculum, in face-to-face sessions or through documentation, audio conferencing, audiocassettes, or online training modules. The use of buddies or learning partners during the training can launch the collaborative approach to system use and provide each student with an online peer for ongoing mutual help and support.

An online Help conference has been found very helpful in encouraging group support. Such a technical assistance conference should be run by students themselves, with students requesting help from and providing help to one another rather than relying on the teacher to provide all of the answers. The teacher or assistant can monitor the information and intervene if corrections are required or if no suggestions are forthcoming by the students. The online Help conference is heavily used, primarily early in the online class and when new activities or applications are introduced.

Customized user documentation and, on occasion, online tutorials on specific problems can be used if there is a group need. A telephone number or hot line to request technical assistance should provided for urgent or difficult problems.

Software difficulties, especially in regard to importing text or uploading messages to the network, are common. One fifth-grade teacher noted: "Our system is very difficult for children because there are so many different commands and instructions." Complex software routines prevent effective use of networks, teachers observe: "I don't know whether it's my fault [but] getting into Dialog and getting into Web … with my grade 7 was very complicated, and no other teachers in my school were even wanting or willing to touch those kinds of areas." One way to simplify the log-on procedures is to obtain help to create macros that automatically log on to one's account and simplify telecommunications: "We have [communication packages set up] now when the kids go on and use Dialog. One click takes them right through to the main menu in Dialog, and the students don't have to do anything—the bell rings when they are there."

With help from one another and from the instructor, users are usually able to gain comfort on the system in four to six hours and confidence and some mastery within eight to twelve hours of use. Nonetheless, it is critical to remember that "every system is harder to use than those who select it imagine, and many participants will drop out rather than report problems, yet will welcome help if it is volunteered" (Feenberg 1991, 99).

8.2 Communication Anxiety

Communication anxiety is a common experience for first-time users. It is, however, a fear of *not* communicating rather than a fear of communicating. This is understandable given just how new and different the experience is and the lack of immediate feedback or referents. This is especially true for asynchronous environments where typically there is no immediate response to entries. Anxiety associated with whether their message was sent properly and arrived successfully is common among novices. A related source of anxiety is whether the message was somehow foolish or inappropriate and thus not worthy of a reply. There are a host of such concerns that grip many novices and even seasoned networkers sending out a message into a new system.

The teacher or facilitator should ensure that all messages are responded to within a reasonable time frame, especially early in an online activity. The teacher might note which comments by students had not received responses and perhaps respond or encourage others to do so. A note about class netiquette might be included to warn students about communication anxiety and encourage them to repeat their message or to flag it if they do not receive a response. Students should also be encouraged to ensure that everyone receives responses to their messages most of the time. Finally, it is also important netiquette to respond to all personal email messages.

8.3   Infoglut

Infoglut—or information overload—is common to all computer networking activities. We are only beginning to learn how to manage communication effectively and efficiently in the online environment. With networking, access to communication, education, and information is no longer the major problem; the key challenge becomes learning how to manage the increased information flows.

Management strategies and tools can help. These depend on the nature of the networking activities. General use of networks, such as joining online special interest groups (SIGs) or clubs, requires judicious consideration and control. With thousands of such groups available on bulletin board services, the Internet, or commercial services, the temptations are many and the range of subjects almost limitless. SIGs offer opportunities to engage in communicating with tens or thousands of other kindred spirits. Yet the results are soon overwhelming; the demands of reading through hundreds or thousands of messages each day are certain to lead to infoglut in short order. Scanning some of the services and perhaps judiciously trying a limited few is advisable. Another advisable strategy is to ask peers for recommendations.

Specific use of networks for course purposes avoids the problem of oversubscription to SIGs, but information overload remains a problem in even a moderately active course conference. The opportunity for or expectation of active student participation generates significant message flows, affecting both teachers and students. Two strategies are advisable. The first is to establish netiquette on standards for length of a message (no more than two screens, for example), and special organizational strategies such as use of advance organizers (keywords) and paragraphing. Second, structuring online class activities helps to organize, if not stem, communication flows. Dyads or small working groups might be introduced to reduce the volume of plenary exchange, or small group discussions could be used when any larger group becomes too active or the topics begin to diverge and the instructor wishes to encourage divergence. Alternatively, the moderator may intervene to help refocus the discussion if the divergences are not appropriate. A few other strategies might be considered as well. The number of messages may be limited. This strategy is not advisable in many cases, but special occasions may warrant this approach. Finally, if the overload problem is extensive, the instructor might consider redesigning the curriculum to reduce the volume of information flows.

A third source of overload is common to being new to a system. Early in the course, as students learn to navigate around the system, the sense of being lost in cyberspace can trigger an experience of information overload. A sense of place has not yet been established, and the conference may feel like a maze. Additionally, students may initially send notes to the wrong conference, creating confusion for readers. Moreover, student enthusiasm is often high in the early weeks of online activity, with some students writing voluminous and numerous messages. With some experience under their belts, students refine their online communicating and navigating skills, and these problems are overcome.

Finally, the nature of the medium is a contributing factor. Most networking systems available today provide few tools to reduce overload. Email networks offer the most limited set of tools for structuring group activities. Computer conferencing enables very active participation and active conferences generate a rich database of information. However, high levels of activity can be a double-edged sword if there are no tools to help manage the information flows. New developments in the area of information management tools hold some promise, and systems with some hypertext or information management features are becoming available.

8.4 Time Management

An increasingly common concern among teachers and students is that the amount of time spent in online classes exceeds equivalent face-to-face classes. One reason may be the initial excitement with the power of networking and the fascination with the diversity and brilliance of human communication. Beyond the initial glow, it is also true that the depth as well as scope of discussion online far exceeds what is possible in face-to-face classrooms. Online discussions can cover more ground, with greater depth of analysis because the online classroom is typically always open. Networks enable each student to be active, demanding much more time to read what is often voluminous discussion proceedings. Moreover, for those with home computers, the accessibility of networking makes it convenient as well as compelling, and thereby also consumes more time.

Teachers need to ensure that the workload for students is manageable and reasonable for the course objectives. Teachers need to attend to their own workload online as well. Given the tremendous accessibility of online class activity and the increased availability of the online teacher, students may begin to expect almost instant responses to any question they pose to the teacher. To help set student expectations, teachers may consider posting "electronic office hours."

8.5   What If You Give a Conference and Nobody Comes?

One of the most common fears of an instructor or moderator of a group activity is that no one will join. Or what if they join but do not say anything? While jitters at each new online class will likely remain as a form of stagefright, there are solutions.

With attention to a few basics, this scenario will never occur for online course activities. The basics are to ensure that everyone has reasonable access, training, and support; be clear about the expected behavior and also about its purpose and its relationship to the curriculum; ensure that the network activity is integrated into the curriculum; and provide a reward (grade) for participation, which includes recognition of adherence to the requisite volume of messaging and the time (and/or regularity) of messaging as well as the quality of the input.

8.6   Getting the Conversation Flowing

Many students may initially be timid and reluctant to make comments for fear of saying something wrong or silly. Also, active group learning is new to many students, and they need to learn and then become comfortable with the norms and expectations.

The best advice is to start the online course (or activity) with a task or topic that is familiar or known to participants and then move to the unknown. The initial set of activities should focus on content that is familiar to students, since they will also be learning a technical and pedagogic system that is likely new and foreign to them. One strategy is to begin by asking students to introduce themselves, their hobbies, and, for online courses, their personal course objectives. This icebreaker helps students to get to know one another. An informal debate, in which the teacher presents a contentious issue and invites response (with some explication of the reasons), is also valuable for generating activity and launching group interaction related to the course.

8.7 Cooperation or Competition?

The instructor faces the challenge of building an atmosphere in which each student will feel that the other students are there to help him or her improve. One way is to have the students view the others' assignments and require that each make constructive criticisms. Any sort of essay or open-ended design problem is a candidate for this exercise. The students might be told that they will be graded on how well they offer constructive help to the other members of the course and that every student will have a period of time to take the suggestions of the other students and rework their assignment before the instructor receives it for final grading.

Once students become used to helping one another improve their individual assignments, the class takes on an atmosphere of a social support group in which no student feels embarrassed at presenting a first draft of an assignment to the rest of the class. Some instructors might view this process as cheating, but it is not. The instructor, by being part of the conference devoted to this process, can see the aid that individual students are contributing; the ability of a student to contribute good ideas to other students says a lot about the truly best students in the course. The best way to reflect this is to give a special grade at the end of the course that sums up the contribution activities of each student.

8.8   Teamwork and Motivation

Many students have never before worked in a group. Even at the college level, students receive little, if any, training on how to work as a team. Only students who have been in a work environment realize that most projects in organizations require a group effort.

The study group model is rare in postsecondary education, found almost only in professional schools. It is also unusual in the school system, except in primary school environments. If there is any one process-type course that should be offered as part of a learning network, it should be a course in the process of teamwork and how to go about it. Short of having such a course available to students on the network, it falls on the instructor to try to ensure an atmosphere that encourages small teams of students to work together effectively.

Depending on the type of assignment, the instructor might prepare a guide of various approaches to carrying out the assignment as a team. Rather than have students divide up the topic, with each person doing a piece and then packaging the pieces together as a final product, the instructor should encourage group interaction at various stages even if some tasks are conducted individually. For example, defining the group activity, identifying the tasks, prioritizing the tasks, and agreeing on the key concepts underlying the project (their significance and validity), procedure (division of labor, identification of a team coordinator, timeline), and, especially, the format and content of the final product might all be group undertakings. Or delegation of final production tasks might be done after material is gathered and reviewed. Nonetheless, all members of the group should be involved in important conceptual, substantive, and procedural issues. Instructor support in organizing the group is essential.

8.9   Group Dynamics

Collaboration offers many important educational benefits, but problems may arise. Group work online is no exception, and the nature of the network medium can sometimes be a constraint. The asynchronous nature of the communication medium can pose particular difficulties for certain aspects of group work, especially when deadlines are near.

When individuals have not previously worked together in teams, motivation for everyone to carry an equal share of the labor is crucial. A member of a team might decide not to work very hard and to let the others carry the load. The instructor cannot afford to get bogged down in being the final manager and evaluator of the relative performance of each team member. It is not possible within the time constraints of a course. Therefore, one approach is to present the operation of the team as a contract with the instructor to do a certain job. It may be desirable to set down explicit rules that are clearly understood beforehand by all members of the class. Here is one set:

1. Each team must have an odd number of people.
2. Each team must designate a team coordinator at the start of the project.
3. The team coordinator may make a decision unless overruled by a majority.
4. The resulting project will receive a grade that applies to every member of the group.
5. The team coordinator will have the final authority to modify any member's grade up or down (except his or her own) provided the average team grade remains the same as that applied by the instructor.

This set of rules includes certain key motivational factors. For reaching closure when necessary, having an odd number of people in the group is preferable. The group itself, not the instructor, chooses the coordinator. The coordinator is motivated to try to obtain the best grade possible for the group as a whole, since his or her grade cannot be better than that. However, the coordinator does have negotiating potential with nonperformers in the group and can downgrade those relative to others who put in more work.

The instructor needs to create an environment in which the team will settle its own problems. Some form of delegation of grading authority to team leaders seems to be a key ingredient to ensuring this situation. Having students do part of the grading might surprise some educators and educational administrators. However, it is an excellent mechanism for encouraging effective group work, given the situation that most students have not had much experience in working with teams.

The issue of group size depends on the nature of the assignment. For writing a joint report or a collaborative programming effort, the range of three to seven members is probably best. For running a company in a management game or undertaking some major technical design projects, it is possible to work with teams in the seven to fifteen range.

8.10 Unequal Participation

A potential benefit of learning networks is that each student can participate equally in class discussions and activities; however, each student may not put in the same volume or quality of material. Differences based on student interest, ability, availability, or other considerations affect the upper and lower levels of participation.

A relatively equitable distribution of communication can be encouraged, but some students may dominate or others refuse to participate. The first step to encouraging active input is to set out expectations for participation. What is the minimum level of messaging required per week per student? Is it a number of messages? Number of log-ons? Length of messaging? How will quality of the message be graded? What kind of activities should be completed? Rewards for participation should be clearly established.

Students who participate very little or not at all should be contacted and the reasons discussed. If they are technical reasons, assistance should be provided. If the reasons are motivational, students can be encouraged by peers or the instructor to increase their level of participation. If that is unsuccessful, teachers in K-to-12 classes may overlook the problem, provide a peer helper, or give that student an alternative assignment. In other cases, particularly with adults, after a certain level of encouragement the instructor may opt to allow the students to choose their own level of participation and grade them accordingly.

Students who are dominating the discussion by sending overly long or too many messages should be sent a personal message that reviews and encourages adherence to the course norms. Grading may take into account excessive input. If the behavior is particularly disruptive, the student may be denied writing privileges for a certain time or even be banned from a topic for a set time.

8.11   Miscommunication

Flaming refers to the use of negative comments, rude or insulting remarks, or other emotionally charged language in a network. It is the network equivalent of yelling at one another, or perhaps a fistfight in the schoolyard. It is called "flaming" because it sometimes seems like a fire out of control: one person's nasty or angry remark fuels an even stronger response by a second person, and so on.

Instances of flaming in educational conferences are rare because the norms of an established group are not fertile ground for it. The most serious form of flaming, intentional disruption, most typically occurs in contexts such as open conferences or SIGs, where the social connectivities are thin and certain individuals seek recognition. Netiquette should address this possibility and discourage negative and hostile exchanges. Rules and repercussions should be clearly established.

Following are excerpts derived from a flaming episode in a student center conference. One member entered an emotional comment about the Los Angeles riots, which had several spelling and grammar errors; this set off an unfortunate exchange:

C 1992 CC 99.5 Dan 5/11/92 1:57 PM Subject: Riots
The L.A. police new what the verdict could be and should have prepared itself for the outbreaks of violence. This was done in Miami were a police officer was acquitted of killing a colored person ... anyway, the majority of the looters stole oly what they could carry. I bet George Bush's sone and his friends couldn't carry all they stole from the S&L crises in their hands. (The Republicans and the Democrats know about the S&L crises. They knew that banks were about to fail but kept it quite because election year was coming up).... The tough talking prosecutors said there going to prosecute the little people but how about the big people?

C 1992 cc 99.5.1 Nan 5/10/92 5:32 PM Subject: Riots
A little grammar here.
Use knew for the verb—not new.
They are—the proper contraction is they're, not there.
To be silent is quiet—quite is incorrect.
Didn't anyone else have old maid English teachers who set them straight?

C 1992 CC 99.5.2 CG 5/11/92 9:10 AM Subject: Grammar
Nan, I'm with you! I know that some of the errors in these comments are just typos that are easier left as is than fixed. BUT it seems that people just don't have a basic command of written English anymore.

C 1992 CC 99.5.3. Dan 5/11/92 Subject: Poor English
The subject was on the L.A. riots, Nan and CG are a thousand miles off the topic.... A person who was truly educated would give a reply in a macro or micro sociological point of view.
C 1992 CC 99.5.6 WG 5/11/92 9:54 PM Subject: Even Poorer Attitudes!
Dear Dan, it was extremely obnoxious of you to criticize Nan and CG for "being a thousand miles off the topic." Who voted you GOD, able to criticize people for free thinking. Yes, the LA riots are awful, but so, too, is the sad state of people. One of their biggest problems is difficulty communicating.... I'm with Nan and CG, by the time you get to a graduate level, either be proficient with English, or get into some remedial classes.

At this point, intervention by an instructor ended the heated argument within the conference, but it simply went to private messages. Below is a message from Nan that ended with her feeling so upset that she felt she did not want to take another online course. Advice from the instructor was necessary in order for her to put the exchange in perspective.

M 1191 Nan 5/13/92 9:34 PM 6 lines
KEYS: /Attachment/Item/ TO: Instructor
Dear Professor,
   I guess what I was, was plain stupid. I never thought I'd upset anyone that much. I'll attach Dan's last mail. Don't look for me on-line next year, I don't feel quite comfortable about it now.
   Nan
ATTACHMENT:
M 1180 Dan 5/13/92 11:23 AM 22 lines
Nan,
   I still find it very hard to believe that you couldn't understand the comment because of grammatical and typo error. I'm a native American and I do have some problems with grammar. I have a spell checker and a grammar checker on my PC. I should have never wasted my time trying to make my point. The subject I posted on Rodney King make me very emotional because it can happen to me. This is why African-Americans men and women view this subject differently. This type of brutality has been brought against my people for generations....
   Other African-Americans have viewed your comment and come to the conclusion that your a racist or a bigot. I rather give you the benefit of the doubt and say that your ignorant. See whenever one our people hold office, speak out against injustice, were usually analyzed under the microscope and subject to ridicule. This is a typical response from people who have full mobility and privileges in a society. The tactic that you have displayed is quite common. It is a shame I fallen for it.

M 1191.1 "Instructor" *5/13/92* 10:00 PM 6 lines
TO: nan R: 1/1
You should not be so discouraged.... Just learn that you need to realize that
people can have their feelings hurt online more easily than off. Did you mention
to him that you could not possibly know his race, so it could not have been a
racist reaction ...?

M 1191.2 "Nan" *5/13/92* 10:46 PM 4 lines
TO: Instructor
Yes, I sent him a reply saying that I didn't know anything about him. Just did it
tonight after I read it. You surely are right about people being more hurt on-line.
Guess I'll consider this a big learning experience. See you on-line next year.

8.12 Administrators and the Environment

One of the ways to understand the importance of the collaborative
approach to learning is to examine the changes it could bring about in
educational practices and institutions. The members of this community
who experience the changes most immediately are the instructors. The
average instructor has fixed hours during the week to engage students in
a classroom setting. For a college or university educator there may also
be a set number of office hours during which the instructor is available
to the students. Whatever this amount of time is, it is secure and com-
forting for many instructors to know that there is a finite and predictable
period of time during which they might be approached by students.

The learning network environment is available to the students and
instructors on a twenty-four-hour-a-day basis. As a result, students expect
regular and ongoing interaction with the instructor. In a college environment, the turnaround time to respond to students can be reduced from a
week to a day. For a public school teacher, this might go from a day to
hours. Clearly not all instructors will welcome this change in the ability
to regulate and control the interaction rate with students.

Networking technology not only affects the pattern of communication
between the students and the instructor; it also expands opportunities
for students to communicate among themselves. It allows the students to
collaborate with one another as a part of the learning process. It makes
it easy for students to work in small groups to exchange information on
assignments and to collaborate on their lessons. In fact, one of the most

effective forms of assignments is giving the students responsibility for providing some of the lesson material for the course. Individual students or small groups of students go out and explore topics that they deliver to the rest of the class. Will this be viewed by administrators as the instructor's shirking his or her duties? Will students feel that this is more work than what is traditionally expected and resist or complain? How will the instructor react when some of the more industrious students come up with material the instructor is not familiar with? Finally, what will the accreditation institutions say about students' doing some of the teaching?

There are thus many challenges confronting educational administrators. For example, team teaching courses becomes easy within the context of a learning network. How do we evaluate and compensate educators in a team-teaching environment? The same effect can be had by mixing courses; that is, two different courses can meet together in a learning network to explore the same topic area from different academic perspectives.

The change in the concept of the time that an instructor spends with students will present an even bigger challenge for the administrator. The time and effort an instructor expends becomes a linear function of the number of students in a class. Administrators can no longer economize on educational effort by increasing class size. The instructor can no longer adapt to class size by allowing less time for individual interaction with the students.

On the other hand, there may be administrative challenges to educators. Administrators might be tempted to take advantage of the complete electronic record that exists of the online class proceedings and all the instructors' notes and materials. Some administrators may contemplate eliminating the instructor, requiring only a lower-level person to play back material in subsequent course offerings. The issues of ownership, academic freedom, and privacy are very real issues for the administration of this technology.

Certainly with this approach to education it becomes much easier for the students, as well as the administrators, to evaluate the instructor. The students can see the work of the other students and the reactions of the instructor to other students' work as well as their own. This makes it much easier for a student to assess consistency in the performance of the instructor.

It is no longer possible for the instructor to dominate the students by the commanding nature of his or her presence in a face-to-face environment. In the electronic environment, the instructor can earn respect only by exhibiting expertise and command of the subject matter. Students may show more of a tendency to challenge instructors in the electronic environment. If students are given the ability to enter anonymous or pen name comments, this tendency can be even more pronounced. Instructors face a much looser ability to control the students online than face to face.

On the other hand, students may not appreciate exposing their performance to fellow students. It is one thing to expose cognitive shortcomings to an instructor but quite another to expose them to fellow students. In a classroom one can always be quiet, but in a learning network the student is forced into participation. How will this requirement affect various types of learners? Will the student tolerate the added effort that equal and active participation implies?

While the network learning process brings impressive benefits to those involved, there is an investment of effort and of learning to be made by students, educators, and administrators to master this approach to learning. It represents a significant change in current approaches and practices at all levels in the educational process.

8.12.1 Lack of Institutional Support and Strategic Planning

Lack of institutional support expresses itself in a variety of ways. Teachers who initiate computing activities on their own may be penalized for being innovative. If the institution does not support their efforts, they are forced to expend their own time to assist students with networking. Administrators may question the value of networking, as "wasting time in computing" rather than "delivering the curriculum." In one case, a teacher who used collaborative approaches to learning networks said, "In my course we socialized and it didn't hurt us. But what happens if a teacher is doing that and the vice principal or the principal walks in? The principal is very conscious of 'on-task time.'" The situation is not unique. School administrators and other school staff might not support the use of computers and impose constraints on their use. Educational institutions, like many other institutions, tend to resist change and the potential impact of computers on schooling.

While schools are increasingly being linked to learning networks, most lack strategic planning to integrate CMC into their daily routine. Network activities are still done before or after school hours or over school lunch hours. Teachers and students involved in networking do the activities on a volunteer basis and do not receive credit for their work. There is a need for appropriate professional recognition and rewards and institutional support for learning network activities.

When innovative teachers have the active support of administration, particularly the principal and vice principal, it is much easier to initiate access to learning networks and integrate learning networks into the curriculum. In schools where teachers lack that type of support, the best alternative is to create a school computing club and then lobby internally for acceptance and use of learning networks. Guest speakers can be invited and demonstrations arranged to help create institutional support.

8.12.2 Lack of Time

Lack of time is the most frequent problem encountered in classroom networks. K-to-12 teachers, more than other educators, are subject to a fixed curriculum that must be delivered in a certain time frame. Learning networks are typically an add-on to the existing curriculum. Online networking requires extra time to learn about the technology, programs available, preparation of the programs, and integrating networking into the established curriculum. Moreover, because most schools do not give students accounts, teachers must also log on and do some of the online work themselves. As teachers are not freed from regular school activities to do online work, these activities represent extra work, often done outside school hours.

This problem is also experienced by teachers in postsecondary education. Christensen (1990), who studied the role of teachers who used CMC as adjuncts to distance education courses at Jutland Open University in Denmark, noted: "CMC gives more work to the teachers, but extra teaching hours have not been added to the courses.... The teachers have to be trained in the technical and especially the educational use of CMC.... [And the] experiences of teachers in previous years must be passed on to new teachers.... I am more and more convinced that many of the problems we are observing are not primarily due to CMC, but in part due to the implementation of it and in part to the way that distance education is organized."

Solutions can be found to reduce the problem. As students are taught to use the system, they can become experts who can help other students, teachers, and school staff to learn the system. Thus, the teacher is no longer the only source of information and gatekeeper to the system, and the time required to help students with technical matters, or to do these activities, should decrease. Teacher networks enable exchange of advice and guidance on integration of networking into traditional curricula, and indeed, some school districts are developing curricula involving networking. Finally, teachers are seeking the development of school policies to assign time for teacher preparation and use of learning networks.

8.12.3 Limited Access to Learning Networks

Hardware set-up and delivery is another common problem encountered in most schools. A student-computer ratio of up to fifteen-to-one leads to frustration among students anxious to get online. One teacher reported, "I think the students can really see the benefits but they also experience the frustration because they can't get the access they'd really like." Access to computers, moreover, does not guarantee access to online networks; a modem, telephone line, and a computer account are still needed. Very few schools have dedicated telephone lines for modems, and when they do, students must share the modem with other students, teachers, and staff. Modem bottleneck is not unusual.

In a study of the use of the Portacom computer conferencing system as a distance education course supplement to facilitate group interaction at Jutland Open University, Denmark, researchers found that student access to computers was a critical factor. In some of the courses, students had the necessary computer equipment at home; in other courses, students had to use the equipment at one of the university's five study centers. Bang and Moller (1990) reported, "The students with home-based personal computers have found that computer conferencing has facilitated communication with their teachers and fellow students. These students completed the arts foundation course with better grades than on similar courses where computer conferencing had not been used.... The conferencing systems has been a very useful addition to their distance education.... It has been harder to motivate students without home-based personal computers to use computer conferencing. They seem unwilling to leave their homes and go to a study center for communication, when they could just as easily grab a phone or mail a letter."

Generally students at the K-to-12 level do not have their own computer accounts to access online networks: they must share the school's or teacher's account. Also, most access is available after class time, and teachers find it difficult to use just one modem to do anything meaningful in a class. Access to equipment is thus a significant factor negatively influencing adoption of learning networks.

8.12.4   Lack of Inservice Training

Inservice training is important in teachers' adoption and use of learning networks. These technical and instructional learning activities require school support. As one teacher noted: "I think we need a better technical support service for the different school districts. Something more formally set up than trying to get help from someone who just thinks they know what they are doing."

The place to begin might be with the development of a half-day workshop format, perhaps offered several times a year. Alumni of this basic orientation session could then conduct advanced online workshops for more experienced teachers. Experienced teachers might also work in a buddy system to support teachers new to networking. Additionally, the opportunity for interested teachers to serve as observers of network activities can supplement inservice training activities.

8.12.5   Integrating CMC with the Curriculum

While many students are excited about computer networks and the options they can find online, school administrators and teachers want to ensure that the activities are curriculum related. At the moment there are no clear guidelines, although a number of examples have been provided in this book to help teachers address this issue.

Other problems are associated with global connections. In school networks, for example, problems arise integrating international activities within the calendar year of each country. Schools also have different semesters in different countries, different curriculum, teaching practices, and, of course, different languages. These issues, if not addressed in the planning stage, can become bottlenecks in school networks.

Perspectives on various issues such as environmental practices, history, culture, or politics may also be not only different but contradictory in different parts of the world and should be anticipated in global learning networks.

8.13 Conclusions

Learning networks imply a significant change to the educational process and to the individuals and organizations making up the educational infrastructure. The more significant the change to a social system, the more likely one will encounter active resistance. Various factors may create resistance to both social and technological change.

• Educators are in general already extremely overworked. The adoption of learning networks requires additional time to learn the technology and to rethink and rework the methods of handling lesson and course material. At issue is whether educators should be expected to expend this added effort over and above their current obligations or whether they will be provided with the necessary support for the transition effort.

• Low wages and years of bureaucratic regulations have drained the willingness of a significant number of educators to deal with change even if improvements in delivery are likely.

• Being an innovator can be lonely. Introducing an educational innovation such as learning networks can be difficult, especially initially. Peer pressure may be exerted against an employee who wishes to promote more innovative approaches.

• Innovation and change cannot be disassociated from a degree of risk. At the very least there will be individual instances of problems and need to change administrative policies and practices. Administrative bureaucracies may resist change.

• Many educators and administrators have been badly burned by experiences with computers in the past decade. They may have invested money or effort in a system, only to discover that it does not live up to the vendor's promises. There are a surprisingly large number of people who justifiably distrust the promises made for the technology. This population may include local businesspersons on school boards.

• Public schools are in a comparable situation to companies in the late 1960s. They have little in the way of technical staff who are computer and information system experts. As a result, they tend to rely on the vendors and often become captive customers of vendors with the best marketing presence. As a result, some so-called educational discount prices for personal computers and mini-computers can be twice the cost of machines just as reliable and just as powerful available in the open market. Equipment and software are often purchased based on the name of the company and not on price or performance considerations.

• Some people still feel that computers are dehumanizing and doubt that communications through a computer can be effective, warm, and inspiring. This belief can be overcome only if these people can be convinced to participate in and observe learning networks.

• It is very difficult for people to conceptualize a new communications medium they have never experienced and to translate what they do into a completely different form of communications. These people need a chance to observe and then experience education through computer-mediated communications.

• In elementary schools, the attitude and support of the parents and the community are key to success. Given a major change that is difficult for the educational community to absorb, how does one gain community support for the effort?

As learning networks become extensions of the school classroom, a number of impacts occur. Students and teachers have increased access to information and share their ideas with a larger audience. The teacher becomes more of a facilitator or resource person rather than a dispenser of information. When the librarian is involved in networking, his or her role expands to help teachers and students access information. In some schools students become "teaching assistants" and work with peers, teachers, and staff to teach them the basics of networking technology.

Networking has not been perceived by any users as a disruption of traditional schooling. These activities, however, have not yet been incorporated into a strategic plan to restructure schooling. They occur as a result of the initiative of some teachers, librarians, and staff. As a result there are no directions on how to integrate these impacts.

III

The Future

9
New Directions

No one can see into the future, at least not very far into the future. However, anyone can help to shape the future. The opportunities that the future presents can be delineated so that people and organizations can take actions to encourage the more desirable alternatives to emerge. In this section we consider some of the more positive directions we see for the technology, the institutions, and the people involved in learning communities. It is our summary blueprint for the future and is clearly based on the values and viewpoints expressed throughout this book:

• The goal of making it possible for anyone, anywhere, at any time, at any age to engage in the learning process.
• The value to the learning process of active and collaborative learning.
• The ability of CMC systems to support the full range of human cognitive and social relationships.
• The belief that improvement of society is tied to a concept of lifelong learning.

9.1 Institutional Changes and Challenges

9.1.1 Kindergarten to Twelfth Grade
The past wisdom for the development of public schools was the larger the school, the better. In a place-dependent school, size of student population could support a wide range of specialized educational services in an efficient manner: special education, counseling services, tutoring services, a large variety of sports, multitrack educational programs, and so forth. Conditions are changing with a declining public school–aged population in many areas and reduced budgets for operating costs, yet the

demands on the education system are increasing. Teachers and administrators find themselves increasingly unable to help socialize and educate their students for life in the twenty-first century. Learning networks can form the basis for reformulating educational services and can assist in creating new options for education.

Among the earliest benefactors of learning networks will be public school teachers. The first and crucial step for the introduction of these networks is support for teachers. Networks provide mechanisms to help teachers cope with declining resources. The key to success will be the improved sense of professionalism and community for teachers who have had a shortage of resources to work with for so long. As the teachers develop their facility with learning network resources, they will quickly learn how to apply them as well for the benefit of their students.

Learning networks should be planned as a service to teachers as well as students. The ability to form peer groups of teachers in given subjects who can exchange the lore and wisdom they have acquired from dealing with the subject holds tremendous opportunity for improvement of the educational process. It also becomes efficient and economical to include experts from higher educational institutions as guides and facilitators for these networks. The delivery of training programs for public school educators via learning networks is a much more efficient and less costly process than current mechanisms, which involve travel and time away from work.

Policies, practices, and procedures must be established to encourage use. Teachers need to be provided with their own computer, especially for home use. Computer resources available in the public schools should be opened to students and teachers after school hours, with computers put in the public libraries for student and teacher use. There are many sensible and possible approaches to making both computer resources and learning networks more accessible. These networks require a new attitude among administrators and administrative bodies: the realization that learning is a twenty-four-hour activity, and students and teachers need that full-time access to the necessary resources.

New forms of learning involve new ways of teaching. What happens when teachers are working from home for a significant portion of the workweek? Administrators and their various accounting regulations will need to adjust to the electronic presence of the worker as in the past they have credited the physical presence. There are still laws on the books of some state and local governments in the United States, for example, that explicitly state a worker must be physically present at a work site.

Private schools and organizations as well can be anticipated to develop learning networks as enrichment options. Private educational institutions can reach anywhere in the world to bring in paying students and to provide top-flight expertise and educators. A proliferation of such offerings will likely emerge; however, only organizations that show results will gain a national or international reputation and clientele. One can even expect to see university professors showing up in some of these offerings to give the children a head start in academic training. Public school teachers may also assume extra teaching assignments on such networks. In addition, many capable educators who have moved to industry because of higher pay scales may find this an attractive second-job option. Added to this are women and men who do not want a full-time job outside the home while raising a family. A ready pool of capable educators can be tapped to support a rapid growth in learning networks for the K-to-12 range.

Networks become efficient if planned on a large scale, and the fragmentation of most school systems within the educational infrastructure in most countries makes this difficult. Many of the synergies possible within teacher communities can occur only when one is talking about thirty or more schools at the same level (elementary schools, junior high schools, or high schools). An adequate peer group size for teachers teaching in the same subject at the same educational level is twenty or more.

9.1.2 Colleges and Universities

The first and foremost impact of learning networks on institutions of higher education is that they will no longer be able to count on a geographical edge. With the growing cost of a college education, even among public institutions, students and parents are becoming far more concerned about the quality of education that they receive. With the continued increase in the percentage of the college-level population that is working or returning to school to train for a second career, there is considerably more discrimination by the student in choosing schools, programs, and instructors. Learning networks will enable students to select the best program for their needs, with considerable savings in transportation and living costs and increased convenience for access to courses and degree programs.

A student could live in New Jersey and take a degree program from a school in California, Japan, or France. Remote learning networks such as NTU (National Technological University) in the United States are demonstrating this phenomenon with graduate education in the technical fields using only video-delivered courses. The remote student in that program can get a master's degree in almost any engineering field and select courses from MIT, Cal Tech, and Dartmouth, among others. The introduction of learning networks will give a competitive edge to those institutions that adopt them.

Learning networks affect educators themselves. Besides basic teaching methods, new types of course offerings are possible. A learning network is a natural environment for team teaching. Multidisciplinary and interdisciplinary views of a subject area are facilitated in the learning network, in which various subject experts can serve as guest lecturers or form part of a teaching team. Different courses can be mixed together when they have overlapping subject areas. It is much easier to support special reading courses for particular students and special project courses. It is also very easy for the teacher to become a student and for faculty to take courses in areas they wish to explore. As well faculty can establish or become part of research communities that are not constrained to close geographical proximity. This latter area is one of the primary activities on higher education networks today. Linkages between educational institutions and both social and professional institutions will also become more fluid and commonplace.

From almost any perspective, the potential impacts of learning networks on institutions of higher education are tremendous. Their introduction has begun. The economic factors are in place to ensure that the driving force is in this direction.

9.1.3 International Training and Education

It is common for governments, organizations, and companies to bring expert trainers to developing countries as a mechanism for attempting to transfer knowledge—a very expensive and all too often ineffective form of educational delivery. The addition of learning networks to improve on-site training can expand student contact with the trainer, especially once the trainee returns to the field. It can also train the trainer, by providing better contact with the field and understanding the problems and conditions in which the trainees operate. Learning networks would represent a minor addition to the costs already present in such programs and would reduce or eliminate the rate of failure in these situations. These networks, once available, would serve as a conduit to a tremendous range of other training opportunities.

Learning networks could become a truly global, multilingual environment through the addition of translators. Discussions in two or more languages could be kept in two or more conferences. Human translators together with machine-translation systems have already proved viable in experiments in Japan. A few simple software tools added to a conference system could help translators to move material around and keep track of what had been translated. The idea of multilingual conferences applies to all forms of international educational activities. Participants do not have to be limited to trying to communicate in a foreign tongue, and linguistic barriers to networking should be reduced or removed as soon and as much as possible.

In many remote areas of the world it is often the recent medical student graduate, or the agriculture student graduate, or the young civil engineer who is sent to do a job. These individuals are very likely to encounter situations not covered by what they learned in the textbooks, and they often lack any sort of local peer support. A learning network would be a significant improvement on the operation in such situations.

Learning networks make possible the ability to place together enough learners who are geographically dispersed (e.g., even worldwide) to have the critical mass for justifying the support costs in supplying the network and an expert in their field. In addition to the aid the expert can supply, the network would allow for collaborative exchange of useful information about the experiences they are encountering.

Moreover, professionals can use learning networks to stay abreast of developments in the field and to gain access to peers and resources relevant to their work. Global learning networks composed of professionals from all parts of the world enrich the world's knowledge, enabling those in the Third World to access information, peers, and expertise and facilitating two-way flows of information and ideas, rather than the one-way flow in which a foreign expert brings or transfers knowledge.

9.1.4 Community Learning

Cable television introduced an array of channels carrying a variety of educational programs, including college courses, "fixit" shows, nature programs, and cooking lessons. Networked neighborhoods, linked by modems and telephone lines, offer an even wider range of publicly available educational and interactive opportunities. We expect that learning networks will support a wide range of seminars and conferences of interest to local community groups. These will no longer be the single meeting or the three-day retreat but an ongoing discussion on a particular topic of interest. Such topics may range from lake conservation practices for communities with lakes to improved elementary school math programs for communities showing poor student performance in math.

There are already special interest public bulletin boards and conferencing systems available devoted to such concerns as ecological activities or discussions of religious topics. A wide range of hobby groups and amateurs have established electronic newsletters or bulletin-board-like services. With fiber-optic possibilities of interactive multimedia there will likely be poetry reading and writing (electronic) circles, a variety of information services for farmers and doctors and businesspeople, and many other special interest groups that are educational in the broadest sense.

Such online learning networks will encompass a much wider range of students in terms of age, nationality, social class, physical challenges, and other characteristics of learners than is typical in traditional face-to-face modes such as adult continuing education programs. We are likely to see precocious preteenagers exchanging ideas with retired people the age of their great-grandparents and more direct interactions among people from very different cultural backgrounds. Such diverse learning communities will require skill and tact on the part of their facilitators.

Another area of network learning in a community context involves personal quality of life on the part of individuals and interest groups.

For example, those in the community who like to hike can now have an ongoing discussion of hiking and local hiking options as well as use the network to plan group hikes. Currently this can only be done on a regional basis by special organizations using a planning cycle that takes months. With learning networks it is possible for small local groups to learn more about their hobbies and local recreational activities as well as plan and execute events efficiently.

Whatever the specialized interest of a group, it is now possible for a meaningful critical mass of local people to maintain contact and engage in a mutual exchange of information that amounts to a sharing and learning process for everyone. The ability of electronic networks to allow small groups to form and become social groups on even the most selective and esoteric of topics makes possible a considerable improvement in the quality of life of the local community. We are very much a social species that learns by exchanging experiences of common interest to one another.

One of the long-term consequences anticipated will be a greater freedom of entry to educators. Who is an educator in a particular topic will be more determinable by performance rather than credentials. One can observe how good an educator is by being invited into one of his or her current virtual seminars and thereby determine if this person should be invited to conduct a seminar in the local community. Potentially this could create a much larger marketplace for learning services by individuals.

9.1.5   Corporate Training and Organizational Development

The 1970s and early 1980s saw a mushrooming of resources invested by major companies in their own corporate training programs. Many corporate educators spoke of their training programs as "our internal college." Recessionary forces have significantly reduced many such programs. A corporation that wants its training programs to survive needs to be prepared to prove their value in much more explicit ways than the indirect acceptance of the necessity of high school and college educational programs. It also has to be distinctive in what it offers and what it accomplishes relative to other educational opportunities.

The typical corporate program usually takes people away from their job for some period of time for training, after which there is rarely further contact with the instructor or with the educational program until the learner "needs" more. In a sense the corporate educational program is isolated from the students and what they are doing or attempting to do. In a larger sense the corporate training program itself is somewhat isolated from the rest of the organization and the mainstream of what is taking place. Learning networks bridge the gap between training and application and facilitate the integration between theory and practice, learning and work.

9.2 New Directions in Technology for Learning Networks

Technology can provide far greater enhancements to learning networks than is currently available to teachers and learners. Much is already demonstrable in the research and development environment, and it is only a matter of cost reduction and attention to careful planning, design, and implementation, that will eventually make these facilities generally available.

Consideration of new directions in technology for learning networks should begin with educational principles and needs. The model presented in this book introduces a shift toward new models of interaction between teachers and learners and new forms of scholarly communication. This model emphasizes active and interactive learning, research, and problem solving. And many technological innovations being studied and developed promise to offer significant and profound changes in this direction. Although many of these changes are revolutionary in their implications, they are solidly rooted in traditional and powerful principles of scholarship: (distributed) learning communities and multiple cross-references. Today these principles are being articulated in new and compelling ways through the development of global networks and hypermedia. It is the technology that is revolutionary: as Lemke (1993) notes, these "principles have been the foundation of scholarship in our culture and many others almost forever."

In this section we consider possible futures for educational practice and scholarship that may be enhanced by or emerge from new technological developments.

9.2.1 Interface Integration

An integrated interface would provide a comprehensive communication capability on a computer; it would provide the methods and metaphor to enable humans to communicate with one another as individuals and as groups as well as providing communications with any other computer resource.

Thus, an interface as a virtual and comprehensive front door to all educational resources, human and archival, should be a primary goal. The educational process ultimately dictates the integration of all computer resources into the communications environment. If some particular material in a database is of interest to a class, the student or teacher should be able to bring it from the database into the conferencing system. This is currently a complex process. There is no ultimate technical bottleneck to integrating all computer resources into a CMC system, so that a user could access any special software as part of the overall communication process. It would also mean ease of transferring material between the communication process and other resources, such as databases, analysis packages, design tools, programming languages, and word processors. The development of integrated interfaces to the complete collection of tools needed by the instructor and the students is the most significant technological goal for the success of learning networks. Achieving this objective will require constant pressure on the technologists by learners and educators.

9.2.2 Multimedia, Graphics, and Animation

The learning networks discussed throughout this book have been generally characterized as text based because the majority of network systems are still text based. However, there is clearly a need for communication involving graphics material as well. Educational communication and research have historically involved multiple media: text, graphics, sound, and various forms of animation. The increasing availability of ISDN and high-bandwidth networks, as well as compression technologies that send video over the Internet, opens important new options for educators, researchers, and learners.

The first level of need in many subject areas is the use of special symbols that occur in just about every technical field. Math, engineering, and scientific symbols are part of the text of those disciplines. This can be handled now as extended icon symbol sets in some editors; however, everyone in a course must be provided the same personal workstation or personal computer editor. At some point, the process of standards setting in the industry will catch up with the needs of the user community. Until that time, the institutions providing the learning network have to do what they can to make sure that every student and instructor has access to a compatible set of software tools for handling symbols in the different learning fields.

Full graphics, the next desirable requirement, necessitates somewhat more powerful software packages. It may also require that everyone involved with a specific learning network have adequate hardware to support the graphics requirements of the fields involved. The current ability in many networks to transmit binary files is not a solution to the communications problem of graphics. Transmitting graphics over long distances on communications networks that charge by the volume of data transmitted is far too expensive. This approach may be acceptable in local area network systems that have no volume charges but not over the long-distance networks operated by communications providers. The need, once again, is for standards to catch up with requirements and to ensure that standards code graphic diagrams at levels higher than binary representations. This lack is more a societal or institutional problem than a technological one.

The area with the most significant potential for learning improvement is animation. Animation is a relatively new area, and good animation systems are still in the R&D stage or are quite expensive. Nonetheless, the implications for education are important and exciting. One type of knowledge that is important to convey but difficult to do outside the face-to-face lecture is the demonstration of thinking processes. When a mathematics professor presents the steps of a proof, he or she is illustrating to the student how to carry out a complex reasoning or problem-solving approach. The same can be said of a literature professor's presenting a complex literary analysis. The learning of the thinking process is aided by the way in which the steps involved are presented and explained. This dynamic timing and sequencing is almost impossible to explain in a comprehensible manner by using plain linear text. However, it would be possible to convey this process if the instructor could add animation to the use of text and symbols, as well as graphics and hypertext.

One can easily imagine parts of an equation moving around the screen to form new relationships each time the student asks to advance the sequence in a derivation being reviewed. There are some poets who have evolved poetry for the computer that involves the dynamic movement of words and phrases as part of the poetic process. The need is to provide systems that will allow instructors to capture the dynamics of the problem-solving processes they wish to get across to students and to allow the students to replay these reasoning processes in an incremental manner. The student could then take as long or short a time to examine and learn these processes as necessary, as well as replay them as often as desired.

Animation provides for the possibility of new art forms. Do the words of a poem have to be motionless? Does an artist's picture have to be static? Does a mystery novel have to be text only? What about collaborative art forms? No one can completely anticipate what types of new art forms might in fact evolve within the networks of the future.

We are not talking about the classic philosophy of CAI approaches. These are not systems intended for a limited set of experts to provide training material for a greater mass of anonymous students. We are talking about the need for systems that allow individual instructors to tailor lectures and learning material to a particular course designed for a particular set and type of student. We are also concerned with the ability of the student to take on the role of instructor for enrichment of the basic course. As a result, the perfection of the interface and the resulting ease of use of these tools are principal concerns.

9.2.3   Hypermedia, Hypertext, and Group Memories

The terms *hypertext* and *hypermedia* refer to the use of the computer to organize, in a nonlinear way, text and other media as bits of information. Although these terms are recent, the concept of cross-referencing among diverse resources is a basic principle and characteristic of scholarly activity. Just as textbooks are typically multimedia—containing words, pictures, graphics, tables, and illustrations—so too do they offer rudimentary tools for cross-referencing: the contents, the index, and the list of figures and illustrations. The student uses these tools to seek the special information required, sometimes in addition to or instead of reading the entire text in a linear fashion from beginning to end. Even when a text is read in a linear fashion, the student may stop to look up a word in a dictionary or seek another resource (atlas, encyclopedia, etc.) for further information.

Casual observance of students in libraries (quickly reading books for their courses) suggests that a student engaged in learning does not read linearly but often flips to other parts of the book or other books to aid in understanding. Students photocopy the material that is particularly important. If they own the material, they make marks with highlighters, adding footnotes or transcribing notes to sheets of paper. These tools for reorganizing the material are also a significant part of any good hypertext facility.

Most users who have experienced only the first generation of commercial hypertext utilization think that hypertext is some sort of mechanism whereby one may choose a highlighted word or other object to jump to more information about the original word or object. This was not the original concept that either Bush (1945) or Nelson (1965) had in mind when they first discussed the concept. Both were emphasizing the process of creating thoughts in language (text or graphics) and the ability to form nonlinear linkages of ideas and concepts. The crux of their insight was that the way we think about things is highly nonlinear and that having to linearize our thinking in order to convey it to others limits our creative function. It also is a fundamental limitation on the ability of groups to function as teams exhibiting "collective intelligence." This is the process whereby the result of a group effort is better than any individual in the group could have produced working alone (Hiltz and Turoff 1978).

In the future, we believe, networks will not be about reading a document but about exploring the thought process or model of a given individual or group. By studying and exploring the hypertext web created by individuals, we will understand the content of the subject and the thought processes that took place on an individual or collective basis to arrive at cognitive relationships expressing the examination of a complex problem. A learner will be able to perceive how the experts in the subject who prepared the material think about and organize the material. A recent study indicates strongly that the degree of structure one imposes on a complex problem is directly correlated with the individual's knowledge of the field (Hopkins, Campbell, and Peterson, 1987). The corollary is that an educator can use the underlying hypertext structure an individual learner or a group of learners create about a topic to measure how much they have learned. This may be a far more holistic approach to measuring knowledge than the reductionist approach of exams made up of a large number of little pieces of the subject. Once we capture the thoughts of learners in electronic form, the ways that we can analyze and gain insights into the learning process are far more open-ended and probably far more informative than current measuring practices.

High-density, rewriteable, and portable optical storage media will one day be commonplace. This will make each instructor capable of publishing her or his own extensive background and lecture-type material for a course. Programs of study that have extensive visual-material libraries (art, architecture, etc.) will be able to publish this library on an inexpensive set of optical disks so that each student will have one. The library can now be brought to the students' homes. The bottleneck here is not technology but institutional practices for copyright and compensation and the cooperation of the publishing industry. These difficulties will impede but not prevent the change that has to come because of the inherent economic and resource efficiencies involved.

Perhaps even more significant than the ability to handle the fixed materials is the ability to begin to accumulate and disseminate the growing body of knowledge that an instructor will collect as a result of working with the same subject matter and numerous sections of a course over time. For example, in a course in which students regularly review professional articles for the benefit of the class as a whole, the article reviews can be incorporated into a growing database that is available to future classes, so that new reviews do not duplicate old ones. In addition to serving the review assignment, they can be a resource for various collaborative projects conducted in the course. The instructor may eliminate poor reviews, and within a few years many hundreds of articles could be present in such a database. An instructor could decide to save outstanding project papers to use with future classes as well.

A useful type of learning assignment is to ask students to develop lesson and practice material and exam questions for other students as a way of learning the material. These could also be accumulated by the instructor. The technology makes it possible for instructors to construct a collaborative memory of course materials derived from their own efforts and the work of the better students. For the university professor, the benefit of being able to stay on top of a large and growing body of literature is a high payoff that cannot be discounted.

One of the most significant enhancements to the learning process would be collaborative knowledge-building structures incorporating hypertext for direct utilization within the class discussion. This means that a person reading a "node" of text can branch off to many different alternative nodes of text. One reader might wish more detail on a sub-topic, while another prefers a more global or summarized explanation. A single node of text can have many different types of linkages to different aspects of the subject. Hypertext is extremely easy to use and allows learners to follow their own interests and concerns while navigating through a large collection of knowledge broken into small-page or screen-size nodes, with numerous linkages among them. A typical hypertext set of choices available for branching off while reading materials might be:

- Provide more detail.
- Explain related global concepts.
- Define terms.
- Present alternative viewpoints.
- Provide references.

There are two key problems associated with hypertext. The first is the ease with which the reader can get lost in a spiderlike network of relationships. There is a trade-off: the microlevel choice flexibility can largely destroy any ability to have a global grasp of where someone is in the knowledge base. This problem is often referred to as getting lost in the spider web of knowledge that characterizes the internal structure. A second and somewhat related problem is that none of us has been taught how to write material for a hypertext document. All our training is in how to write linear documents. We spend a great deal of educational effort forcing students to learn to express thoughts in a linear manner.

One potential approach to the solution of these problems is the development of knowledge structures appropriate to the type of subject matter. One could be given a set of alternatives for the types of content that nodes can have and the types of relationships that can exist between nodes, that is, fitted to the nature of the subject matter. Then the process of knowledge building by a group of people can become one of collaboration to fit together a complex jigsaw puzzle, with the instructor taking on the role of referee or critic with respect to the resulting composition. The instructor can also develop and define templates or patterns of information for which the students have to develop the content collaboratively. There are a host of possible approaches for using a versatile hypertext system for knowledge building. For learning purposes, the most effective use is the process of learners' formulating the knowledge they are acquiring into a coherent whole rather than as a way of presenting knowledge gathered by experts for dissemination to nonexperts. Hypertext computer conferences are being developed.

Most hypertext systems emphasize the presentation of material and devote too little consideration to the ease of structuring and acquiring material. Hypertext systems do not in themselves overcome the basic information retrieval problem. There is still a need for adequate methods of indexing material. Hypertext satisfies a different need from both the top-down organization of material (the outline) and the totally lateral organization (the index). Both of these are necessary adjuncts of the use of hypertext. This is especially true if the instructor views knowledge acquisition as a process that is cumulative over time, involving the integration of the efforts of many different offerings of the same or related courses.

The evolution of standards for multimedia and hypertext will play an important role in creating an atmosphere in which educational institutions and individual learners and educators can share large bodies of knowledge. The recent emergence of the World Wide Web via the General Markup Language approach is an example of how universal this can become. A great many universities on Internet are now making general hypertext databases available throughout the network using this software implementation of a hypertext capability.

9.2.4   Class Management Tools

A course of twenty students can be taught using a simple bulletin board or a simple conferencing system; managing more than a hundred students in four or more different courses is a very different challenge—and the typical course load in many public school systems, junior colleges, and even some universities. It is even more complicated to manage a complete learning network made up of hundreds of instructors, tens of thousands of students, and hundreds of courses. As the population of students and instructors goes up, everyone can quickly become a victim of information overload (Hiltz and Turoff 1986).

We begin first with the individual class. A host of tools for instructors and students aid in reducing the amount of communications traffic that is not a productive part of the learning process. One is the electronic gradebook, which reduces the amount of communication the instructor must manually generate to keep students informed about their performance. An extension to that concept is an analysis package, which provides the instructor with a summary of the communications activity for each student. The package would provide information on the number of new discussion threads each student has started, how many replies or responses they have made to the contributions of other students, what specialized activities they have engaged in, and the frequency of their interaction and participation in the system. With large populations of students such analysis support could be critical to aiding the instructor in recognizing which students may be falling behind or having trouble in keeping up.

A more sophisticated approach might incorporate various forms of linguistic analysis, such as concordance analysis, to aid the instructor in determining the atmosphere in the class discussion and how well the students are beginning to adopt and use the terminology that characterizes the subject matter being taught. Such a system would give tremendous insight into how each child is developing a basic vocabulary capability. It would help to identify children who need special help much more quickly and more accurately than an instructor could by merely reviewing the total flow of communications. Such analysis routines could allow teachers to direct students to special computer-assisted instructional

(CAI) packages to augment their learning activities. The state of the art of grammar checkers is such that these can be incorporated readily into analysis routines to evaluate grammar knowledge as well as vocabulary. Students would use grammar checkers to analyze and improve their own writing projects.

Many current CAI packages track student performance with respect to preset question-and-answer-type dialogue, so the knowledge exists to develop content analysis tools that will be able to gauge the progress of students in terms of their decision making, creative processes, and mastery of concepts and language. A host of artificial intelligence and expert system techniques under development today may be adopted and adapted to educational activities.

These potential developments in assessment systems imply certain difficulties and even dangers. In a networking world, it is quite clear that there will be packages developed for people engaged in negotiation of deals to aid them in analyzing the psychology and positions of other parties. There will probably also be packages for aiding in formulating the content of one's communications to convey "the right" impressions. Even today's generation of grammar checkers has the ability to differentiate between many different styles of writing (e.g., formal or informal). We do not yet have the norms, policies, regulations, or laws to cope with the possible privacy issues that can arise in the teacher-student relationship. Regulations that govern psychological testing and the privacy of the data do not by definition have any applicability to what can be done with psycholinguistic and psychological scaling techniques in a network environment.

Clearly there is also a need to train and upgrade the ability of teachers to understand and use tools of this type. This ultimately implies a world in which the teacher is a very highly skilled professional in the techniques of facilitating the learning process. This will not happen overnight and will be a gradual transition. Initially there will probably be special professionals who are concerned with conducting sophisticated student evaluations for feedback to teachers and also for brokering information through the networks (similar to a reference librarian in concept). However, one day we can expect the status of public school educators to equal that of college educators over the long term. Education at any level will be viewed more as a sophisticated craft on the part of the practitioner as opposed to a person delivering programs and curricula developed by others as merely a mechanic of the delivery process. We have gone through many generations of a trend that has reduced the status of educators at the lower levels because of the approaches of the delivery of canned educational processes; networking gives the opportunity for a completely different direction for the members of this profession.

9.2.5   Discussion Management

Managing and facilitating the class discussion is a prime responsibility of the instructor. An open-ended set of tools should be available to the instructor to support the guidance of the discussion. Many of these tools may reflect techniques used in face-to-face classes, but they may perform differently, and in some cases better, in a computer context. For example, the process of asking a discussion question can be set up on the computer so that students cannot see others' responses until they have made their own answer. Each student thus has to think through an answer and avoid being swayed by the thoughts of other students. It is also possible to set this up in levels, so that after viewing the initial responses of other students, they then are asked to comment and reflect on whether those have caused any changes in their own viewpoint. These secondary responses could also be hidden from the students until they have made their secondary response. At some level, the process can be opened for general discussion.

The ability to control the phasing of the discussion in a computer conference has certain characteristics of the techniques used in the Delphi process (Linstone and Turoff 1975). Delphi is the design of paper-and-pencil-based communication processes for allowing groups to explore complex issues through a structured communication format. Many of the methods designed for improving communications among experts are also applicable to aiding a group in learning about a complex topic. Another area that has also developed a large number of face-to-face discussion aids is the design of nominal group techniques (Delbec, Vande Ven, and Gutafson 1975). A number of special versions of these techniques have been popularized (e.g., brainstorming, synergistics,

T-groups) and sold as special problem-solving methods to organizations. Many are quite easy to learn and straightforward enough for an instructor to incorporate as tools to aid collaborative learning activities.

To facilitate a case study discussion of possible decision options in a management course, students might be confined to following a Policy Delphi structure. Each entry in the discussion is designated a potential resolution, a con argument, or a pro argument. The incorporation of an argument must be given a link to the resolution it addresses. The computer automatically attaches voting scales to each item; resolutions are voted on by scales of desirability and feasibility, and the arguments are voted on by scales of importance and validity. The computer conference version of a Policy Delphi tool for resolving an issue thus restricts the types of entries that can be made, reorganizes them so that arguments are linked to the resolutions they are addressing and the counterarguments, collects and tabulates the votes, and announces when votes are available for viewing.

A simpler example for elementary school students might be a structure to facilitate the writing of a collaborative story by the class as a whole. The teacher could supply an outline that represents a sequence for the plot of the story; this might have resulted from general discussion with the class on the nature of the plot. Then any child can contribute a piece for some part of the story by linking that text to the appropriate place in the plot. If two children enter conflicting pieces of the story, there could be a simple voting procedure to allow the class to decide which version to retain. This type of collaborative story for the class as a whole is difficult to manage in a face-to-face environment. It is simple and straightforward in the computer conferencing environment with just a few simple tools such as the preset outline to fill in and a voting process. Students could even make initial entries on an anonymous basis and have the computer announce the author only when a contribution is accepted, a method that encourages students to make contributions.

Besides concentrating the efforts of the students and regulating the flow of communications, such Delphi or polling structures have the merit of eliminating unnecessary effort. The ability to vote means that there is no need for separate comments from each student merely to express how much they agree or disagree. Think of the number of independent comments that would be necessary for a class of thirty students to collect the same profile of classwide opinion.

Most of the current research in group support systems is associated with how to design tailored and specialized communication structures for large groups of people to deal with a complex problem more effectively than they could ever do in a face-to-face meeting. These designs borrow heavily from earlier work in the Delphi area. When we restrict education to single learners, we are excluding the real-world types of complexity that reflect how people deal with problems in organizations. Clearly there is much in the literature about how we are not teaching students, even at the university levels, to work in teams. However, this is a limited view of the problem. There is also the key issue of how a particular type of complex problem is best decomposed and structured to be worked on by a group. These techniques go far beyond the forms of problem solving we now teach students.

Given the effort to develop and capture these techniques in software, we can project that eventually there will be many of these group problem-solving approaches available to educators to incorporate into their set of learning tools. These communication structures will be merged with current and future simulation packages so that educators can conduct complete mock-ups of real-world situations. For example, the typical business computer game might be extended to have a gaming-communications overlay, so that the students use the communication structures that exist in a typical business and between businesses in carrying out the simulation of the company. Educators could set up realistic simulations of the political and economic structures of their local community as a part of teaching students how the local political process works. Such local simulations might involve family members and local community leadership. Another type of simulation would be the ability to represent the political and social structure of a foreign country or a particular ethnic community or go back in time to relive an ancient civilization. Learners will be able to participate in gaming situations that mimic principles and concepts not only from business but from civics, history, sociology, anthropology, political science, and psychology as well as from the pure and applied sciences.

9.2.6 Network Approaches to Class Assignments

Learning networks will give rise to new approaches to the organization of assignments given to students. For example, it is possible to give unique assignments to each member of the class. A simple software tool that allows the instructor to list assignment alternatives and allows students in a course to choose one of the alternatives is a valuable feature. Each student can view the list at any time to see what has been taken or what is available for choice.

Certain types of assignments might not be entered into the conference for the class as whole but would go to the instructor to review and grade separately. A well-designed learning network could allow a student to trigger an Assignment function whereby he or she is asked to indicate which assignment is being handed in. The instructor would have pre-programmed the system to file the different types of assignments from a course in specific places. The same software would track who has or has not completed an assignment and could be used to generate automatic notifications to those who have not yet completed the assignment.

It is possible to give quizzes online. In one implementation of such a facility, once the student starts the quiz, it is timed and he or she cannot shut it off and start again. We do not yet know all of the specialized communication structures that might evolve as desirable for learning networks. At this time, we have been extrapolating from our prior experiences with the face-to-face environment. However, even some of those extrapolations, such as the Assignment function, behave entirely differently in the computer environment. The process of learning is a unique application of CMC that will evolve a host of new communications structures appropriate for learning networks. They will have embedded in them all the other capabilities we have discussed, such as hypertext.

Integration with other computer tools can be extremely important in some courses. In a programming course in which the students are required to work collaboratively on a large programming assignment, they must be able to exchange code and documentation in their own private conference. They should also be able to move the code to be compiled, interpreted, and/or run on the programming language system they are used to. The results must be easy to move back into the conference for the benefit of all. In some cases special-purpose program-language-oriented editors and precompilers must be integrated as well to make collaborative approaches to education a reality. As students begin to work collaboratively on large-scale programming problems, they will need specialized data structures and communications structures to aid them in managing the team effort and keeping the overall specifications and requirements organized.

For business students, the same may be said of spreadsheets, business graphics, business models, and games. For various courses, the need to share results of data searches and data analysis from statistical packages is also crucial. While it is true that a great deal of this can be accomplished by having the student master various uploading and downloading procedures, it can get to be quite a problem for the instructor if the students are not already computer sophisticated and are not using the same communications package.

The control of processes and assignments is just as important for the collaborative work groups made up of the students as it is for the instructor. For the job of composing a jointly authored report, group members have to be provided with a tracking mechanism that allows them to coordinate their changes to a document and agree on what revisions are final. Merely taking a report and dividing it up among the collaborators does not foster true collaboration. A well-designed system should enable an individual to suggest rewordings or changes that are linked to the place in the text where they would go. The group would then be able to compare the current version and proposed change and discuss it. Also, any member of the group should be notified whenever changes have been made to a portion of the document that has been seen or reviewed.

There is an open-ended set of convenient tracking facilities possible for any type of collaborative group effort. If a course requires a significant amount of a certain activity by groups (e.g., composition, programming, budget estimation, data analysis), then tools to minimize the effort needed and time wasted in the coordination process should be developed and utilized. The coordination effort could be more usefully employed in the learning process. Certainly for the instructor, every minute spent on doing the routine work of tracking detracts from the effort that can be devoted to the substance of what the students are doing.

9.2.7   Voting Methods

Voting methods are numerous and lead to a large number of candidates for incorporation in the tool box to support learning-oriented conferences. For example, when the students in a senior or graduate class are asked to review different professional articles, the teacher might allow the class as a whole to rank-order the article reviews for significance. Peer ratings might motivate the students more than the instructor grading, and they provide the instructor with significant insight into how the students are viewing the issues and concepts in the field. It can also lead to some insightful comments on the part of the instructor to aid the students in their views of the field.

In a simple conference system, each student could send a message with rankings to the instructor, who would then compile the results. But this places an unnecessary communications load on the instructor, who must compile and analyze rank orders (or any other voting process). Instead, the computer can do it.

This area can become much more sophisticated with the incorporation of powerful scaling and social choice methods for the analysis of voting patterns. The use of factor analysis and multidimensional scaling would allow instructors to identify social and value biases. The ultimate example here is the ability to teach a class in survey design, with the students able to design and experiment on one another with surveys designed within the learning network and integrated with the conferencing capability.

Given the right software support, it becomes possible to introduce the ideas and capabilities of techniques such as survey design into the high school curriculum. The tools this provides can be used to augment courses in history, civics, and the environment.

Voting is a significant way of reducing information overload; it provides a compact summary of what a large group of people think about a particular topic or issue. Its first benefit is identifying where there is agreement and disagreement, so that the group can determine where further investigation and discussion are warranted. This is often forgotten in the news media emphasis on polling. It is not a desirable outcome for people to feel that a single round of voting should resolve their uncertainties about an issue. It is desirable for voting to influence people and communities of people in deciding where they need to explore an issue and what they need to discuss to feel confident about the resolution.

Different voting processes can produce different outcomes and can aid in highlighting what needs to be explored. In particular, when voting processes are coupled with forms of statistical correlation analysis among related issues and the backgrounds of voters, one can gain tremendous insight into what is happening and why. The only reason this is not taught at earlier grade levels is that it requires a high degree of computer support and computer resources for the analysis process. These tools become extremely easy to integrate into a computer-based learning network. Given the tools, preliminary understanding of such empirically based assessments can be taught at junior high levels in the educational process as regular parts of social studies courses.

While the combination of voting techniques and empirical analysis sounds like a rather specific area, their introduction at lower educational levels will profoundly influence the ability of the average citizen to be a fully aware and active member of a democratic political system. If our aspirations are to produce citizens who can readily deal with the complex issues facing society, this area becomes a necessity for the future of our educational systems.

9.2.8   Anonymity and Pen Names

The ability to enter anonymous comments or to use consistent pen names allows students to make comments from which they might otherwise shy away. In situations dealing with psychological and sociological reactions, students may prefer anonymity to speak about experiences they have encountered. For certain assignments, the ability to use anonymity might be under the control of the instructor. There are instances when the instructor as well can benefit from anonymity.

In management courses, students working for a specific company might be reluctant to relate case histories of bad decisions they have seen in their company, unless they can protect their identity and that of their companies. In other instances, it is sometimes useful to bring managers or professionals into the course under pen names so they can relate disaster tales. In courses dealing with pragmatic instances of why bad decisions and bad situations occur, it is difficult to find such material in the literature. One of the real potentials for learning networks is the ability to fertilize course conferences with the experiences of relevant nonstudents.

Pen names allow a person to develop an alternative identity. Many forms of educational exercises are based on role playing in which students are asked to answer or discuss a given issue as if they were someone else. How would this philosopher or that world leader have reacted to a certain situation? For example, each member of the class might assume the role of a different former prime minister of Britain and explain what they would do and how they would react to some current world situation.

A final point is the potential for anonymity and pen names in learning networks at the K-to-12 level to facilitate the handling of areas such as child abuse, drug addiction, and associated problems that the school systems have some responsibility for dealing with. The concept of a crisis hot line may also be incorporated into these systems. Young children might be willing to bring up problems and discuss them in special-purpose conferences that are monitored and facilitated by people with the proper training than they would be to approach adult authority figures in person.

Clearly, abuse of anonymity is possible. However, there are ways to deal with this situation, and the potential for abuse is not sufficient reason to forgo the potential benefits. In many conference systems, the actual author of an anonymous message or pen name is in fact stored, and there may be conditions under which the computer systems people will be asked to violate anonymity or pen name protection and disclose to the administration the real author—for example, if laws are violated. This includes sending sexually harassing communications or making threats against others. With a clear, open and publicly stated policy, forbidden types of communication occur infrequently. The policies governing the privacy, security, and ownership of communications in a learning network need to be clearly spelled out. Where there is some legal confusion with respect to such issues as ownership of electronic messages, there is nothing preventing the organization running the facility from setting the policy it wishes.

The following policies, we suggest, are desirable, simple, and straightforward:

• Any technical person having the ability to violate the privacy and security of communications and who does so without a written directive from the responsible administrator will be fired, with a description of the violation placed on that person's record.

• If a valid complaint is made by a recipient of an anonymous or pen name communication and the communication item is not a clearly illegal item (e.g., only insulting), a warning will be sent the first time to the author. For a second offense, the person loses their network ID. If the act is clearly illegal, such as a threat, the receiver will be informed of who has sent it and will be free to file a complaint with the appropriate authorities.

• The author of a communication item is the owner of the item. However, in a conference, the owner of a private conference has the right to establish a different policy, provided it is announced to the membership. In general, educators reserve the right to reuse material that students supply to a class discussion to enrich later versions of the course.

The anonymity of pen names offers opportunities for learners to expose situations they would not otherwise. It also opens the ability to bring into a course people from outside who could not relate certain things unless they had this protection. These facilities open the real world to incorporation in the classroom. The more a subject has pragmatic content, the more desirable this is for providing a fundamental improvement to the learning process. When managers can talk about mistakes a company has made, when people who have had psychologically difficult experiences can present them, when people can relate unpleasant or embarrassing legal, political, or discriminatory experiences, then we have the atmosphere of learners' being able to prepare to deal with their own futures in a far more secure manner.

9.2.9   Gaming and Role Playing

While it has been demonstrated that role plays and simulation games are powerful learning techniques that can be readily used in the CMC environment, there are no general support tools as yet available for gaming on these systems. There could be a conference with a structure specifically designed to conduct games. It would allow the instructor to establish a set of roles to be assigned to individual students and restrict them to contributing only in those roles. It would also allow the instructor to designate the parameters for what each role may and may not do. The same structure would allow the instructor to set up lists of potential events that can occur in the game and to set the conditions (e.g., probabilistic, deterministic, etc.) that determine how and when these events can occur. In other words, support for gaming would provide tailored communication structures that allow any instructor to create a role-and-event-oriented game.

When games and role playing have been used successfully in the CMC environment, instructors have largely been forced to exercise control manually over the flow of the game. This involves a sizable amount of process tracking and creation of material on a dynamic basis, which could instead be managed by a computer program—to reduce the workload of the online teacher.

There are two startling characteristics of gaming in the CMC environment: It is possible to enforce realistic communication channel limitations, and games can be conducted in real time or prolonged over very long periods. In face-to-face games it is difficult to impose communication restrictions on individual group members. In fact, one usually designs the face-to-face games largely to ignore this real-world complication. Also, in the face-to-face environment, having a class engage in a three-hour game either greatly compresses the time scale of the real-world situation or inhibits the amount of realism that can be incorporated into the game. Real management, psychological, social, or political situations can be drawn out over more realistic time scales of a week to a semester in the CMC environment.

The success of management games in the CMC environment (Hsu 1992) has led to the hypothesis that one could have a set of companies that went on year after year. Students in a beginning course in management would qualify for lower-level positions; as they advanced in the educational program, they could take on higher and higher positions.

Accomplishing this through a computer system requires that tracking and maintaining the corporate identity and state between course offerings can easily be handled by the computer. Political science and public administration courses could function with mock governments instead of mock companies.

The spread of games over time, the ability of people to work on their roles in a more realistic asynchronous manner, the communications control offered by the CMC approach, and the accounting ability offered by the computer and its memory indicate that there is an opportunity to open up a new world of gaming as an educational tool.

9.2.10   Televirtual Learning Networks

Three-dimensional virtual reality has fired the imagination of many in terms of the possibility of participation in three-dimensional simulated environments. The prospect of televirtual systems, or networked virtual reality, is a promise of the not-too-distance future. The example of the plans in New Zealand for televirtual seminars in the year 2000 illustrates the adoption of virtual reality by education.

Experience with text-based virtual reality has already reached classrooms around the world. MUSEs and MUDs on the Internet, such as those of the MIT Media Lab, bring virtual laboratories into K-to-12 classrooms and offer educational role plays and simulations available to all Internet users. These constructed worlds take gaming and role playing to a more sophisticated level. The implications for educational virtual reality and televirtual learning networks are only beginning to be explored, and with research and evaluation, their merit and role will be better understood.

9.3   Global Learning Networks

In most commercial organizations that have gone heavily into networking, fundamental changes are taking place in the organizational structure. Education around the world is becoming strongly networked, and we are beginning to see fundamental changes taking place in the organization of education too. A large number of regional and national organizations have emerged that represent an almost reluctant pooling of talent and resources of individual college and university environments. In the United States this has been driven in part by declining enrollments from the high school graduate population and the need to service an older population of working and adult learners. Today, working students can get a master's degree in all the classical engineering fields by taking a variety of remote courses from dozens of different universities through the National Technological University program.

We no longer have geographical isolation or geographical monopolies at the college and university level. As this book is being written, the Internet is expanding to provide the ability for member institutions throughout the world to share information. Network-accessible databases are being made available without prior approval of accounts from local institutional suppliers. The recent changes in Eastern Europe are opening those countries to the same network access. It may not be obvious yet, but the long-term implications are a worldwide network and a real marketplace for university and college level education. This will expand naturally into vocational and adult training as well. Education will become a major export factor between countries.

Today the messaging between an elementary school class in Canada and one in Russia is still an item worthy of note in the local newspaper. In five years this will be so commonplace that no one will consider it newsworthy. The time scale may be longer, but networking among public schools will be common on a worldwide basis. Areas of the world that cannot afford to import a native English-speaking instructor physically will be able to import one electronically at far less cost. A teacher in physics at a local high school will no longer feel isolated from other physics teachers and will have an electronic community of peers for exchanging information and ideas about teaching physics. The parent who feels that the local math teacher is not doing a good job for a high- or low-IQ student will be able to enroll the child in a private school offering of an appropriate math course. That private school might be ten thousand miles distant.

Networking ultimately will change the character of education at all levels. Economically it will counteract monopolies and facilitate people accessing the educational services that best suit their needs. Local townships that cannot afford to put in place special educational programs for certain classes of learners could find it very economical to buy such services electronically. No one knows what might be the final infrastructure for education twenty or thirty years from now, but whatever results, it is likely to be much more effective and stimulating for the learner and provide enormous variety of choice.

10

Network Learning: A Paradigm for the Twenty-first Century

Learning networks are transforming teaching and learning relationships, opportunities, and outcomes. Traditional educational structures are being dramatically altered by new communication and information technologies. As Brand (1987) has noted "Communications media are so fundamental to a society that when their structure changes, everything is affected" (xiii). Networking, the convergence and maturation of computing and telecommunications, has become a force for a new form of education, creating a paradigm shift: a change to a new model and set of expectations and rules for how to function successfully within a new learning environment.

10.1 Network Learning: Toward A New Educational Paradigm

Computer networks both require and enable new forms of teaching and learning, and this creates the basis for changes in how education will be conceptualized and practiced. One of the basic requirements for education in the twenty-first century will be to prepare students for participation in a knowledge-based economy in which knowledge will be the most critical resource for social and economic development. Curricular content and approaches to twenty-first-century society are being forged through discussion and debate in the public, business, and academic sector. What is increasingly clear is that current educational models, structures, and approaches are inadequate. Students need new and different information resources, skills, roles, and relationships. The traditional educational model, based primarily on the concept of the school and the teacher/classroom as islands, standing alone and not interconnected with society or other educational institutions, will not generate competence in a knowledge society. School librarians find they cannot provide the wide-ranging and changing resources that students need for participation in a global learning environment. Libraries cannot respond to the need for up-to-date information. Schools are limited in their ability to provide the range of expertise that students need. The concept of education as internal to the school, moreover, is outdated, inappropriate, and incorrect. This shift extends as well to the model of the learner. The concept of education is changing from one based on individualism and competition (with collaboration and exchange among students viewed as disruptive or cheating), to one in which teamwork and networking are valued, mirroring changes in society and the work force.

Network technologies provide the means whereby learners can interact with peers, resources, and experts to build knowledge and develop skills. Networks enable the teacher to become a facilitator, providing educational structures, and guiding the learner in accessing the data and organizing the information into knowledge. Teachers need no longer serve as the font of information and knowledge. While recognizing the role of authoritative information and teacher guidance, many new networked learning systems aim to give learners increased control and agency in the knowledge-building process (Scardamalia and Bereiter 1991). Networks also enable education to become interinstitutional, tremendously extending the access of the student and the teacher to information resources and expertise around the world, at the best facilities available.

The attributes of networking thus enhance the opportunities and resources available to learners and teachers. Users are not geographically limited. Outside experts (poets, scientists, social groups, or professors) can be easily accessed, regardless of where they are geographically located. Students can tap into the best libraries and databases in the world electronically; peers and learning resources may be located tens or thousands of miles apart. Today's learners and teachers can form linkages with counterparts in other parts of the world with relative ease. And they are doing so. The asynchronous nature of networking further expands access; not only are international interactions facilitated, but teachers and learners have control over the time and pace of their participation. The quality of the exchange is enhanced through increased opportunities to reflect on the message received or being composed.

Many aspects of network learning are new and have not been available in the traditional classroom. The opportunity for each member of a group to participate actively and frequently is not possible in the time-dependent, face-to-face classroom, nor is it always possible to reflect and compose a response to a discussion or for students to work at their best learning readiness times. These new opportunities that characterize network learning promise improvements in cognition and social interaction. Moreover, as the technologies that support network learning improve, the opportunities to augment educational collaboration will increase. The nature of network learning is still being shaped; nonetheless, the outlines of a new way of teaching and learning are already visible.

10.2 Characteristics of Network Learning

The use of networking technologies alters the relationship of the learner and the teacher to educational resources and processes. The learner has more options and more control over the nature of interaction. Access is expanded across time, place, and subject. Network learners of the future will have access to formal and informal education of their choice, wherever they are located, whenever they are able to participate—early morning, during the day, or late at night. The network learner will be an active participant in the learning process rather than a passive recipient, learning with and from experts and peers wherever they are located. The curriculum will be more interdisciplinary and integrated, with links between theory and practice becoming common. Moreover, the concept of who is a teacher and who is a learner will become more fluid.

10.2.1 Expanded Educational Access
Network learning is education without borders. Students can link with other students or access experts, regardless of where they are located. Students in remote areas are no longer denied access to the kind of education that they want or need because of their location. Nor are people who are housebound (whether due to age, physical ability, or family

responsibilities) out of bounds for education. Network learning provides not only courses, credit, and curricula but the opportunity to engage with others, to share and build knowledge together. This is the essence of education.

Restrictions of time are dissolved by networks. The opportunity for asynchronous interaction facilitates communication across time zones and increases control by the user over the time and pace of participation. Network learning thus enables participants to engage at their best learning-readiness time and supports thoughtful consideration of the interaction, both messages received and sent.

Networks enable linkages of home and school and work. Experiments that gave public school students their own computers and modems for home use and involved teachers and parents have demonstrated network learning to be a tremendously powerful agent for enhancing educational effectiveness for all participants.

Linkages between school and work have proved valuable. Nontraditional students have been given access to learning opportunities. Adults with full-time jobs who have taken courses online report that network learning helps to dissolve the dichotomy between theory and practice, a disjuncture common to professional development courses and training programs. Networks help to make those connections, and learning becomes integrated into the rest of life.

Network learning is a framework for lifelong learning. There is a tremendous need for ongoing educational opportunities. Life in the twenty-first century promises to be increasingly demanding in terms of the pace of technological changes, with a need for relevant information and skills in group problem solving to deal with global and local economic, political, social, professional, and environmental problems. Network learning will facilitate access to the best resources as needed.

Finally, boundaries of school subject and discipline will be challenged by the demands of life in the next century. New interdisciplinary, problem-solving approaches to the curriculum will become common, and network learning will be both a catalyst and a response to that need.

10.2.2   Collaborative Learning and Group Work
The fundamental characteristic of network learning is the premise of collaborative approaches to learning. Networks are group communica-

tion environments that augment social connectivity. Network learning enables unprecedented forms of collaboration, based on shared interest rather than shared geography.

Learners work together to support one another in problem solving, information sharing, knowledge building, and social communication. Collaboration has both motivational and intellectual benefits. Peer learning is among the most effective approaches to cognitive and social learning that humans have developed. Writing skills are improved through writing to real audiences; mathematics learning is enhanced through group approaches; scientific collaboration reflects real-world practice. Working collaboratively introduces multiple perspectives on an issue or topic. And it can be more enjoyable than working alone.

Learning networks enable global collaborations. The opportunity for cross-cultural global contact can help to build mutual respect, trust, and the ability to work together. Through network learning, the interconnectivity among learners of the world can contribute to developing approaches for addressing today's problems: global, political, social, and environmental. Moreover, in addition to enhancing global understanding, global communication can enhance local understanding.

10.2.3 Active Learning

The network encourages, even requires, active rather than passive learning. Active participation is required because in a text-based environment it is necessary to make a comment in order to be seen as present. Once an idea is articulated and presented to the group forum, it becomes part of an ongoing interaction in which it may be challenged or expanded by peers in the process of knowledge building.

Learning networks are unique in their ability to support active learning by all participants. Air time is not limited and not easily controlled by a few individuals. In the traditional classroom, class size precludes input by some or most students; there is not enough time for everyone. Learning networks, based on asynchronous communication, offer unique opportunities for active participation. Students in online courses have access to the air time they want or need, enabling everyone to participate. Network environments such as educational computer conferencing do not entirely eliminate domination by a few more vocal participants.

What is new and different is that conferencing ensures that dominance by a few does not exclude others.

The quality of participation can also be improved online. Asynchronicity provides each user time to formulate ideas and contribute responses. Students who characterize themselves as timid, passive, or unable to think quickly on their feet in face-to-face situations report that asynchronicity enables them to participate more actively and effectively. Asynchronous communication provides participants the opportunity to comment immediately or to reflect and compose a response thoughtfully. Together with the opportunities for composing (and editing) a response in the text-based medium, asynchronicity can contribute to improving the quality of student interaction and participation.

10.2.4   Learner-Centeredness and Fluid Roles

Today anyone can become an information provider for others, thereby both democratizing information access and enabling new roles for network users. In the most successful online courses, students assume some of the roles that traditionally belong to the instructor. Unlike didactic or teacher-centered models that view the learner primarily as a passive recipient of knowledge or information transmitted from an expert, network learning is premised upon a learner-centered model that treats the learner as an active participant, interacting with others in the group. The learner actively constructs knowledge by formulating ideas into words, and these ideas are built upon through reactions and responses of others to the formulation (Harasim 1990a). There is an effort to facilitate students' ability to guide their own study. Students are encouraged to focus on problems (on how things work and the underlying causes) and respond constructively and actively to one another's work, thereby viewing ideas from multiple perspectives and contributing to the construction of collective knowledge (Scardamalia and Bereiter 1994).

The most successful online courses also include some meta-communication to discuss the content and process of the course and offer suggestions for changes. Rather than follow a fixed syllabus and schedule, there is more fluidity; learners introduce new questions and new problems, and the group can explore those areas in which they are interested.

10.2.5   Learning Networks as Online Learning Communities

Computer-mediated communication is capable of supporting socio-emotional communication as well as task-oriented communication; in fact, without personal, emotional communication, the group will not be nurtured (Rice and Love 1987; Hiltz and Johnson 1990). There should be places to play and socialize online, as well as places to work.

Those who are not experienced with online communication will need guidance about appropriate and inappropriate behavior, and there will need to be some discussions about netiquette and possible misunderstandings. Personal socializing should be confined mainly to private messages and to conferences or spaces set up specifically for these activities. But it needs to be encouraged as a way for learners to build a supportive peer community online that will extend beyond a single course, to create a kind of cohort that takes many courses together as part of a program.

In building learning communities, Peter and Trudy Johnson-Lenz (1991) speak of the need for "rhythms, boundaries, and containers" for interaction. All life, and all social interaction, tends to be characterized by certain rhythms (breathing in and breathing out; planting and harvesting; the workweek and the weekend; the semester and the vacation). The natural rhythms of interaction should be reflected in the establishment of some predictable regularities, such as activities or assignments that last for a prespecified amount of time. "Containers" and their "boundaries" for interaction can be established by a combination of software features, facilitator actions, and instructional designs or metaphors. The more the software has features to support educational designs for online interaction, the less work the instructor must do to create these boundaries, rhythms, and containers for interaction.

10.3   Conclusions

Networks are social spaces with the potential to be more egalitarian than other media for social interaction. The nature of networking technologies tends to democratize participation and enable increased interaction among learners and between learners and their facilitators/teachers. But the democratic potential of networks is not guaranteed. A tremendous investment in infrastructure will be required if this potential is to be realized. The information highways in the form of fiber-optic or other backbones that can give free or reasonably priced connectivity to anyone, anywhere, need to be built. Equipment will need to be available to students, their families, and teachers. Network learning requires that policies be established in relation to such issues as cost and access, so that it becomes accessible to all who can benefit, regardless of their ability to pay, just as universal free public school education has been provided to all children.

Moreover, network learning requires that cultural and organizational structures be developed to support collaboration and that participants, especially teachers, be taught how to design and implement network learning approaches. These steps must be taken in order to realize the potential that networking systems provide.

Profound changes at all levels of society and technology demand new educational responses. The paradigm for education in the twenty-first century that is emerging is network learning. Based on global interactivity, collaborative learning, and lifelong access to educational activities and resources, it provides an approach that emphasizes international connectivities and engenders new ways of working, studying, and problem solving. Network learning provides a model and approach to meet the challenges of the twenty-first century, enriching educational processes and resources. Most important, in an age of scarce resources and rapidly expanding knowledge, when "knowledge is power," network learning offers the possibility of bringing equal learning opportunities to learners whenever they need them and wherever they may be.

11

Epilogue: Email from the Future

UNINET TIMES   MAY 14, 2015

THE ELECTRONIC NEWSLETTER OF THE WORLD ASSOCIATION OF
COLLEGE, UNIVERSITY, AND PUBLIC SCHOOL EDUCATORS (WACUPSE).

**UNIVERSITY ADMINISTRATORS AWASH IN UNUSED CLASS-
ROOM FACILITIES**   University administrators are having difficulty in
finding productive uses for the growing mass of unused classroom space.
Many of those located in prime metropolitan areas have converted
classrooms to studio apartments, but for the vast majority of universities
and colleges this does not seem to be a viable option. A number of leading university donors have complained about their names being attached
to or associated with vacant blocks of concrete and are insisting that
these facilities be put to some productive use.

**UNIVERSITY OF MICHIGAN IN COURT OVER FIRING OF
PROFESSOR**   A University of Michigan professor has gone to court to
block his firing and removal of tenure for his decision to live in Hawaii.
The professor claims that since he offers all of his courses via networks,
there is no longer any need for his physical presence in Michigan to be
able to carry out the obligations of his position. The university has
refused to comment publicly on the case in progress. The issue of state
employees' not living in Michigan has not yet been addressed by the
state legislature in terms of workplace insurance, cost-of-living increases,
and other place-dependent policies.

UNIVERSITY OF NEW MEXICO SUED BY STUDENT FOR DIVULGING GRADING   The main complaint by a New Mexico student is that many subjects are taught totally by collaborative learning techniques, which imply both group grading and the exposure of grading and criticism by instructors about individual students to the other students in the course. The student claims this to be a violation of privacy in that the concept of a student's grades being confidential is well established. Furthermore this practice by a state-supported institution denies her right to seek a meaningful alternative institution at similar cost. The university claims that the privacy of final grades does not apply to the intermediate grading in a course, nor does it limit the right of instructors to provide constructive criticism of the work of individual students publicly within class discussion groups. The university views such approaches to student work as beneficial to the class as a whole.

INCREASING DEBATES ABOUT HOW MUCH OF PUBLIC SCHOOL EDUCATION IS TO BE VIRTUAL   The heated meetings of the Trois Rivières School Board in Québec are symptomatic of that which is occurring all over Canada. Providing high school students with electronically based courses is estimated to be half the cost of providing the same course with a local teacher. It is estimated that 30 percent of high school courses are currently delivered electronically, and many taxpayers view this as an approach to reducing local taxes. On the other side of the debate are many parents who feel that at the public school level all courses should be taught with the physical presence of an instructor.

ADMINISTRATORS OF MAJOR UNIVERSITIES ON THE EDGE OF THEIR CHAIRS   The case of Dr. Johnson versus the Pacific Accreditation Association begins trial tomorrow. Dr. Johnson is suing the association to force it to provide college accreditation to the courses she teaches electronically on various mathematical and statistical topics. Dr. Johnson is presenting evidence that her students score higher on standard national tests than those from most major accredited universities. Therefore, her students should be receiving college-level credits that can be applied to degrees at regular institutions. Many university and college administrators are extremely concerned that this could further erode the viability of traditional institutions of higher education. This concept of accreditation's resting with individual faculty members rather than institutions has received endorsement from the Association of University Professors. It is argued that educators should have the same professional status and license to practice that doctors and lawyers have.

PROFESSOR MAVERIK OF SIMON FRASER UNIVERSITY NOW HOLDS WAITING LIST RECORD   There is now a five-year waiting list for Professor Maverik's course in investment policies. As a result of strict limitations on the number of students who can be enrolled in any network-offered course, the waiting lists for many nationally acclaimed instructors continue to grow. A recent statistical analysis conducted by the International Network Student Association (INSA) has shown a direct correlation between waiting list length and the INSA ratings of instructors. The same study also indicated some correlation of poor ratings with the closing in recent years of a number of institutions that seemed incapable of drawing significant numbers of students over the network. Despite these findings, the Association of College and University Professors continues to ignore the student-conducted rating system and to seek policies to even enrollments through all course offerings. A proposal suggesting that tuition charges for a given course be based on the length of waiting list, so that a free enterprise approach to tuition charges would even out the waiting lists, was recently rejected.

LUIZA LEITE OF THE AMAZON STATE, BRAZIL, ATTENDED THIRTY UNIVERSITIES   Ms. Leite, who received the first learning network master's degree in the field of criminology, now holds the record for the number of different institutions of higher learning attended. When interviewed by this reporter, she said her biggest current problem was the fact that she had received application forms from the alumni offices of twenty-five of these institutions! With over half of the student enrollment at many institutions now comprised of remote students, there is considerable uncertainty about which institution a student is an alumnus of. Alumni offices are, of course, very concerned about maintaining the alumni population. Ms. Leite stated that she has decided to join the newly organized Internet alumni organization.

IFIP ANNOUNCES CERTIFICATION EXAM FOR UNDERGRAD-UATE DEGREES   The International Federation of Information Processing is the third professional association in the past five years to announce a certification exam. It will be required of all individuals holding an undergraduate degree in computer science who wish to obtain a software engineering license and a membership in the society. A spokesperson for the society indicated that with the growth of network-based undergraduate programs in computer science, the governing board felt it had to ensure that these degrees were really earned by those having obtained the degree. With the growth of networks, the underground market in homework has spread from a limited number of large universities to any campus where someone is willing to pay for answers.

CHURCH VS. STATE IN LOCAL NETWORKS GOES TO SUPREME COURT   The case of Union County public schools in New Jersey versus the Mormon Church of Latter Day Saints has been accepted for review by the U.S. Supreme Court. Union County operates a county-wide network for its public school system. A number of community groups, including the local Mormon church, requested access to the network to provide their own bulletin board services. Originally Union County authorized the Mormons' use of the network, considering it similar to the standard policy of letting community groups hold meetings in public schools in the evening. After a period of operation for the Mormon Bulletin Board, the school system received a number of complaints from parents that their children were participating in some of the Mormon-oriented discussions of religious principles, which were contrary to the beliefs of the families complaining. As a result, the Union County public school system ordered the Mormon Bulletin Board to terminate its access to the network in order to maintain a clear separation of church and state and to remove any possibility that the school system could be viewed as subsidizing or encouraging the spread of the Mormon religion. The Mormon church has sought to overturn this ruling in the courts by claiming that the denial of access to this network is an undue limitation on its freedom to practice its religion and outlawing use by religious groups, when the network has become a primary form of community communications, is a case of religious discrimination. The church further stated that it would not bar the doors of its electronic conference to those who sought entry.

RECENT RECESSION SEES THE DEMISE OF MOST CORPORATE TRAINING PROGRAMS   One of the major casualties of downsizing during the recent U.S. recession has been corporate training programs. Most major corporations now contract for training with both individuals and organizations. In some corporations employees needing specialized training are given an allowance and allowed to choose their own source of external training.

Spokespersons for a number of educational associations have stated that a positive outcome of the recession has been to redress the imbalance that had occurred in the education field. Corporations had built up elaborate internal training programs, rather than financing employees to attend established educational institutions such as colleges and universities. Union spokespersons have stated that to a large extent this change has been a response to the demands of employees to be able to choose their own educational alternatives and the observation that network-based courses allow employees to obtain the best training and educational options available, regardless of location.

NEW JERSEY CLOSES TWO-THIRDS OF ITS COUNTY COLLEGE SYSTEM   After five decades of building up an extensive county college system that resulted in a separate community college in practically every county in the state, the state of New Jersey has indicated that it is terminating subsidies to approximately two-thirds of these institutions. Faculty members holding tenured positions will be moved to the surviving educational institutions. It is almost surprising that this has occurred without any outcry from the affected communities. However, it was expected, since most of the campuses had been reduced to serving very small numbers of students. Now that accredited university courses are available electronically anywhere in the country, the concept of the local community or county college makes no sense for those seeking an education leading to employment or serious academic pursuits. The cost of university courses provided electronically is less than the real costs of supporting the same course at a local community college, and most students seem to feel they have a wider choice of outstanding faculty on the networks than they do at local community institutions.

The number of college students living within New Jersey and taking courses electronically at out-of-state universities has now exceeded the number taking courses at New Jersey institutions. The governor warned that unless a sizable investment is made, the state-funded universities could disappear in another decade. He also pointed out that the introduction of "marginal" priced tuition rates by private universities to remote students has seen course offerings at places like Harvard and Princeton financially competitive with on-campus offerings at Rutgers and NJIT, the leading state universities. The concept of marginal tuition pricing is rapidly eating into enrollments at many state universities throughout the country. The problem has become significant enough to be on the agenda for the next governor's conference.

EC DEBATES EDUCATIONAL STANDARDS   Rarely in recent years has a debate about education attracted such a diversity of lobbyists and interested parties. The mushrooming of remote educational and training opportunities throughout Europe has led to a totally confused marketplace. A large number of training scams that transgress national boundaries has raised a hue and cry for EC regulations that require those who advertise across national boundaries to meet certain disclosure conditions, such as clearly stating the accreditation status of any degree program advertised. The debate extends to requiring public disclosure of the performance of students on standardized EC tests. Many representatives from the growing commercial training market are seeking to derail the current push for these standards. Also a number of leading universities have expressed concern about a trend to the same level of control over university education that the national governments now exercise over public school systems.

Appendix A
Learning Networks Resource List

Academy One Affiliated with the National Public Telecomputing Network (NPTN) and the Cleveland Free-Net, this program aims to create a national on-line information cooperative for K-to-12 telecomputing activities. Internet access to Academy One is offered through the Cleveland Free-Net Telnet to

freenet-in-a.cwru.edu
freenet-in-b.cwru.edu or
freenet-in-c.cwru.edu

6330 Lincoln Avenue, Suite 117, Cypress, CA 90630; (714) 821-4427. Program contact: Linda Delzeit, NPTN Director of Education. Internet: AA002@nptn.org (For information about NPTN, contact T. M. Grudner, President, Box 1987, Cleveland, OH 44106; (216) 368-2733; Internet: tmg@nptn.org)

American Open University See On-line Campus of New York Institute of Technology.

AppleLink This official online information resource of the Apple Computer community offers a K-to-12 Education Area with special information for classroom teachers and computer coordinators. Access is through general AppleLink membership, which now includes more than 40,000 Macintosh users worldwide. Information is available from Apple sales representatives. Program contact: Lisa Bauer, Mail Stop 41-D, Apple Computer, 20525 Mariani Avenue, Cupertino, CA 95014; (408) 996-1010.

AT&T Learning Network This curriculum-based telecommunications program for grades K to 12 matches students and teachers in learning circles with eight to ten other classes around the world. The program reinforces collaborative learning through a structured, committed partnership between all matched classes. PO Box 6391, Parsippany, NJ 07054; (800) 367-7225. Program contact: Joan Fenwick.

Big Sky Telegraph (BST)   This is a rural educational, business, and individual telecommunications support service. Rural teachers take active part in online activities to facilitate information sharing and learning in their communities. BST also offers online courses, teacher in-service for recertification, online databases, and access to the Internet. Contact: Frank Odasz, Western Montana College, 710 South Atlantic, PO Box 11, Dillon, MT 59725.

Boise State University   Students can earn master's of science degree in instructional and performance technology, online. Boise, Idaho; (800) 824-7017, ext. 1312 or (208) 385-1312.

British Open University   Contact: Jim Borrows, Director of Academic Computer Services, Open University, Milton Keynes, Walten Hall, MK7 6AA, UK; 44-908-65-3193.

California Technology Project   This project, operated collaboratively by the California State University system and the California Department of Education, sponsors the California Online Resources for Education (CORE). CORE provides K-to-12 teachers with access to email, the Internet, and education-related curriculum materials. In California, call (800) 272-8743; outside California, call (310) 985-9631. Program contact: Keith Vogt. Internet: kvogt@eis.calstate.edu

Center for Children and Technology   This research center also serves as the National Center for Technology in Education, a project of the Office of Educational Research and Improvement, U.S. Department of Education. Bank Street College of Education, 610 West 112th Street, New York, NY 10025; (212) 875-4560. Program contact: Margaret Honey. AppleLink: CTE.BCS. Internet: mhoney@prime.bnkst.edu

Computer Supported Intentional Learning Environment (CSILE)   CSILE runs on networked computers, providing a single database into which students can enter various kinds of text and graphic notes, which can then be retrieved, commented on, or linked to other notes. CSILE-mediated discourse can be used in all academic areas. Contacts: Marlene Scardamalia and Carl Bereiter, Ontario Institute of Studies in Education (OISE), 252 Bloor Street West, Toronto, Ontario M5S 1V6, Canada; (416) 923-6641.

Connected Education,™ New School for Social Research   92 Van Cordtlandt Park South, #6F, Bronx, NY 10463; (212) 548-0435. Offers a master's degree in communications plus various credit and noncredit courses.

Consortium for School Networking (CoSN) CoSN is a community of organizations, government agencies, corporations, and individuals with an interest in K-to-12 education. PO Box 65193, Washington, DC 20035-5193; (202) 466-6296. Internet: cosn@bitnic.bitnet   Program contact: Connie Stout.

EDUCOM K-12 Networking Project This project aims to link practitioners in primary and secondary education through computer-mediated communication networks and, with this connectivity, to develop networked resources to support curriculum reform and institutional restructuring. EDUCOM, 1112 16th Street NW, Suite 600, Washington, DC 20036; (202) 872-4200. Program contact: John Clement. AppleLink: EDUCOM. Internet: clement@educom.edu

Electronic Frontier Foundation (EFF) This membership organization focuses on policy issues related to national networking. EFF publishes a free newsletter, *Effector Online*, on general Internet topics. 666 Pennsylvania Avenue SE, Washington, DC 20003; (202) 544-9237. Internet: eff@eff.org

Electronic University Network, Division of Open Learning Systems EUN is a federation of colleges, universities, and businesses that use telecommunications to deliver college courses and business training. About twenty colleges and universities are affiliated with the network, which supplies the software and the host system to enable member institutions to offer courses online. EUN also handles administration; the individual colleges supply instructors and course content. EUN offers over 150 courses in a variety of disciplines, but the major emphasis is on business-related courses. At the undergraduate level, students may enroll for degrees through Thomas A. Edison College in New York; at the graduate level, an M.B.A. is offered through John F. Kennedy University near San Francisco, which requires attendance at several week-long on-campus seminars during the program. 4104-B California Street, San Francisco, CA 94118; (415) 221-7061 or (800) 552-6000.

Electronic University Network, Telelearning Systems 505 Beach Street, San Francisco, CA 94133; (800) 225-3276.

ERIC Clearinghouse on Information Resources (ERIC/IR) ERIC/IR is one of sixteen clearinghouses in the ERIC system, which is sponsored by the Office of Educational Research and Improvement, U.S. Department of Education. ERIC/IR specializes in educational technology and library/information science and processes documents in these areas for the ERIC database. 030 Huntington Hall, Syracuse University, Syracuse, NY 13244-2340; (315) 443-3640. Internet: eric@suvm.acs.syr.edu   Program contact: Nancy Preston.

Florida Information Resource Network (FIRN)   FIRN posts curriculum guides for using media resources in the classroom and provides teachers and administrators in Florida with free accounts for email. Users can also access the ERIC database and library card catalogs of several colleges and universities in Florida through the network. Florida Education Center, Room B1-14, 325 West Gaines Street, Tallahassee, FL 32399; (904) 487-0911.

FrEdMail Network   This cooperative consortium maintains a distributed and low-cost telecommunications network for public agencies such as schools, libraries, cities, and community service organizations. FrEdMail Foundation, PO Box 243, Bonita, CA 91908; (619) 475-4852. Program contact: Al Rogers. Internet: arogers@bonita.cerf.fred.org

IBM/National Education Association (NEA) School Renewal Network   Dedicated to school reform, this electronic network is intended to create a research base by a community of actively engaged practitioners and researchers. NEA National Center for Innovation, 1201 16th Street NW, Washington, DC 20036; (202) 822-7783. Program contact: Shari Castle.

I*EARN   International Education and Resource Network, 345 Kear Street, Yorktown Heights, NY 10598; (914) 962-6472. Email contact: ED1@IGC.ORG

International Society for Technology in Education (ISTE), Special Interest Group for Telecommunications (SIG/Tel)   The largest international nonprofit professional organization serving computer-using educators, ISTE is dedicated to the improvement of education through the use and integration of technology. ISTE-Net, an online computer network for ISTE members, is available through GTE Education Services; (800) 927-3000. 1787 Agate Street, Eugene, OR 97403-1923; (503) 346-4414. Internet: iste@uoregon.edu   Program contact for SIG/Tel: Lynne Schrum. Internet: schrumlm@splava.cc.plattsburgh.edu

K12NET   This network is a system of more than 250 linked bulletin boards carrying thousands of messages each week among sites around the world. Contact: Janet Murray, 1151 SW Vermont Street, Portland, OR 97219; (503) 280-5280. Internet: jmurray@psg.com

Learning Link National Consortium   Learning Link is a computer-based, interactive communication system for K-to-12 educators, students, adult learners, and public television viewers. It features databases and information resources, message centers, and mail and gateways to remote sites. WNET/13, 356 West 58th Street, New York, NY 10019; (212) 560-6613.

Merit/NSF Information Services Merit Network, which operates the NSFNet backbone, also provides information support services to the networking community through email or telephone. Merit publishes a free newsletter, *Link Letter*, which can be requested through email to nsfnet-linkletter-request@merit.edu To obtain hard copies, write to the organization. Merit Network, 2901 Hubbard Pod G, Ann Arbor, MI 48105-2016; (800) 66-MERIT or (313) 936-3000. Internet: nsfnet-info@merit.edu

National Aeronautics and Space Administration NASA has created Spacelink, a computerized electronic bulletin board that enables teachers and students to receive information about NASA programs, historical and astronaut data, lesson plans, and classroom activities. NASA, 300 E Street SW, Washington DC 20546. For document distribution, contact: Committee on Education and Human Resources, Federal Coordinating Council for Science, Engineering and Technology, (202) 453-1287. Spacelink (electronic bulletin board number): (205) 895-0028.

National Geographic Kids Network Kids Network is an international telecommunications-based science and geography curriculum for fourth through sixth graders created by the National Geographic Society and Technical Education Research Centers Inc. For prices and session dates, contact National Geographic Society, Educational Services, Washington, DC 20036; (800) 368-2728.

National Science Foundation's Network Service Center (NNSC) The mission of NNSC is to collect, maintain, and distribute information about NSFNet and provide assistance to networking end users. NNSC maintains the *Internet Resource Guide*, which is available through anonymous file transfer protocol at nnsc.nsf.net, directory resource guide. This and others can also be obtained by sending email to info-server@nnsc.nsf.net and typing in the body of the message:

Request: info
Topic: help

NNSC offers network assistance through email and a telephone hot line. 10 Moulton Street, Cambridge, MA 02138; hot line: (617) 873-3400. Internet help: nnsc@nnsc.nsf.net Program contact: Corinne Carroll.

National Technological University (NTU) NTU offers satellite broadcast–based courses from over thirty colleges and universities. Included are several master's-level courses in computer and information science from NJIT that combine video delivery of lectures with computer conferencing. 700 Centre Avenue, Fort Collins, CO 80526-9903.

New Jersey Institute of Technology, Distance Learning Program   The program offers online courses on videotape plus the Virtual Classroom™ on EIES 2; fall and spring course offerings are fifteen weeks long; summer courses are 8 to 12 weeks long. Several courses in computer science are offered via this method each semester; many other courses are offered via video alone. A B.S. in information systems is available through distance education. Accredited by Middle States Association. Distance Learning, NJIT, University Heights, Newark, NJ 07102; (201) 596-3000.

New York State Education and Research Network (NYSERNet)   NYSERNet is a regional network of the National Science Foundation's NSFNet and the Internet. The network includes a K-to-12 networking interest group. 111 College Place, Syracuse, NY 13244-4100; (315) 443-4120. Internet: info@nysernet.org

NKI College of Computer Science   NKI Forlaget, Hans Burums vei 30, Postboks 111, 1341 Bekkestua, NORWAY; (02) 122950.

Northwest Regional Educational Laboratory (NWREL)   A program of the Office of Educational Research and Improvement, U.S. Department of Education, NWREL seeks to improve schools and classroom instruction in the Northwest states. With a special interest in education technology and networking. NWREL offers publications and a free newsletter, *Northwest Report*. 101 Southwest Main Street, Suite 500, Portland, OR 97204; (503) 275-9500. Program contact: Jerry Kirkpatrick.

Nova University, Center for Computer-Based Learning   NOVA offers educational courses with a real-time component: the entire class logs on simultaneously. 3301 College Avenue, Fort Lauderdale, FL 33314; (305) 475-7047.

On-Line Campus of New York Institute of Technology (formerly known as the American Open University)   CoSy computer conferencing. Courses are offered in six overlapping terms per year. The degrees offered are a B.A. in interdisciplinary studies, and a B.S. in interdisciplinary studies, business administration (management option), or behavioral sciences (options: psychology, sociology, community mental health and criminal justice). Accredited by the Middle States Association. Many specific degrees are also accredited. On-Line Campus, Enrollment Services, Sunburst Center, New York Institute of Technology, 300 Carelton Avenue, Central Islip NY 11722-4597; (800) 222-6948.

Ontario Institute for Studies in Education   The institute offers several graduate-level courses (M.A. and Ph.D.) online, in the field of education. 252 Bloor Street West, Toronto, Ontario M5R 1S6; (416) 923-6641.

Open Learning Agency   A variety of undergraduate credit courses as well as noncredit courses are offered online. 4355 Mathissi Place, Burnaby, BC V5G 4S8; (604) 431-3196.

SchoolNet   SchoolNet services are based on the Internet information distribution system Gopher and are freely available to all schools, provided they have the requisite technology and access through an Internet node. The address of the English language gopher is ernest.ccs.carleton.ca 419. The address for the French language gopher is ernest.ccs.carleton.ca.415. SchoolNet can also be found on the National Capital Freenet (telnet freenet.carleton.ca) in the Science and Engineering Technology Centre (#8) and in the Schools, Colleges and Universities section under Academy One (#1). Schools without an Internet Gopher server can Telnet to freenet.carleton.ca and log on as a guest (at the password prompt, press the Return key). National SchoolNet Office, Industry Canada, Room 805F, 235 Queen Street, Ottawa, Ontario K1A 0H5 Canada; (613) 991-6057; fax: (613) 941-2811. Internet: schoolnet_admin@carleton.ca

SENDIT   SENDIT is a pilot K-to-12 computer network for North Dakota educators and students developed by the North Dakota State University (NDSU) School of Education and Computer Center. More than seventy forums have been established. Educators also have limited access to the Internet. Box 5164, NDSU Computer Center, Fargo, ND 58105; (701) 237-8109. Program contact: Gleason Sackman. Internet: sackman@plains.nodak.edu

SouthEastern Regional Vision for Education (SERVE)   A program of the Office of Educational Research and Improvement, U.S. Department of Education, SERVE focuses on improving education in the Southeast. Nonmembers with telecommunications software and a modem can get limited access to SERVE-Line through (800) 487-7605. For more information or a membership, contact SERVE, 41 Marietta Street NW, Suite 1000, Atlanta, GA 30303; (800) 659-3204.

Southern Interior Telecommunications Project (SITP)   SITP uses various learning methods, including online games, simulations, and role playing, by which learners collaborate and work with network mentors, tutors, peers, and experts to learn the curriculum. The curricular areas supported by the SITP networked classroom are science, environmental studies, law, creative writing, history, geography, and computer studies. For information, contact: Education Technology Centre of British Columbia, PO Box 2040, 1515 McTavish Road, Sidney, British Columbia V8L 3Y3 Canada.

SpecialNet   In operation since 1981, this information network offers educators and administrators email, bulletin boards, conferencing, and databases that address various topics in special education. For subscription information, contact GTE Education Services, GTE Place, West Airfield Drive, PO Box 619810, Dallas/Fort Worth Airport, TX 75261-9810; (800) 927-3000.

Technical Education Research Centers (TERC)   This program researches, develops, and disseminates innovative programs for educators with a special interest in curriculum projects involving telecomputing. TERC publishes a free newsletter, *Hands On!* 2067 Massachusetts Avenue, Cambridge, MA 02140; (617) 547-0430. Program contact: Ken Mayer. Internet: ken_mayer@terc.edu

Texas Education Network (TENET)   TENET links more than 150,000 K-to-12 educators and administrators who use the network for email, resource sharing, and access to databases via the Internet. Texas Education Agency, 1701 North Congress Avenue, Austin, TX 78701; (512) 463-9091.

University of Phoenix   Students can earn a B.S. in business administration, an M.B.A., or an M.A. in management entirely online. 101 California Street, Suite 505, San Francisco, CA 94111; 1-800-388-5463, (800) 888-4935 or (415) 956-2121.

Virginia's Pen   Approximately 6,000 educators have accounts on Virginia's statewide network. Network offerings include various discussion groups, topical news reports, study skills guides, and curriculum resources. Virginia Department of Education, 101 North 14th Street, 22d Floor, Richmond, VA 23219. Program contact: Harold Cathern, Internet: hcathern@vdoe386.vak12ed.edu

Writers in Electronic Residence (WIER)   The WIER program links writing and language arts students in Canada with writers, teachers, and one another, for an exchange of original writing and commentary. Contact: Trevor Owen, Faculty of Education, York University, 4700 Keele Street, North York, Ontario, M3J 1P3, Canada; (416) 978-6900.

Appendix B
Commercial Services

America Online
8619 Westwood Center Drive
Vienna, VA 22182
(800) 827-6364
Offers education discussion groups, online homework help for students, a software library, and computer access to National Geographic's educational resources.

American Productivity and Quality Center
123 North Post Oak Land
Houston, TX 77024
Offers ongoing conferences on topics related to total quality control and improving organizational productivity via its own tailored version of EIES 2.

America Tomorrow
PO Box 2310
West Bethesda, MD 20827-2310
(800) 456-8881
America Tomorrow's Leadership Network and Information Service is set up to allow education, business, and community leaders to share information and to work collaboratively online.

APC Network (Association of Progressive Communications)
PeaceNet, EcoNet, ConflictNet, IGC
18 De Broom Street
San Francisco, CA 94107
(415) 442-0220
Offers conferencing and email. The APC Network has its main nodes at London (GreenNet), Stockholm (NordNet), Toronto (Web), and San Francisco (PeaceNet/IGC Networks) and, with links to Internet, provides a global community of discussion oriented toward environmental, peace, and local and international development issues. There are approximately 900 conferences on hundreds of specific issues, most of them open to all users, from all over the world.

Awakening Technology
695 Fifth Street
Lake Oswego, OR 97034, USA
(503) 653-2615

Compuserve Information Service
Customer Service Ordering
Department
(800) 848-8199
Online services, conferencing, and email.

GTE Education Services
GTE Place
West Airfield Drive
PO Box 619810
Dallas/Fort Worth Airport,
TX 75261-9810
(800) 927-3000
Offers several education-related databases, including the ERIC database, ERIC Digests Online, a calendar of 500 education-related conferences, and a database of 350 education information centers.

META Network
Conferencing and email.
Metasystems Design Group, Inc.
2000 North 15th Street, Suite 103
Arlington, VA 22201
(703) 243-6622 (voice);
(703) 841-9798 (fax)
Set-up fee and monthly charges.

PEN Action Group
Information Systems Department
Santa Monica City Hall
1685 Main Street
Santa Monica CA 90101
(213) 458-8383
The People's Electronic Network Action Group, an electronic city hall set up by the city of Santa Monica. PEN is an illustration of the use of computer conferencing for community development and education.

Prodigy
445 Hamilton Avenue
White Plains, NY 10601
(800) 776-0840
Offers many specialized bulletin boards as well as news, weather, financial and political updates, and consumer reports. Educational offerings for children include *Grolier's* encyclopedia; the geography game Where in the World Is Carmen Sandiego? and science experiments from Nova.

The WELL
27 Gate Five Road Sausalito,
CA 94965
(415) 332-4335 (voice);
(415) 332-6105 (modem)
Conferencing and email. Membership is free to credit-card customers. Monthly fees and usage fees are billed by the minute.

Appendix C

Vendors of Computer Conferencing Systems

Caucus
Metasystems Design Group
2000 North 15th Street, Suite 103
Arlington, VA 22201, USA
(703) 243-6622

CLAS System Software
Financial Proformas Inc.
1855 Olympic Blvd., Suite 200
Walnut Creek, CA 94596, USA
Voice: (510) 945-1005
Fax: (510) 945-1162

COCONET Software
Coconut Computing
7946 Ivanhoe Avenue, Suite 303
La Jolla, CA 92037, USA
Voice: (619) 456-2002
Fax: (619) 456-1905
Email: info@coconut.com

COM/SuperCOM
Stockholm University Computing
Center
Linnegatan 89
Box 27322
S-102 54 Stockholm, Sweden
+46-8-665-4500

CONFER II
Advertel Communication Systems
2067 Ascot
Ann Arbor, MI 48103, USA
(313) 665-2612

Convene International
591 Redwood Highway, Suite 2355
Mill Valley, CA 94941-6004, USA
(415) 380-0510

CoSy
Softwords
4252 Commerce Circle
Victoria, British Columbia,
CANADA, V8Z 4M2
(604) 727-6522

EIES 2
Virtual Classroom™
Computerized Conferencing and
Communications Center
New Jersey Institute of Technology
University Heights
Newark, NJ, 07102, USA
(201) 596-3437

FirstClass Systems
SoftArc Inc.
805 Middlefield Road, Suite 102
Scarborough, Ontario, CANADA,
M1V 2T9
Tel: (416) 299-4723
Fax: (416) 754-1856

Lotus Notes
Lotus Development Corporation
1-800-346-1305, or contact your local
Lotus sales division.

PARTICIPATE (Parti)
Eventures Limited
2744 Washington Street
Allentown, PA 18104, USA
(215) 770-0650

Porta COM
Komunity Software AB
Sveavagan 114
S-113 50 Stockholm, SWEDEN
+46-8-34-20-40

VAXNOTES
Digital Equipment Corporation
1-800-267-5251; or contact your local
DEC sales division.

The VIRTUAL UNIVERSITY
University-Industry Liaison Office
Simon Fraser University
Burnaby, B.C. V5A 1S6, CANADA
(604) 291-4292

Women's Wire
P.O. Box 191490
San Francisco, CA 94119-1490, USA

Appendix D
Lists of Free-Nets

Via Telnet

Buffalo Free-Net
Telnet freenet.buffalo.edu
or 128.205.3.99
Log in: freeport

CalState Free-Net
Telnet swrl36.calstate.edu
or 130.150.108.36
Log in: guest
Password: guest

Cleveland Free-Net
Telnet hela.ins.cwru.edu
or 129.22.8.38
Log in: visitor

Denver Free-Net
Telnet freenet.hsc.colorado.edu
or 140.226.1.8
Log in: visitor

Heartland Free-Net
Telnet heartland.bradley.edu
or 136.176.5.114
Log in: bbguest

Lorain County Free-Net
Telnet freenet.lorain.oberlin.edu
or 132.162.32.99
Log in: guest

National Capital Free-Net
Ottawa, Canada

Telnet freenet.carleton.ca
or 134.117.1.12
Log in: guest

SENDIT
North Dakota's K-12 Educational
Telecommunications Network
Telnet sendit.nodak.edu
or 134.129.105.1
Log in: bbs
Password: sendit2me

Tallahassee Free-Net
Telnet freenet.fsu.edu
or 144.174.128.43
Log in: visitor

Tri-State Online (Cincinnati)
Telnet cbos.uc.edu
Enter User ID:visitor
Enter PIN:9999
Enter Password:(Press return)

Victoria Free-Net
Telnet freenet.victoria.bc.ca
or 134.87.16.100
Log in: guest

Youngstown Free-Net
Telnet yfn.ysu.edu
or 192.55.234.27
Log in: visitor

Via the National Public Telecomputing Network Affiliate Systems

For more information about NPTN or information on how to start a community computer system, access the anonymous FTP site at: nptn.org (go to: /pub/info.nptn); or send email to: info@nptn.org

Big Sky Telegraph—Dillon, Montana
Modem: (406) 683-7680—1200 baud
Internet: 192.231.192.1

Buffalo Free-Net—Buffalo, New York
(Demo System)
Modem: (716) 645-6128
Internet: freenet.buffalo.edu

Cleveland Free-Net—Cleveland, Ohio
Modem: (216) 368-3888—300/1200/2400 Baud
Internet: freenet-in-a.cwru.edu

Denver Free-Net—Denver, Colorado
Modem: (303) 270-4865
Internet: freenet.hsc.colorado.edu
(140.226.1.8)

Heartland Free-Net—Peoria, Illinois
Modem: (309) 674-1100
Internet: heartland.bradley.edu
(136.176.5.114)

Lorain County Free-Net—Elyria, Ohio
Modem: (216) 366-9721—300/1200/2400 baud
Internet: freenet.lorain.oberlin.edu
(132.162.32.99)

National Capital Free-Net—Ottawa, Canada
Modem: (613) 780-3733
Internet: freenet.carleton.ca
(134.117.1.25)

Tallahassee Free-Net—Tallahassee, Florida (Demo System)
Modem: (demo system, Internet access only)
Internet: freenet.fsu.edu
(144.174.128.43)

Tristate Online—Cincinnati, Ohio
Modem: (513) 579-1990
Internet: cbos.uc.edu

Victoria Free-Net—Victoria, British Columbia
Modem: (604) 595-2300
Internet: freenet.victoria.bc.ca
(134.87.16.100)

Wellington Citynet—Wellington, New Zealand
Internet: kosmos.wcc.govt.nz
(192.54.130.39)

Youngstown Free-Net—Youngstown, Ohio
Modem: (216) 742-3072—300/1200/2400 baud
Internet: yfn.ysu.edu (192.55.234.27)

Appendix F

Sample Course Description and Letter to Online Students

Course Description for Computers and Society via Video Plus Virtual Classroom

As a result of a generous grant, we are able to experiment with trying to create a "twenty-first century" model for computer-supported learning, using a computer-mediated communication system to allow class members to participate in the coursework at whatever times and places are most convenient for them. Before enrolling for this class, however, you should understand what will be required of you in order to pass the course.

You will need to spend eight to ten hours a week on this course in order to obtain a good grade. This is broken down approximately as follows:

1. One hour: Watch the weekly broadcast or videotape (instead of attending class).

2. Two to three hours: Read required text and articles, take notes, study notes to understand the material (same as in traditional section).

3. About two hours: Work on a term project, which will consist either of doing twenty-five hours of volunteer work in a community service agency or of preparing and presenting a term paper about twenty-five pages in length (same as in traditional section).

4. Two to three hours: Using a computer and modem at home or in your dormitory room, or a computer laboratory on campus, to log into the "Virtual Classroom" on EIES 2. You are expected to log on at least three times a week. There you will read additional lecture-type material in written form, discuss issues related to the video and readings, and do your homework assignments, many of which will involve working with or sharing information with other students in the online "class conference." There will be an assignment due online almost every week. (Replaces the other two hours of classroom lecture and discussion time and handing in homework on paper.)

We will be studying and discussing many topics that can be very interesting and fun to study via computer communication, including computers and medicine, computers and privacy, computer crime, and ethical and legal issues related to computer applications. Even though you can choose which hours a week to "attend class," you must do this regularly, every week. If you do not have access to computer equipment or the self-discipline to do this, do not take this section!

In addition, you will be asked to attend an initial training session and to take the midterm and final exams on campus. If there are reasons why this would be very difficult for you, you can make alternative arrangements with your instructor. Finally, you will be asked to fill out some questionnaires or answer questions to help us to evaluate and improve this mode of course delivery.

If you would like more information about this course before deciding whether to enroll, see the professor.

A Sample Orientation Letter for Enrolled Students

A Note from Your Teacher. Please Read It!

Dear Student,

You might have noticed already that this is not a class like all other classes.

This letter, which you are holding in your hands, should be part of a large package that you have received. All the materials in this package are for preparing you for taking this unique class.

Let me explain for a moment why this class is unique.

You are not going to see me

Well, maybe you will see me once at an orientation session, once at your midterm, and once at your final. If you really WANT to see me, you can also come to my office hours.

But the fact remains, that you are never going to sit in a room with me and hear me lecture. Instead, you are going to:

• See me on CTN TV (or on videocassette).
• Talk to me and your classmates by using an electronic conferencing system.

The two other letters in this package explain why we are doing this, and many of the technical details. Let me not repeat too much of this information. I will concentrate on the few facts you need to know, so that you can pass this class (and get a good grade in it).

In a traditional class (the kind you have been taking for the last 12 + years) two things are supposed to happen:

1. You listen to an instructor and take notes.
2. You ask questions of and answer questions posed by the instructor.

Unfortunately, as class time is severely limited, many students never get to ask or answer questions. Some students are also shy or uncomfortable to talk in front of 30 other people.

In this class, or any other Virtual Class, you listen to your instructor on TV. You ask questions (and answer them) by typing questions and answers into a computer system. Your questions and answers will be read by your instructor and all your classmates.

Now we have eliminated all the problems listed above!!! There is no time limit. Students type questions whenever they arise. There is also less of a problem with being shy. Nobody sees you, nobody hears your voice, and you can edit and change and improve your message until you like it!

There is also a downside to this new form of education. As you are missing the regularity of class sessions, you might be tempted to "skip a couple of weeks." To avoid this, there will be "electronic homework" due every week.

Now, please do the following:

1. Read the other letters that you have received in this package.
2. Carefully read the syllabus.
3. Read Homework 1, so that you don't miss the first due date.

At this time, I would like to wish you good luck in this class, and I hope that you will find it as exciting an experience as we do.

Your Professor,

Appendix G
Annotated Excerpts from an Online Course

Following are some extracts from the use of a conferencing system to support the discussions of a graduate course in the management of information systems offered in the spring 1992. It provides an illustration of some of the phases of an online course, from the instructor's active responsiveness at the beginning of the course, to letting the students take over some of the teaching and moderating role by the end of the course.

This was an evening course that met one night a week for three hours. It had twenty-two students, and over two-thirds were working full time. The typical student was either in the master's in management or the master's in computer science program at NJIT, with a few students in the Ph.D. in management program.

The subject of management contains a great deal of pragmatic material, and the area of information systems has evolved so rapidly that the wisdom of management in this area is under considerable flux. There is not enough time in the lectures, given the material that needs to be covered, to allow for adequate discussion. The discussion from which the following material is taken was about three hundred comments long, many of them too long to include here. What can be observed is the students' sharing knowledge among themselves, with the instructor playing a purely facilitative role.

In addition to the main discussion conference, there was a second conference for the students to contribute the longer items they were asked to generate as assignments. These included a review of a recent and different professional article by each student, the independent review of chapters from the textbook, and the executive summary and reference list for the individual course project. The students made initial proposals for the topic they would investigate for the course project report. This ensured that the students did not overlap one another and gave the professor a chance to make suggestions on the proposed topic, abstract, and outline. It was not uncommon for the students to make suggestions on each others' proposals. Based upon their readings of the literature and the formal lectures, the students were also requested to suggest questions that could be used on the class midterm exam.

The conference was used to track each student's status on assignments and to answer questions the students had about the assignments. The conferencing system used was EIES 2 with various Virtual Classroom features (described in chapter 3) to support and organize the process. With twenty students, there tended to be an average of five entries every weekday, and over half were more than two screens long. The use of key words to index the items and the self-organizing nature of the comments in the conference were critical to tracking and reviewing what was happening for the students and the instructor. Note that comment 2.5 denotes that this comment is the fifth reply to root comment 2.

Initially students are asked to provide some background on themselves and to express their objectives for what they hope to obtain from the course. The following is an example supplied by a student to that particular Question activity. We have eliminated any identification of any particular student but include the comment titles to show how these comments are formatted. The first "C 103.3" indicates the conference ID number from which the comment was taken. The "XXX" field is where the name, nickname, and ID number of the author were placed.

C 103.3 CC 2.5 XXX 1/30/92 12:48 PM 7 lines
SUBJECT: background and objectives KEYS: /Question/Introduction

I have 5 years experience in business applications development, with some experience in management of small-scale information systems. I hope to gain some insight into information systems management as it applies to my work. I do NOT plan on becoming an IS manager; I prefer the more technical aspects of computer science, but I recognize the importance of proper management.

The next request the students responded to was to provide an example of a situation they had encountered that could be viewed as a management problem. Given the many years of work experience in this class, this produced quite a few nontrivial examples. It also placed the instructor in the role of having to show if he had the knowledge to respond intelligently to some of these examples. It provided the students an opportunity to gauge their instructor. We are showing the instructor's response to each of these; since this was the first assignment, it was important for the instructor to respond. Some of the twenty examples generated by the students ended up involving questions being asked by the instructor and other students to explore and clarify each situation. The first example was of just such a nature and led to a long discussion. The second two were easier to respond to in a direct comment.

C 103.3 CC 3.2 XXX 2/ 1/92 9:18 PM 25 lines
SUBJECT: examples of management problems KEYS: /question/problem

In my department, upper-level management had decided that selective mainframe applications must be rewritten in order to process on smaller non-IBM machines. Their objective was to drastically reduce data processing costs. In order to begin this major work effort, one financial MVS application system was selected for the re-engineering effort. The development group was staffed and retrained in UNIX and C. Unfortunately, the users of the mainframe application were not consulted. The application group worked independently in order to build a new state-of-the-art system. In fact, the new mini-application could not handle the volume of data from the current environment and demonstrated significant performance problems. Since the requirements stage of the system development life cycle had been bypassed, the users were dissatisfied and refused to use the system. Another difficulty was that the final new system processed longer than the mainframe application since the new system was maintaining the same amount of data and functionality. As a result, the overall project failed.

C 103.3 CC 3.2.1 INSTRUCTOR 2/ 2/92 4:15 PM 5 lines
SUBJECT: raises questions

An interesting, and I am afraid very typical, example. Is there any insight into the organizational structure and management culture that would explain why the users were not consulted? Is this typical? Are upgrades!! considered or handled differently than new systems? Is there any sort of steering committee?

C 103.3 CC 3.6 XXX 2/ 3/92 10:14 PM 17 lines
SUBJECT: examples of management problems KEYS: /question/problem

We were recently asked to develop a prototype for a new rating system at the insurance company for which I work. There was little available staff. We agreed to do it as an R&D effort to see if we could build a rating system on a PC using some new software that we had in house. The user agreed but did not understand the nature of an R&D effort. They wanted something quick to test a new methodology and thought that using the PC instead of the mainframe would mean it would be quick. They wanted something within three months. We ran into some difficulties and because the technology was new, no one could give good estimates of how long it would take. The final test system was delivered 2 months late.

The programming staff felt the R&D effort was a success because we proved we could use the technology. But the user was disappointed and only seemed to care that it was late. These are unfortunate results that can happen when the purpose of a project is not fully communicated at the outset of a project.

C 103.3 CC 3.6.1 INSTRUCTOR 2/ 4/92 9:16 PM 17 lines
SUBJECT: Impact of being late

You have got to remember that the user is not just viewing that YOU were two months late. The user was two months late to whoever evaluates him or her (or group) because of you—that is why they had difficulty viewing it as a good system even if it was. The user group cannot separate the two factors. I have the same feeling about TURBO TAX and the fact that what they delivered to me as a 1991 package is missing one of the new forms I need. It is Feb. now and they have not released an update yet for a project I have to complete by April 15th. The IRS will not accept from me any excuses about the delivery schedules of Chipsoft. You always have to ask in the use of deadlines, "what is the penalty to the user if you are late?" In cases of real bad relations between users and developers, at the end of the project there is this little game of who was responsible for being late: the developers with their performance or the users with all the changes they wanted!!!

C 103.3 CC 3.7 XXX 2/ 4/92 12:33 PM 23 lines
SUBJECT: examples of management problems KEYS: /question/problem

I am currently directly affected by an interesting situation involving a large application development project. I work for a large manufacturing firm with three consumer product divisions. Plans are under way for consolidation of the three divisions into one division to be located in Connecticut. I am faced with relocation or looking elsewhere for a new job.

The situation that eventually brought this about was, ironically, over-specification for a new order management system (OMS). Originally, OMS was intended for one division only. It was designed to be a state-of-the-art masterpiece using IBM's new philosophy of joint applications development and the very latest in new technology. This overblown vision required more resources than were currently available, so a large software consulting firm was brought in. It was agreed that their existing package would be rewritten to make use of the latest technologies (DB2, et al), and they could market the final product. This new vision now had a price tag of several million dollars, so approval was required from higher than the division-level management. The president of all three consumer divisions thought to himself "Why pay all this money for just one division? Let's consolidate OMS for all consumer divisions ... and while we're at it, why do we need three finance departments? Why not consolidate everything into one consumer products division?" And the rest is history.

C 103.3 CC 3.7.1 INSTRUCTOR 2/ 4/92 9:27 PM 5 lines
SUBJECT: Examples of runaway projects

Nothing like a "runaway" project to bring about the involvement of upper management. Sounds like this guy needs to prove it was not a runaway project; the logical first step in what is going to be a major cost saving undertaking? It is sort of interesting in organizations how a "failure" can be turned into a "success."

Later on in the course, the students began taking much of the initiative, and the instructor could mainly plan a facilitating role. A course in management is designed to induce the students to examine critically much of the academic material and to realize there are considerable disagreements in the literature. When the students begin to realize this, there are always some who begin to suggest how they think the course should be changed:

C 103.3 CC 34 XXX 2/12/92 8:43 PM 19 lines
SUBJECT: Dynamic systems and Static models

As far as I am concerned (and correct me if I am wrong), organizations are dynamic systems. IT within the organization is a part of such a system. That part is dynamic as well. What's interesting about those systems is that they never reach equilibrium (unless the organization dissolves). Despite that, Nolan, Cash and others try to describe such systems using ... static models, or dynamic models that always reach equilibrium. For heaven's sake, this is never going to work. If you agree, then the course has to take a drastic change. Instead of reading bulks of material that would fall into the above category (i.e., describing dynamic systems with static models) we should concentrate on an attempt to build such a dynamic model that never reaches equilibrium. (AND, I don't mean to say that the course has to become a Ph.D. dissertation....)

Instructors are gratified to see students reinterpret the concepts being taught in the context of their own environments. The following is an excellent example:

C 103.3 CC 38 XXX 2/13/92 9:54 PM 12 lines
KEYS: /steering committees

Seems like quite a coincidence that we discussed steering committees and operational committees in class tonight, and that the steering committee should be translating business goals to information technology goals.

The reason I missed class last week was because I was at a National Sales Training Conference, and during the conference I got to hear 4–5 VP's and Directors talk about their goals and objectives, and LOTS of those goals related to INFORMATION. The only problem was that there were only about 10 lower level "information" type people there to hear what they were saying. The rest of the attendees were from sales. There is no steering committee in our organization and little interest on the part of those in information systems to give the users a formal voice.

There were a number of Questions that the instructor provided in the conference as official assignments. Following are a few of the shorter answers provided:

C 103.3 CC 43 INSTRUCTOR 2/21/92 11:41 AM 9 lines
SUBJECT: determining professionalism of a technical organization
KEYS: /Question/professionalism

This is a "question" activity, so you cannot see the answers of the other students till you supply your own. You are about to go for interviews for a possible job with a company in some part of their Information Systems operation. What would you try to observe and ask (of whom) in order to determine how "professional" the technical staff is and the associated morale or attitude they have to their work? Explain the rationale for your specific questions and observations.

C 103.3 CC 43.4 XXX 2/27/92 6:55 AM 12 lines
SUBJECT: determining professionalism of a technical organization

The things I would look for to determine professionalism of an organization I might join are: Ask how the projects in progress or proposed are related to the corporate business. Determine if possible, the process for reporting to upper management about the progress of a project. Find out what education is normally provided to keep the staff technically literate. Check the area to see if there are technical journals and books available. Find out if there is a technical library on site or readily accessible by staff.

C 103.3 CC 43.6 XXX 3/ 4/92 11:44 PM 28 lines
SUBJECT: determining professionalism of a technical organization

Determining the morale of a company would be very important to me as a potential place that I would spend two thirds of my awakening hours. Some of the clues that I would look for are the employees appearance and facial expressions, their interpersonal encounters and their communication style. For example, in an unprofessional shop people are more inclined to shout to one another (disrupting others). People may look harried or stressed out by their facial expressions or sloppy dress. However, I don't feel that a casual dress code is any indicator of professionalism. Interpersonal encounters like two people passing in the hall can show if it is a friendly company. I don't feel people need to stop and chat but, if they don't acknowledge each other it's not a good sign. I would also be interested in hearing other employees converse. People often talk about how it's going, so I might hear if things are going bad.

I would also look for presence of necessary supplies and equipment. Many sweat shops don't provide proper office supplies and require employees to sit in uncomfortable chairs. That can be a major problem as most IS jobs require you to sit working on a PC or terminal. It is also bad if you don't have the tools to do your job (necessary hardware/software).

As a job applicant, I would be careful bringing up subjects like employee moral, benefits and salary potential with the hiring manager. However, most companies have candidates interview with technical people and Personnel representatives. I would use those opportunities to determine how progressive the company is with benefits, are the employees satisfied and what the policies are concerning salary and performance review frequency.

One sign of success in a course like this is that students continue to bring up material for discussion even when there is no request from the instructor to do so. It is even better when the other students jump in to provide insight before the instructor has to. In this example the student chose to use the Anonymity feature to enter this comment so that it would not be obvious which company had gotten itself into this situation:

C 103.3 CC 44 (ANONYMOUS) 2/23/92 11:57 AM 17 lines
SUBJECT: Systems Development

Recently our company purchased a new development methodology system. We are currently implementing this system throughout the corporation. The goal of implementing 'x' methodology was to provide standards so that the different development groups within the company could read and speak the same language when developing systems. The problem however is that the modeling aspects are so complicated that we now are finding that on every large project we need to go back to the vendor of 'x' methodology and ask for consulting services. I get the feeling the vendor knew this.

C 103.3 CC 44.1 XXX 2/23/92 4:38 PM 11 lines
SUBJECT: Systems Development

Would you really expect to be able, as an organization, to master a new technology/methodology without assistance? One way of learning is by having dedicated training sessions. It's like learning how to swim using a correspondence course. The other way is to learn from the experience of others. As a new methodology, there aren't too many people with experience out there. Probably the only resource is the vendor. But, looking at the long run, wouldn't you expect to be independent? (I mean within 6 months to a year). Then the organization will be in a position (hopefully) to maximize its benefits from the product/methodology.

Following are additional examples of students' relating the material in the course to their own experiences:

C 103.3 CC 49 XXX 2/28/92 4:35 PM 11 lines
SUBJECT: computers-first use KEYS: /computers/management

The discussion in last night's class regarding famous bad decisions in computer management reminds me of the first experience I and my company had with computers. At the time, I was in the preliminary design group at Reaction Motors, a rocket engine design and manufacturing company, now defunct. We were considering our first computer, a tape driven machine that was supposed to replace our slide rules. The head of the department set forth a heat transfer problem. It was a race between manual calculation (on the slide rule) and someone on the computer. The computer beat the man by 6 hours, and Reaction entered the computer age! Management needed concrete proof of what should have been obvious.

C 103.3 CC 56 XXX 3/ 9/92 4:18 PM 16 lines
SUBJECT: IS Champions KEYS: /Champion

Shortly after I finished reading the chapter "Champions," I found that one of my most intimate acquaintances was faced with an interesting situation in which she seemed to be facing the consequences of affecting the environmental culture as a result of implementing an innovation. She fell somewhere in the category between pioneer and innovator. Reading the chapter permitted her to understand better what was going on in the Administration and possibly how to cope. A copy of this chapter is being submitted to the Administration Chairman.

In the final weeks of the course, the instructor started to feel fairly drained, but the students were still going strong with the introduction of new material and problems. The following example led to an extensive class discussion. A few replies are presented.

C 103.3 CC 76 XXX 4/13/92 10:37 PM 50 lines
SUBJECT: Impact of new IS on team members KEYS: /team/question

A Question to the INSTRUCTOR & everyone else.

Background: I'm currently involved in the introduction of a new system to a group of users in a financial organization. Up to this date they have been using manual procedures to accomplish their work. They would some times use a mainframe terminal to retrieve information, but it's used just as the telephone is being used: for retrieval purposes only, for a narrow scope of information.

A key point to note is, that at this point of time, only their manager knows and sees the complete picture. The team members do not know what other members have accomplished, and how much they have progressed in the cycle. Neither are they aware of each other's workload, in terms of # accounts handled and the complexity of each account.

The system that is going live on May 1st, 1992, will change that. All group members will share a common database. (PC based, on LAN, on-line 24 hours a day). Each member could and would see the status of all accounts during the cycle. (Update access is somewhat more restricted). Suddenly, each member of the team will have information unavailable to him/her previously: the work load, the complexity, and especially timely progress of each one of the team members.

The Question: What is your opinion as to the potential impact of such a system on the individual team members? What would be some of the benefits for having the new knowledge? What are the dangers of having the new knowledge if any? Is there any literature (Besides the Star Ledger of course ...) that addresses similar situations? Thanks, XXXX

C 103.3 CC 76.3 XXX 4/22/92 12:47 PM 8 lines
SUBJECT: Impact of new IS on team members

A question: My experience has been that people who think their workload is larger than others will complain loudly to anyone who will listen. Being able to view other worker's workloads might shut them up or even make them louder. The fact that everyone completes a cycle monthly may ease any problems caused by viewing other's progress. Hopefully a month isn't long enough for large discrepancies to accumulate.

C 103.3 CC 76.3.1 XXX 4/22/92 4:19 PM 2 lines
SUBJECT: Impact of new IS on team members

Has any consideration been given to having a pool of "extra" work that any member can do when they have a lull in their own workload?

C 103.3 CC 76.6 XXX 5/2/92 7:30:52 PM 15 lines
SUBJECT: Impact of new IS on team members

I think the behavior of the workers who now will know how each is doing relative to the others, will take the lead from the actions of managers. If the difference in work performance leads to different treatment (observable treatment) by management, I think this will steer the reactions of the employees. Is it important that they know how each other is doing? Is that a management ploy to set up a kind of competition among them? Usually such things are kept private between the employee and the manager. There are usually ways to protect controversial data if so desired. It's interesting that this information will now be open to all. Is it a side product of the system design that the information is available?

It should be evident from the examples that instructors can gain significant insight into the thinking processes of students—far more insight than is obtained by the typical verbal quick-reaction response to face-to-face questions. Clearly the students spent considerable time thinking about the content of their entries into the conference environment. The examples here illustrate the richness of the class discussion and sharing of information that is possible.

References

Bang, J., and Moller, M. (1990). Computer conferencing in Danish distance education. In A. W. Bates, ed., *Media and Technology in European Distance Education* (249–252). Milton Keynes, UK: Open University.

Barker, J. A. (1992). *Paradigms: The Business of Discovering the Future*. New York: HarperCollins.

Bates, A. W. (1991). Third generation distance education: The challenge of new technology. *Research in Distance Education* 3 (2).

Beath, C., Mathis, G., and Ives, B. (1988). The information champion: Aiding and abetting, care and feeding. In R. H. Sprague, Jr., ed., *Proceedings of the 21st Annual Hawaii International Conference on Systems Science* 4: 115–124. Washington, DC: IEEE Press.

Bellman, B., Tindimubona, A., and Arias, A. Jr. (1993). Technology transfer in global networking: Capacity building in Africa and Latin America. In L. Harasim, ed., *Global Networks: Computers and International Communication*. Cambridge: MIT Press.

Bouton, C., and Garth, R. Y. (1983). *New Directions in Teaching and Learning*. Learning in Groups (no. 14). San Francisco: Jossey-Bass.

Brand, S. (1987). *The Media Lab: Inventing the Future at MIT*. New York: Viking.

Brasher, M. (1992). A publisher's perspective on telecomputing. In R. F. Tinker and P. M. Kapisovsky, eds., *Prospects for Educational Telecomputing: Selected Readings*. Cambridge: TERC.

Brookfield, S. D. (1986). *Understanding and Facilitating Adult Learning*. San Francisco: Jossey-Bass.

Brown, J., Collins, A., and Duguid, P. (1989). Situated cognition and the culture of learning. *Educational Researcher* 18 (1): 32–42.

Bruffee, K. A. (1986). Social construction, language and the authority of knowledge: A bibliographical essay. *College English* 48 (8): 773–790.

Bush, V. (1945). As we may think. *Atlantic Monthly* (July): 101–108.

Christensen, B. (1990). Teachers and CMC at Jutland Open University: A case study. In A. W. Bates, ed., *Media and Technology in European Distance Education* (253–258). Milton Keynes, UK: Open University.

Clifford, J. (1981). Composing in stages: The effects of a collaborative pedagogy. *Research in Teaching English* 15 (1): 37–44.

Cohen, M., and Riel, M. (1989). The effect of distant audiences on students' writing. *American Educational Research Journal* 26 (2): 143–159.

Collins, A., Brown, J., and Newman, S. (1989). Cognitive apprenticeship: Teaching the crafts of reading, writing, and mathematics. In L. Resnick, ed., *Knowing, Learning and Instruction*. Hillsdale, NJ: Erlbaum.

Coombs, N. (1989). Using CMC to overcome physical disabilities. In R. Mason and A. Kaye, eds., *Mindweave: Communication, Computers, and Distance Education* (180–185). Oxford: Pergamon Press.

Critical Connections: Communications for the Future. (1990). Washington, DC: Office of Technology Assessment.

Daloz, L. (1986). *Effective Teaching and Mentoring*. San Francisco: Jossey-Bass.

Davie, L. (1989). Facilitation techniques for the online tutor. In R. Mason and A. Kaye, eds., *Mindweave: Communication, Computers and Distance Education* (74–85). Oxford, UK: Pergamon Press.

Davie, L., and Wells, R. (1991). Empowering the learner through computer-mediated communication. *American Journal of Distance Education* 5 (1): 15–23.

Delbec, A. L., VandeVen, A. H., and Gutafson, D. H. (1975). *Group Techniques for Program Planning: A Guide to Nominal Group and Delphi Techniques*. Glenview, IL: Scott-Foresman.

Deutschman, B. W. (1984). Computer teleconferencing and independent study. In J. J. Manock, ed., *Proceedings of the Exxon Conference on Computer-Mediated Conferencing Systems and Their Potential* (13–23). Wilmington, NC: Office of Research Administration, University of North Carolina.

Ehrmann, S. (1988). Assessing the open end of learning: Roles for new techologies. *Liberal Education* 71 (3): 5–11.

Eisenberg, M. B., and Ely, D. P. (1993). Plugging into the net. *ERIC Review* 2 (3) (Winter): 2–10.

Faris, R. (1975). *The Passionate Educators: Voluntary Associations for Control of Adult Educational Broadcasting, 1919–1952*. Toronto: Peter Martin.

Feenberg, A. (1987). Computer conferencing and the humanities. *Instructional Science* 16 (2): 169–186.

Feenberg, A. (1989a). The future of teaching in the planetary classroom. In D. Whittaker, ed., *Proceedings of the Tenth Annual Conference of the Pacific Region Association for Higher Education, University of California at San Diego*.

Feenberg, A. (1989b). The written word: On the theory and practice of computer conferencing. In R. Mason, and A. Kaye, eds., *Mindweave: Communication, Computers and Distance Education* (22–49). Oxford, UK: Pergamon Press.

Feenberg, A. (1991). CMC in executive education: The WBSI experience. In A. Fjuk, and A. E. Jenssen, eds., *Proceedings Nordisk Konferanse om Fjernundervisning, Opplæring of Dataformidlet Kommunikasjon* (95–100). Oslo: NKS Ernst G. Mortensens Stiftelse and Universitets Senter for Informasjonsteknologi (USIT).

Feenberg, A. (1993). Building a global network: The WBSI experience. In L. Harasim, ed., *Global Networks: Computers and International Communication.* Cambridge: MIT Press.

Feenberg, A., and Bellman, B. (1990). Social factor research in the design of educational computer networking. In L. Harasim, ed., *Online Education: Perspectives on a New Environment* (67–97). New York: Praeger.

Ferguson, M. (1980). *The Aquarian Conspiracy.* Los Angeles: J. P. Tarcher.

Fullan, M. (1991). *The New Meaning of Educational Change.* London: Cassell.

Grint, K. (1989). Accounting for failure: Participation and non-participation in CMC. In R. Mason and A. Kaye, eds., *Mindweave: Communication, Computers and Distance Education* (189–192). Oxford, UK: Pergamon Press.

Hahn, H. A., Ashworth, R. L., Phelps, R. H., Wells, R. A., Richards, R. E., and Daveline, K. A. (1990). *Distributed Training for the Reserve Component: Remote Delivery Using Asynchronous Computer Conferencing.* Alexandria, VA: U.S. Army Research Institute for the Behavioral and Social Sciences.

Hansen, A. G. (1992). A buddy computer in the home: Five year progress report. *Technological Horizons in Education Journal* 19 (9) (April): 61–65.

Harasim, L. (1986). Computer learning networks: Educational applications of computer conferencing. *Journal of Distance Education* 1 (1): 59–70.

Harasim, L. (1987a). Computer-mediated cooperation in education: Group learning networks. In *Proceedings of the Second Guelph Symposium on Computer Conferencing, June 1–4* (171–186). Guelph, Ontario, Canada: University of Guelph.

Harasim, L. (1987b). Teaching and learning on-line: Issues in designing computer-mediated graduate courses. *Canadian Journal of Educational Communications* 16 (2): 117–135.

Harasim, L. (1988). *Online Group Learning/Teaching Methods.* Technical Paper 7. Toronto: Ontario Institute for Studies in Education.

Harasim, L. (1989). Online education: A new domain. In R. Mason and A. Kaye, eds., *Mindweave: Communication, Computers and Distance Education.* Oxford: Pergamon Press.

Harasim, L. (1990a). Online education: An environment for collaboration and intellectual amplification. In L. Harasim, ed., *Online Education: Perspectives on a New Environment* (39–64). New York: Praeger.

Harasim, L., ed. (1990b). *Online Education: Perspectives on a New Environment.* New York: Praeger.

Harasim, L. (1991a). Designs and tools to augment collaboration in computerized conferencing systems. In J. Nunamaker and R. Sprague, eds., *Proceedings of the Hawaiian International Conference on Systems Science* (4: 379–385).

Harasim, L. (1991b). Researching online education: Perspectives and methodologies. Paper presented at the AERA conference, Chicago.

Harasim, L. (1993a). Networlds: Networks as social space. In L. Harasim, ed., *Global Networks: Computers and International Communication*. Cambridge: MIT Press.

Harasim, L. (1993b). Collaborating in cyberspace. *Interactive Learning Environments* 3 (2): 119–130.

Harasim, L.. (1994). Computer learning networks. In T. Husen and T. N. Postlethwaite, eds., *The International Encyclopedia of Education*. 2d ed. Oxford: Pergamon Press.

Harasim, L., and Johnson, E. M. (1986a). Computer conferencing and online education: Designing for the medium. *Canadian Journal for Information Science* (Winter).

Harasim, L., and Johnson, E. M. (1986b). *Educational Applications of Computer Networks*. Ontario Ministry of Education Publication Series on Education and Technology. Toronto: Queen's Printer.

Harasim, L., and Teles, L. (1994). Developing The Virtual Interactive Environment for Workgroups. In A. Stahmer, L. Van den Brande, and T. Riveste, eds., *New Media Learning Technologies: Perspectives on Developing an International Collaboration for Flexible and Distance Learning*. Ottawa: Industry Canada.

Harasim, L., and Yung, B. (1993). *Teaching and Learning on the Internet*. Burnaby, BC: Department of Communication, Simon Fraser University.

Hardy, G., Hodgson, V., McConnell, D., and Reynolds, M. (1991). *Computer Mediated Communication for Management Training and Development*. Lancaster, UK: Centre for the Study of Management Learning, Management School, Lancaster University.

Hart, R. (1987). Towards a third generation distributed conferring system. *Canadian Journal of Educational Communication* 16 (2): 137–152.

Hedegaard, T. (1992). *Online Education Programs for MBA, MA, BSc*. Phoenix: University of Phoenix.

Hiltz, S. R. (1984). *Online Communities: A Case Study of the Office of the Future*. Norwood, NJ: Ablex Publishers.

Hiltz, S. R. (1986). The virtual classroom: Using computer-mediated communication for university teaching. *Journal of Communication* 36 (2): 95–104.

Hiltz, S. R. (1988a). *A Virtual Classroom on E.I.E.S.* Vol. 1: *Learning in a Virtual Classroom*. Research report 25. Newark, NJ: Center for Computerized Conferencing and Communication, NJIT.

Hiltz, S. R. (1988b). *A Virtual Classroom on E.I.E.S.* Vol. 2: *Teaching in a Virtual Classroom*. Research report 25. Newark, NJ: Center for Computerized Conferencing and Communication, NJIT.

Hiltz, S. R. (1988c). Collaborative learning in a virtual classroom. In *Proceedings of the Conference on Computer-Supported Cooperative Work, Portland, Oregon* (282–290).

Hiltz, S. R. (1989). Productivity enhancement from computer-mediated communication: A systems contingency approach. *Communications of the ACM* 31 (12): 1438–1455.

Hiltz, S. R. (1990). Evaluating the virtual classroom. In L. Harasim, ed., *Online Education: Perspectives on a New Environment* (133–185). New York: Praeger.

Hiltz, S. R. (1994). *The Virtual Classroom: Learning Without Limits via Computer Networks*. Human-Computer Interaction Series. Norwood, NJ: Ablex Publishing Corp.

Hiltz, S. R., and Johnson, K. (1990). User satisfaction with computer mediated communication systems. *Management Science* 36 (6) (June): 739–764.

Hiltz, S. R., Shapiro, H., and Ringsted, M. (1990). Collaborative teaching in a virtual classroom. *Proceedings of the Third Symposium on Computer Mediated Communications* (37–55). Guelph, Ontario: University of Guelph.

Hiltz, S. R., and Turoff, M. (1978, 1993). *The Network Nation.: Human Communication via Computer*. Reading, MA: Addison-Wesley. Rev. ed., 1993: Cambridge, MA: MIT Press.

Hiltz, S. R., and Turoff, M. (1986). Remote learning: Technologies and opportunities. In *Proceedings, World Conference on Continuing Engineering Education*, Vol. 2, (754–764). New York: IEEE.

Honey, M., and Henriquez, A. (1993). *Telecommunications and K–12 Educators: Findings from a National Survey*. New York: Center for Technology in Education, Bank Street College of Education.

Hopkins, R. H., Campbell, K. B., and Peterson, N. S. (1987). Representations of perceived relationships among the properties and variables of a complex system. *IEEE Transactions on Systems, Man and Cybernetics* 17 (1).

Hsu, E. (1992). *Management games for management education: A case study*. Unpublished doctoral dissertation, Rutgers University.

Humphrey, C. (1985). Getting a turnout: The plight of the organizer. *Iassist Quarterly* 9 (2): 14–27.

Hunter, B. (1992). Linking for learning: Computer-and-communications network support for nationwide innovations in education. *Journal of Science Education and Technology* 1 (1).

Hunter, B. (1993). NSF's networked testbeds inform innovation in science education. *T.H.E. Journal* 2 (3).

Johnson, D., Maruyama, G., Johnson, R., Nelson, D., and Skon, L. (1981). The effects of cooperative, competitive, and individualistic goal structures on achievement: A meta-analysis. *Psychological Bulletin* 89 (1): 47–62.

Johnson-Lenz, P., and Johnson-Lenz, T. (1990). Islands of safety for unlocking human potential. In *Proceedings of the Third International Guelph Symposium* on Unlocking Human Potential via Computer-Mediated Communication, University of Guelph (304–325).

Johnson-Lenz, P., and Johnson-Lenz, T. (1982). Groupware: The process and impacts of design choices. In E. B. Kerr and S. R. Hiltz, eds., *Computer-Mediated Communication Systems: Status and Evaluation* (45–56). New York: Academic Press.

Johnson-Lenz, P., and Johnson-Lenz, T. (1991). Post-mechanistic Groupware primitives: Rhythms, boundaries and containers. *International Journal of Man-Machine Studies* 34: 395–417.

Kane, P. (1991). *Prodigy Made Easy*. Berkeley, CA: Osborne McGraw-Hill.

Kaye, A. (1991). Computer networking in distance education: Multiple uses, many models. In A. Fjuk and A. E. Jenssen, eds., *Proceedings of the Nordic Electronic Networking Conference* (43–51). Oslo, Norway: NKS.

Keen, P. (1981). Information systems and organizational change. *Communications of the ACM* 24 (1): 24–33.

Kehoe, B. P. (1993). *Zen and the Art of the Internet*. 2d ed. Englewood Cliffs, NJ: Prentice-Hall.

Kidd, J. R., ed. (1963). *Learning and Society*. Toronto: Canadian Association for Adult Education.

Knox, A. B. (1974). Life-long self-directed education. In R. J. Blakely, ed., *Fostering the Growing Need to Learn*. Rockland MD: Division of Regional Medical Programs, Bureau of Health Resources.

Kort, B. (1993). The MUSE as an educational medium. Available on musenet. bbn.com in the anonymous FTP Directory.

Krol, E. (1992). *The Whole Internet: User's Guide and Catalog*. Sebastapol, CA: O'Reilly & Associates.

Kurshan, B. (1990). *Statewide Telecommunications Networks: An Overview of the Current State and the Growth Potential*. Roanoke, VA: Educorp Consultants.

LaQuey, T. (1993). *The Internet Companion: A Beginner's Guide to Global Networking*. Reading, MA: Addison-Wesley.

Lemke, J. L. (1993). Hypermedia and higher education. *Interpersonal Computing and Technology: A Journal for the 21st Century* 1 (2) (April).

Levin, J. (1990). *Teleapprenticeships on globally distributed electronic networks*. Paper presented at the meeting of the American Educational Research Association, Boston.

Levin, J., Kim, H., and Riel, M. (1990). Analyzing instructional interactions on electronic message networks. In L. Harasim, ed., *Online Education: Perspectives on a new Environment* (185–213). New York: Praeger.

Levin, J., Riel, M., Rowe, R., and Boruta, M. (1984). Muktuk meets jacuzzi: Computer networks and elementary school writers. In S. W. Freedman, ed., *The*

Acquisition of Written Language: Revision and Response (160–171). Norwood, NJ: Ablex.

Levinson, P. (1989). Media Relations: Integrating computer telecommunications with educational media. In R. Mason and K. Kaye, eds., *Mindweave: Communication, Computers and Distance Education.* Oxford: Pergamon Press.

Linstone, H. A., and Turoff, M. (1975). *The Delphi Method: Techniques and Applications.* Reading, MA: Addison-Wesley.

McGreal, R. (1993). Exemplary programs of secondary distance education in Canada. *DEOSNEWS (The Distance Education Online Symposium)* 3 (6).

Markoff, J. (1993). Building the electronic superhighway. *New York Times,* January 24, 1993.

Mason, R. (1989). An evaluation of CoSy on an Open University course. In R. Mason and K. Kaye, eds., *Mindweave: Communication, Computers and Distance Education.* Oxford: Pergamon Press.

Mason, R. (1990). Conferencing for mass distance education. In *Proceedings of the Third Guelph Symposium on Computer Conferencing.* Guelph, Ontario: University of Guelph.

Mason, R. (1993). Computer conferencing and the new Europe. In L. M. Harasim, ed., *Global Networks: Computers and International Communication.* Cambridge, MA: MIT Press.

Mason, R., and Kaye, A., eds. (1989). *Mindweave: Communication, Computers and Distance Education.* Oxford: Pergamon Press.

Mason, R. and Kaye, T. (1990). Toward a new paradigm for distance education. In L. Harasim, ed., *Online Education: Perspectives on a New Environment* (15–38). New York: Praeger.

National Geographic Kids Network. (1992). *Year 4: Final Annual Report.* Cambridge: TERC.

Nelson, T. H. (1965). A file structure for the complex, the changing and the indeterminate. In *ACM 20th National Conference Proceedings* (84–99).

Nelson, T. H. (1974). *Dream Machines.* Chicago: Hugo's Book Service.

Newman, D. (1990). Cognitive and technical issues in the design of educational computer networking. In L. Harasim, ed., *Online Education: Perspectives on a New Environment* (99–116). New York: Praeger.

Newman, D. (1993). *The National School Network Testbed at BBN.* Proposal to the NSSFnet.

Owen, T. (1989). Computer-mediated writing and the writer in electronic residence. In R. Mason and A. Kaye, eds., *Mindweave: Communication, Computers and Distance Education.* Oxford: Pergamon Press.

Owen, T. (1991). *On-Line Learning Links Are Language Learning Links.* Toronto: ECOO Output.

Owen, T. (1993a). Wired writing: The Writers in Electronic Residence Program. In R. Mason, ed., *Computer Conferencing: The Last Word*. Victoria, B.C.: Beach Holme Publishers Ltd.

Owen, T. (1993b). High teach: Learning from the experiences of wired writers. Master's thesis, Simon Fraser University.

Paulsen, M. F., and Rekkedal, T. (1990). *The Electronic Cottage: Selected Articles from the EKKO Project*. Norway: SEFU, Norwegian Centre for Distance Education.

Peters, O. (1983). Distance education and industrial production: A comparative interpretation in outline. In D. Sewart, D. Keegan, and B. Holmberg, eds., *Distance Education: International Perspectives*. London/New York: Croon Helm/St. Martin's Press.

de Presno, O. (1991). Children help change the online world. *Matrix News* 1 (5): 1, 13–16. (Available from Matrix Information and Directory Services, MIDS, Austin, Texas.)

Peyton, J. K., and Batson, T. (1986). Computer networking: Making connections between speech and writing. *ERIC/CLL New Bulletin* 10 (1): 1–7.

Quarterman, J. S. (1993). *The Global Matrix of Minds*. Cambridge, MA: MIT Press.

Quinn, C. N., Mehan, H. Levin, J. A., and Black, S. D. (1983). Real education in non-real time: The use of electronic message systems for instruction. *Instructional Science* 11 (4): 313–327.

Resnick, L., ed. (1989). *Knowing, Learning, and Instruction*. Hillsdale, NJ: Erlbaum.

Resta, P. (1989). Educational communications: The good, the bad, and the ugly. In *Proceedings of the International Symposium on Telecommunications in Education (Jerusalem)*. Eugene, OR: ISTE.

Rheingold, H. (1993). *The Virtual Community: Homesteading on the Electronic Frontier*. Reading, MA: Addison-Wesley.

Rice, R. E., and Love, G. (1987). Electronic emotion: Socio emotional content in a computer-mediated communication network. *Communication Research* 14 (1) (February): 85–108.

Rich, M. (1992). *The Use of Electronic Mail and Conferencing Systems in Teaching Management Students*. Working Paper Series. London: City University Business School.

Riel, M. (1983). Education and ecstasy: Computer chronicles of students writing together. *Quarterly Newsletter of the Laboratory of Comparative Human Cognition* 5 (3): 59–67.

Riel, M. (1990). Learning circles: A model for educational telecomputing. Paper presented at the meeting of the American Educational Research Association, Boston.

Riel, M. (1993a). Global education through learning circles. In L. Harasim, ed., *Global Networks: Computers and International Communication.* Cambridge, MA: MIT Press.

Riel, M. (1993b). The SCANS Report and the AT&T Learning Network: Preparing students for their future. *Telecommunications in Education News* 5 (1): 10–13.

Roberts, N., ed. (1990). *Integrating Telecommunications into Education.* Englewood Cliffs, NJ: Prentice-Hall.

Rosenthal, B. (1991). *Computer-mediated discourse in a writing workshop: A case study in higher education.* Unpublished doctoral dissertation, New York University.

Sayers, D. (1989). Bilingual sister classes in computer writing networks. In D. Roen and D. Johnson, eds., *Richness in Writing: Empowering Minority Students* (120–133). New York: Longman.

Scardamalia, M., and Bereiter, C. (1991). Higher levels of agency for children in knowledge-building: A challenge for the design of new knowledge media. *The Journal of the Learning Sciences* 1 (1): 37–68.

Scardamalia, M., and Bereiter, C. (1993). Technologies for knowledge-building discourse. *Communications of the ACM* 36 (5): 37–41.

Scardamalia, M., and Bereiter, C. (1994). Computer support for knowledge-building communities. *The Journal of the Learning Sciences* 3 (3): 265–283.

Scardamalia, M., Bereiter, C., Brett, C., Burtis, P. J., Calhoun, C., and Smith Lea, N. (1992). Educational applications of a networked communal database. *Interactive Learning Environments* 2 (1): 45–71.

Schepp, B., and Schepp, D. (1990). *The Complete Guide to CompuServe.* New York: Osborne McGraw-Hill.

Sharan, S. (1980). Cooperative learning in small groups: Recent methods and effects on achievement, attitudes, and ethnic relations. *Review of Educational Research* 50 (20): 241–71.

Shneiderman, B. Education by engagement and construction: Experiences in the AT&T Teaching Theater. Keynote for ED-MEDIA 93, June 1993, Orlando, FL.

Slavin, R. E. (1983). *Cooperative Learning.* New York: Longman.

Smith, R. C. (1988). Teaching special relativity through a computer conference. *American Journal of Physics* 56 (2): 142–147.

Sproull, L., and Kiesler, S. (1991). *Connections: New Ways of Working in the Networked Organization.* Cambridge, MA: MIT Press.

Sterling, B. (1992). *The Hacker Crackdown: Law and Disorder on the Electronic Frontier.* New York: Bantam Books.

Strangelove, M. (1991). *Directory of Electronic Journals and Newsletters.* Ottawa: University of Ottawa.

Teles, L. (1988). The adoption of word processing by graduate students in education. *Education and Computing* 4 (4): 287–299.

Teles, L. (1993). Cognitive apprenticeship on global networks. In L. Harasim, ed., *Global Networks: Computers and Communications*. Cambridge: MIT Press.

Teles, L., and Duxbury, N. (1992). *The Networked Classroom: An Assessment of the Southern Interior Telecommunications Project (SITP) Report of Phase 1.* Burnaby, BC: Faculty of Education, Simon Fraser University.

Teles, L., and Duxbury, N. (1992). *The Networked Classroom: Creating an Online Environment for K–12 Education*. Burnaby, BC: Faculty of Education, Simon Fraser University (ERIC ED348 988).

Thompson, D. P. (1988). Interactive networking: Creating bridges between speech, writing, and composition. *Computers and Composition* 5 (3): 2–27.

Tifflin, J., Rajasingham, L. (1993). Telelearning research in New Zealand: The search for the virtual classroom. Unpublished paper, Victoria University, Wellington, New Zealand.

Tinker, R. F., and Kapisovsky, P. M., eds. (1992). *Prospects for Educational Telecomputing: Selected Readings*. Cambridge, MA: TERC.

Turoff, M. (1990a). The anatomy of a computer application innovation: Computer mediated communications (CMC). *Technological Forecasting and Social Change* 36: 107–122.

Turoff, M. (1990b). Computer mediated communication requirements for group support. *Organizational Computing* 1 (1).

Turoff, M., and Rao, U. (1991). Collaborative hypertext in computer mediated communications. In *Proceedings of the 24th Annual HICSS* (357–366). Washington, DC: IEEE.

Turoff, M., Rao, U., and Hiltz, S. R. (1991). Collaborative hypertext in computer-mediated communications. *Proceedings of the Twenty-Fourth Annual Hawaii Conference on System Sciences* (4: 357–366). Washington DC: IEEE.

Umpleby, S. (1986). Online educational techniques. *ENA Netweaver* 2 (1): article 6.

Vygotskii, L. (1978). *Mind in Society: The Development of Higher Psychological Processes*. Cambridge: Harvard University Press.

Waggoner, M. D., ed. (1992). *Empowering Networks: Computer Conferencing in Education*. Englewood Cliffs, NJ: Educational Technology Publications.

Webb, N. (1982). Group composition, group interaction, and achievement in cooperative small groups. *International Journal of Educational Psychology* 74 (4): 475–484.

Webb, N. (1989). Peer interaction and learning in small groups. *International Journal of Educational Research* 13 (1): 21–29.

Wells, R. A. (1990). *Distributed Training for the Reserved Component: Remote Delivery Using Asynchronous Computer Conferencing*. Report 2Q263743A794. Idaho Falls, ID: Idaho National Engineering Laboratory.

Wells, R. A. (1992). *Computer-Mediated Communication for Distance Education: An International Review of Design, Teaching, and Institutional Issues.* Research Monographs 6. American Center for the Study of Distance Education, State College, PA, Pennsylvania State University.

Winkelmans, T. (1988). *Educational computer conferencing: An application of analysis methodologies to a structured small group activity.* Unpublished master's thesis, University of Toronto.

Wolfe, R. (1990). Hypertextual perspectives on educational computer conferencing. In L. Harasim, ed., *Online Education: Perspectives on a New Environment* (215–227). New York: Praeger.

Index